THE
HISTORY OF
ARGENTINA

ADVISORY BOARD

John T. Alexander
Professor of History and Russian and European Studies,
University of Kansas

Robert A. Divine
George W. Littlefield Professor in American History Emeritus,
University of Texas at Austin

John V. Lombardi
Professor of History,
University of Florida

THE
HISTORY OF
ARGENTINA

Second Edition

Daniel K. Lewis

The Greenwood Histories of the Modern Nations
Frank W. Thackeray and John E. Findling, Series Editors

AN IMPRINT OF ABC-CLIO, LLC
Santa Barbara, California • Denver, Colorado • Oxford, England

Copyright © 2015 by ABC-CLIO, LLC

Library of Congress Cataloging-in-Publication Data

Lewis, Daniel K., 1959–
    The history of Argentina / Daniel K. Lewis. — Second edition.
      pages cm. — (The Greenwood histories of the modern nations)
    Includes bibliographical references and index.
    ISBN 978-1-61069-860-3 (hard copy : alk. paper) — ISBN 978-1-61069-861-0 (ebook)
  1. Argentina—History. I. Title.
    F2831.L69 2015
    982—dc23   2014026892

ISBN: 978-1-61069-860-3
EISBN: 978-1-61069-861-0

19 18 17 16 15   1 2 3 4 5

This book is also available on the World Wide Web as an eBook.
Visit www.abc-clio.com for details.

Greenwood
An Imprint of ABC-CLIO, LLC

ABC-CLIO, LLC
130 Cremona Drive, P.O. Box 1911
Santa Barbara, California 93116-1911

This book is printed on acid-free paper ∞

Manufactured in the United States of America

Contents

Series Foreword

The Greenwood Histories of the Modern Nations series is intended to provide students and interested laypeople with up-to-date, concise, and analytical histories of many of the nations of the contemporary world. Not since the 1960s has there been a systematic attempt to publish a series of national histories, and as series editors, we believe that this series will prove to be a valuable contribution to our understanding of other countries in our increasingly interdependent world.

Some decades years ago, at the end of the 1960s, the Cold War was an accepted reality of global politics. The process of decolonization was still in progress, the idea of a unified Europe with a single currency was unheard of, the United States was mired in a war in Vietnam, and the economic boom in Asia was still years in the future. Richard Nixon was president of the United States, Mao Tse-tung (not yet Mao Zedong) ruled China, Leonid Brezhnev guided the Soviet Union, and Harold Wilson was prime minister of the United Kingdom. Authoritarian dictators still controlled most of Latin America, the Middle East was reeling in the wake of the Six-Day War, and Shah Mohammad Reza Pahlavi was at the height of his power in Iran.

Since then, the Cold War has ended, the Soviet Union has vanished, leaving 15 independent republics in its wake, the advent of the computer age has radically transformed global communications, the rising demand for oil makes the Middle East still a dangerous flashpoint, and the rise of new economic powers like the People's Republic of China and India threatens to bring about a new world order. All of these developments have had a dramatic impact on the recent history of every nation of the world.

For this series, which was launched in 1998, we first selected nations whose political, economic, and socio-cultural affairs marked them as among the most important of our time. For each nation, we found an author who was recognized as a specialist in the history of that nation. These authors worked cooperatively with us and with Greenwood Press to produce volumes that reflected current research on their nations and that are interesting and informative to their readers. In the first decade of the series, more than 40 volumes were published, and as of 2014, some are moving into second editions.

The success of the series has encouraged us to broaden our scope to include additional nations, whose histories have had significant effects on their regions, if not on the entire world. In addition, geopolitical changes have elevated other nations into positions of greater importance in world affairs and, so, we have chosen to include them in this series as well. The importance of a series such as this cannot be underestimated. As a superpower whose influence is felt all over the world, the United States can claim a "special" relationship with almost every other nation. Yet many Americans know very little about the histories of nations with which the United States relates. How did they get to be the way they are? What kind of political systems have evolved there? What kind of influence do they have on their own regions? What are the dominant political, religious, and cultural forces that move their leaders? These and many other questions are answered in the volumes of this series.

The authors who contribute to this series write comprehensive histories of their nations, dating back, in some instances, to prehistoric times. Each of them, however, has devoted a significant portion of their book to events of the past 40 years because the modern era has contributed the most to contemporary issues that have an impact on U.S. policy. Authors make every effort to be as up-to-date as possible so that readers can benefit from discussion and analysis of recent events.

In addition to the historical narrative, each volume contains an introductory chapter giving an overview of that country's geography, political institutions, economic structure, and cultural attributes. This is meant to give readers a snapshot of the nation as it exists in the contemporary world. Each history also includes supplementary information following the narrative, which may include a timeline that represents a succinct chronology of the nation's historical evolution, biographical sketches of the nation's most important historical figures, and a glossary of important terms or concepts that are usually expressed in a foreign language. Finally, each author prepares a comprehensive bibliography for readers who wish to pursue the subject further.

Readers of these volumes will find them fascinating and well written. More importantly, they will come away with a better understanding of the contemporary world and the nations that comprise it. As series editors, we hope that this series will contribute to a heightened sense of global understanding as we move through the early years of the twenty-first century.

Frank W. Thackeray and John E. Findling
Indiana University Southeast

Preface

I wrote this text to provide a brief overview of Argentina's complicated history. It was a rewarding challenge. I first traveled to Argentina in 1986. During that time, the country was in the midst of rapid change. I found myself in a deeply divided society. Debates over the past and its legacy had revived, but the damage wrought by decades of political strife and economic chaos created enormous problems for Argentina's citizens and leaders.

Since the fall of the military dictatorship and the country's return to civilian rule, Argentina has experienced cycles of economic expansion and contraction. The last three decades have shown that Argentina faces significant challenges.

Fundamentally, its fortune is still based on the export of its agricultural products. During periods of increasing international demand all things seem possible. When markets stagnate or prices drop, the resources that once supported prosperity and innovation disappear. Economic and political crises, often accompanied by popular protest, ensue.

History does not provide any clear lessons for us to follow. It does, I think, help us best understand the world that we live in. Argentina's present is limited in fundamental and frustrating ways by its past. In some way I hope that the text that I have written helps those unfamiliar with this country gain an appreciation of its trials and its promise.

I am grateful for the opportunity that the editorial staff at ABC-CLIO has granted me. The first edition went to press before one of Argentina's most confusing periods of political shifts and turns. The consolidation of a new generation of Peronist rule is the main topic of the final chapter that addresses the country's recent experience. The competition between the Kirchner and Fernández de Kirchner administrations and their rivals within and beyond the Peronist movement has many facets. If one can step back from the events, one notes that the fundamental challenges that confronted past generations remain unresolved. Its urban population, especially in Greater Buenos Aires, is politically engaged and dominant. Although the government continues to promote economic diversification in hopes of lessening the country's dependence on the exports of primary products, its rural industries remain crucial. With increasing difficulty, the government channels resources toward the support of those at the base of Argentine society. Global economic shifts appear to be undermining efforts to defend local industries.

Thanks to its organizational strength, Peronism dominates. While many predict disaster, international conditions might allow the movement to hold onto power. If its leaders can effectively forge an economic partnership with China and Asia and extend the integration of established partnerships with Mercosur, they may command the resources needed to fulfill the promises that they make to their supporters.

The History Department and the Dean's Office of the College of Letters, Arts, and Social Sciences at the California State Polytechnic University in Pomona provided reassigned time and funds for me to work on the original version of this text and for a visit to Argentina just as I began work on this project. I remain grateful for my college's support in the years since.

In Argentina, I have had help from a number of patient and insightful individuals. Although I cannot mention all of those who helped me complete my work here, I again thank Dr. José Fernandez Vega for his friendship and support. Finally, I thank my family for their patience and encouragement.

ARGENTINA

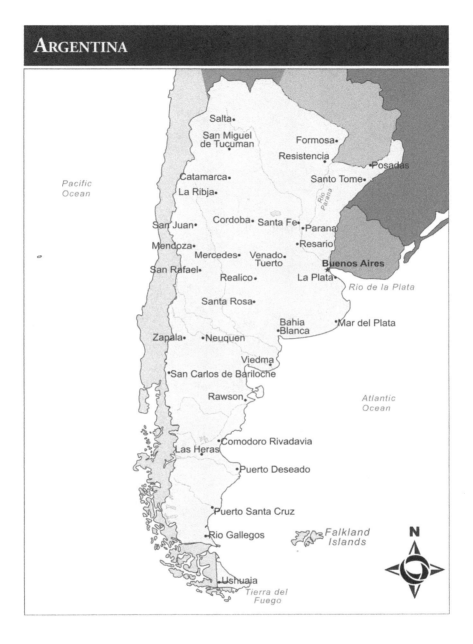

Salta

San Miguel de Tucuman

Formosa

Resistencia

Posadas

Catamarca

Santo Tome

La Ribja

Pacific Ocean

Cordoba

Santa Fe

Parana

San Juan

Rio Parana

Mendoza

Resario

Mercedes

Venado Tuerto

Buenos Aires

San Rafael

Realico

La Plata

Rio de la Plata

Santa Rosa

Bahia Blanca

Mar del Plata

Zapala

Neuquen

Viedma

San Carlos de Bariloche

Rawson

Atlantic Ocean

Comodoro Rivadavia

Las Heras

Puerto Deseado

Puerto Santa Cruz

Rio Gallegos

Falkland Islands

N

Ushuaia

Tierra del Fuego

Timeline of Historical Events

1516	A Spanish expedition under the command of Juan Díaz de Solís arrives at the Río de la Plata estuary and claims the territory in the name of the Crown.
1520	Magellan's search for the southwest passage continues the exploration of Argentina's southern coasts.
1527–1529	An expedition under Sebastian Cabot's command explores the Parana River and establishes the first Spanish settlement—Sancti Spiritus.
1536	Fearing Portuguese expansion into the region, the Spanish Crown sponsors the creation of a settlement on the banks of the Río de la Plata. The expedition commander, Pedro de Mendoza, names the city Nuestra Señora de Santa María del Buen Aire. Expedition survivors abandon the city, now known as Buenos Aires, and travel to Asunción (Paraguay).
1543–1565	Expeditions establish settlements in Argentina's northwest and in Cuyo.
1573	Jerónimo Luis de Cabrera establishes the town of Córdoba. Juan de Garay establishes Santa Fe.

1578–1579	Franciscans build missions in Río de la Plata region.
1580	Supplied by Santa Fe and Asunción, Juan de Garay rebuilds the settlement of Buenos Aires.
1595	The sale of African slaves, operating from the market of Buenos Aires, begins in Argentina.
1605	First shipment of salted beef is sent from Buenos Aires.
1610	The first Jesuit mission is established at San Ignacio Guazú.
1622	Authorities open the University of Córdoba.
1713	British merchants gain control of the slave trade in Spanish American ports.
1767	The Spanish Crown orders the Jesuits' expulsion from its colonies.
1776	The Spanish Crown establishes the viceroyalty of the Río de la Plata, and names Buenos Aires as its capital.
1795	The first *saladero* is established in Argentine territory.
1806	Santiago Liniers leads a counterattack that pushes British invaders from Buenos Aires.
1807	The militia of Buenos Aires defeats a second British invasion force.
1810	On May 25, the *cabildo abierto* assumes political authority over the viceroyalty.
1811	Military losses at Paraguarí, Tacuarí, and Huaquí separate Paraguay and Upper Perú (Bolivia) from Buenos Aires.
1816	The Congress of Tucumán formally declares Independence.
1817	General José de San Martín leads the Army of the Andes into Chile and begins the final phase of the Independence wars.
1818	San Martín defeats the Spanish at the Battle of Maipú.
1820	The "Terrible Year Twenty," when Independence armies splinter into regional, rival forces and political disagreements shatter the unity of the revolutionary government in Buenos Aires.
1821	Authorities open the University of Buenos Aires.

1824	The Battle of Ayacucho effectively ends the Independence struggle in Perú and ends Spanish ambitions in South America.
1825	Great Britain formally recognizes the United Provinces of the Río de la Plata.
1825–1828	War with Brazil over the *Banda Oriental* ends with the creation of an independent Uruguay.
1829	Federalist armies challenge *Unitario* rule. Military conflict splinters the United Provinces of the Río de la Plata.
	Juan Manuel de Rosas becomes governor of Buenos Aires and asserts the province's independence.
1844	British immigrant rancher Richard Newton imports barbed wire for use on his properties. The spread of barbed wire will later allow the modernization of sheep and cattle ranches as landowners transform their operations to take advantage of growing foreign demand.
1845–1848	British and French forces mount a naval blockade of Buenos Aires.
1852	Rosas's army is defeated at the Battle of Caseros. The dictatorship ends.
	The San Nicolás Agreement creates the Argentine Confederation on May 31.
1856	The Santa Fe government sponsors the first agricultural colony, "La Esperanza."
1859	On October 23, Confederation armies win the Battle of Cepeda. The leaders of the defeated forces of Buenos Aires agree to join the Confederation.
1861	Battle of Pavón, on September 17, once again blocks Buenos Aires's efforts to remain independent.
1862	Following the adoption of a new constitution, Bartolomé Mitre is elected as the first president of the Argentine Republic.
1865–1870	War of the Triple Alliance pits Argentina, Brazil, and Uruguay against Paraguay.
1877	The first shipment of frozen beef from Argentina to Europe takes place.
1878–1879	Julio Roca, minister of war under President Nicolás Avellaneda, launches the "Conquest of the Wilderness"

that annihilates the Native American communities in the Argentine Pampa and northern Patagonia.

1878   Merchants ship wheat from the port of Rosario to Great Britain.

1880   The city of Buenos Aires is transformed into the Federal Capital of the Argentine Republic.

1890   The Baring crisis creates financial panic and recession in Argentina. Political dissatisfaction leads to the "Revolution of 1890" and the resignation of President Miguel Juárez Celman.

1912   Sáenz Peña Law, which mandated universal male suffrage and secret ballots in elections, is approved by the national government.

1916   Hipólito Yrigoyen and the *Unión Cívica Radical* (UCR) soundly defeat their conservative rivals in national elections.

1919   January 7–13 is marred by fighting between striking workers and army units in Buenos Aires and other urban districts. The bloody repression of the worker protests is later named the "Semana Trágica" (Tragic Week).

1924   UCR splits into pro- and anti-Yrigoyen factions.

1930   Military units under the command of Jose´ F. Uriburu mount a successful coup against the Yrigoyen government.

1932   Fraud and violence rig Agustín P. Justo's election as president. The *Concordancia* begins its reign over the *Decada infame* (Infamous Decade, 1932–1943).

1933   Roca-Runciman Pact, also known as the Treaty of London, grants Great Britain special economic privileges in exchange for trade regulations in defense of Argentine interests.

The Justo government puts in place its *Plan de Acción Económica* (Plan of Economic Action), designed by Economics

Minister Federico Pinedo and Agricultural Minister Luis Duhau. By placing controls on foreign exchange and by setting minimum prices for agricultural exports, the plan helps Argentina adjust to the impact of the Great Depression.

1943	Army officers, declaring themselves loyal to the country's national interests, topple the provisional government of Ramón Castillo and create a military dictatorship.
1946	Juan Domingo Perón is elected president.
1946–1949	The Peronist government nationalizes key industries and services.
1947	After a campaign spearheaded by María Eva Duarte de Perón, the government grants Argentine women the right to vote.
1952	Taking advantage of the constitutional reform of 1949, Juan Perón successfully wins direct reelection and begins his second term in office. María Eva Duarte de Perón—Evita—dies of cancer.
1955	The armed forces force Perón from power. General Pedro Aramburu assumes the title of provisional president.
1958	Popular pressure and military factional strife leads to a return to civilian rule. Arturo Frondizi is elected president.
1962	Frondizi promises to allow Peronist participation in the coming elections. To block this move, the armed forces remove Frondizi from power and assume control of the government in March.
1963	With the Peronists banned from participation, Arturo Illia is elected president.
1966	Economic and political turmoil encourage the military to move against Illia. General Juan Carlos Onganía is named president in June.
1969	The *Cordobazo:* Rioters and protesters overwhelm police and military forces in Córdoba and briefly take charge of the city on May 29 and 30.
1970	Guerrilla unit loyal to the *Montoneros* kidnaps and assassinates Pedro Aramburu. Escalating political violence and economic instability lead elements within the armed forces to demand a greater voice in government. Onganía's refusal leads to his dismissal from office in June.
1972	Provisional president Alejandro Lanusse begins the process of returning Argentina to civilian rule. He

approves the pardoning of Juan Perón and allows the ex-president to return briefly to the country.

1973   The Peronist Party, united behind Héctor José Cámpora, sweeps the elections on May 25. Cámpora's planned resignation triggers the scheduling of new elections. On September 23, Juan Perón is elected to an unprecedented third term as president.

1974   Juan Perón dies on July 1. María Estela Martínez (Isabelilta) de Perón, his wife and vice president, succeeds him.

1975–1983   The *Guerra sucia* (Dirty War), the government's campaign of censorship, violence, and terror against real and suspected enemies of the state, leads to the death and disappearance of tens of thousands of Argentines and foreign nationals.

1976   The military pushes Isabelita from power. Jorge Rafael Videla, commander-in-chief of the armed forces, becomes president and officially launches the "Process of National Reorganization."

1977   The "Mothers of the Plaza de Mayo," often called *las madres,* begin their silent protests against the dictatorship.

1981   Viola succeeds Videla as provisional president.

1982   Leopoldo Galtieri assumes the presidency. Hoping to build popular support and nationalist enthusiasm, Galtieri orders the invasion of the Falkland and the South Georgian Islands. The British, who claim authority over the islands, defeat the Argentines in a brief war. Revelations of the military's incompetence lead to Galtieri's resignation. General Reynaldo Bignone assumes the presidency and begins negotiations with civilian leaders to orchestrate the end of the dictatorship.

1983   Raúl Alfonsín wins a surprising victory in the presidential elections.

1985   The government announces the Austral Plan to combat inflation and stabilize the economy.

1986   Alfonsín government approves the *punto final* legislation that blocks investigations of and indictments against officers and individuals involved in the Dirty War.

1987   The "Easter Rebellion" by army units challenges President Alfonsín's authority.

1989   Deteriorating economic conditions and disapproval of
                        the government's handling of human rights cases un-
                        dermine political support for the Alfonsín government.
                        After the UCR loses the national elections, Alfonsín
                        negotiates an immediate transfer of presidential au-
                        thority to Carlos Saúl Menem, the victorious Peronist
                        candidate.

1991–1994   The Menem administration authorizes the privatiza-
                        tion of most public industries and companies as part
                        of its program to reduce public deficits and stabilize
                        the economy. Corruption and poor supervision mar
                        the privatization process.

1994   Menem and Alfonsín lead negotiations that produce
                        a constitutional reform. Allowed to run for reelection,
                        Menem captures a second term in office.

1999   Fernando de la Rúa, at the head of a center-left alliance
                        of opposition parties, defeats the Peronist candidate
                        Eduardo Duhalde in presidential elections.

2000   Popular protests and strikes in transport and indus-
                        trial sectors disrupt the country. Massive deficits and
                        mounting debt restrict the national government's abil-
                        ity to address public concerns.

2001   The imposition of budget cuts leads to a general strike
                        in July.

                        In October, the Peronists win majorities in the na-
                        tional Chamber of Deputies and the Senate. Economic
                        minister imposed restrictions on bank withdrawals
                        and currency trading, which leads to a new round of
                        strikes and protests. In the wake of clashes between
                        rioters and police, President de la Rúa resigns from
                        office on December 20.

                        Senator Adolfo Rodríguez Sáa becomes interim presi-
                        dent on December 23. He resigns after seven days.

2002   Senator Eduardo Duhalde is elected by the Argentine
                        Congress as president. *Los Piquiteros*, an urban protest
                        movement of unemployed industrial and service sec-
                        tor workers, organizes roadblocks, factory occupa-
                        tions, and other actions in opposition. In November,
                        negotiations with the International Monetary Fund
                        (IMF) break down. Argentina defaults on its debt
                        payments.

2003   Nestor Kirchner is elected president. Congress re-
                scinds laws that restricted prosecution of military
                and government officials implicated in crimes against
                humanity during the "Dirty War." In September, the
                government negotiates a settlement with the IMF.

2005   Argentine Supreme Court nullifies laws granting mili-
                tary and police officers amnesty for crimes committed
                during the "Dirty War."

                After renegotiating a debt service plan, President
                Kirchner announces the full payment of the country's
                debt owed to the IMF on December 15.

2007   Cristina Fernández de Kirchner is elected president.

2008–2009   Proposed tax increases on and caps on profit margins
                generated by farm exports, aimed at taking advantage
                of the strong demand and high market prices for soy
                beans and other grains, creates confrontation between
                the government and farmer organizations. Farmer
                organizations organize a strike that threatens the
                economy.

2009   The Argentine government presents formal claims to
                the mineral rights over the seabeads surrounding the
                Falkland Islands. President Fernández de Kirchner
                calls for the return of the islands to Argentina.

2010   The death of Nestor Kirchner undermines plans to
                orchestrate his re-election.

2011   Fernández de Kirchner is re-elected president.

2013   Cardinal Jorge Mario Bergoglio is named Pope Fran-
                cis. He is the first Latin American pope in the history
                of the Catholic Church.

2014   Economic instability, fuelled by falling export revenues
                and increased government expenditures, leads to ris-
                ing inflation and the devaluation of the *peso*.

                Court Ruling in New York City voids debt reduction
                and repayment agreements between the Argentine
                government and its international creditors. After
                months of attempted negotiations, Argentina falls into
                default in December.

1

Argentina Today

At the end of the nineteenth century, international opinion predicted that Argentina would develop into one of the world's leading nations. Its natural resources, its size, and its lucrative trade with Europe provided what seemed to many to be a solid foundation. These predictions did not come true. Commentators now characterize its nineteenth century as a period of decline. Argentina's nineteenth-century champions and twenty-first-century detractors exaggerate, respectively, the country's apparent wealth in the past and its decline since 1900. The paradox of the country's early potential and its actual failings make the presentation of its history both fascinating and challenging.

ITS PLACE IN THE WORLD

Physically, Argentina spans much of the southern half of the Western Hemisphere. It is the eighth-largest country in the world and, behind Brazil, the second-largest country in South America: Its recognized boundaries surpass 1.1 million square miles. The Argentine government also claims possession of the Falkland Islands, known locally as the Malvinas, in the South Atlantic Ocean and a portion of Antarctica.

Stretching 2,170 miles in length, the country's geography is as diverse as any other in the Americas.

Argentina shares borders with Chile to the west, Bolivia to the north, and Paraguay, Brazil, and Uruguay to the northwest. Geographers generally divide Argentina, with its 23 provinces, into six distinct zones with unique climates and characteristics. Its northeastern region is called the country's "Mesopotamia." Located within this region are Misiones, Corrientes, and Entre Ríos. Defined by the course of the Paraná and Uruguay Rivers, this region has a tropical climate. Much of the region is near sea level. Rainfall is frequent and plentiful. Temperatures are usually warm.

The land and the climate support the production of *yerba mate*. Argentines use the dried leaves of the plant to make *mate*, a hot, caffeine-rich drink. At the point where Argentina's border meets those of Brazil and Paraguay is Iguazú Falls, which is one of the world's largest. In the relatively drier areas of the south, landowners focus on sheep herding, cattle ranching, and the production of forage crops, which are used as cattle feed.

In the center of northern Argentina is the Chaco. This region, which borders on Bolivia, is a section of a much larger plateau that runs north and west through Bolivia and Paraguay into Brazil. It has a number of rivers and a warm climate marked by seasonal rainfall. The provinces of Chaco, Formosa, and Santiago del Estero, along with the northern edges of Santa Fe and Córdoba, form the territory. The region's vegetation varies. Scrub forests give way to jungles to the north and deserts to the west. In the forest areas grows the *quebracho* tree, which is used for firewood and to produce a resin used to process leather.

The high peaks of the Andes and the sub-Andean mountain range define the northwestern corner of Argentina. Within the Andean region are the provinces of Catamarca, Jujuy, La Rioja, Salta, and Tucumán. Here, where some of Argentina's oldest towns and cities are located, the weather is cold. The high mountain peaks give way to valleys where cotton, sugar, and tobacco production share the land with sheep herding and small ranches. To the east, the mountains give way to the Puna, a cold desert with sparse vegetation.

South of the Andean region is the Cuyo. The Andes mountain range forms the western edge of this region. It includes the provinces of San Juan, San Luís, Mendoza, and part of La Pampa. In the shadow of the mountains, despite the relative lack of rain, a number of rivers make the climate favorable for a variety of agricultural activities. The heart of the Cuyo supports Argentina's noted wine industry. The highest mountain peak in the Western Hemisphere, Cerro Aconcagua (23,034 feet), is located in this region.

Patagonia begins farther south, across the Río Colorado. Sparsely populated, it holds almost a quarter of the country's surface area. Irrigation has allowed the development of fruit orchards and limited farming in its northwestern corner; at the same time, mining operations have become increasingly important in the regional economy. Dry and cold, the territory remains an important area for sheep herding. The glaciers and vast plains are Patagonia's main features. It includes the provinces of Chubut, Neuquén, Río Negro, and Santa Cruz and the territory of Tierra del Fuego. Ushuaia, the designated capital of Tierra del Fuego, is the world's southernmost city. It serves as a base for tourism in the region and into Antarctica.

Argentina's heart is the Pampa, the rolling territory located in the center of the country. The region is a massive alluvial plain. Only one small mountain range, the Sierras de Córdoba, breaks the region's mostly flat and open character. During the colonial period, it was a vast grassland that supported rapidly expanding herds of wild horses and cattle. Today, it includes the country's most populated provinces: Buenos Aires, Córdoba, Santa Fe, and the eastern half of La Pampa. The eastern core of the region receives more rainfall. The western and southern sections are drier and colder. The temperate climate of this region has helped foster the country's "Mother Industries": ranching and grain farming.

Within the Pampa are the country's largest cities and industrial centers: Mar del Plata, Rosario, Córdoba, and Buenos Aires. Buenos Aires, the national capital, and the *partidos* (counties or districts) closest to it are referred to as *Gran Buenos Aires* (Greater Buenos Aires). It is one of South America's largest urban zones. Córdoba developed during the 1600s into the region's cultural and political center. The University of Córdoba is one of the oldest in the Americas. It is still regarded as the institutional center of the Catholic Church in the country. Rosario, located in Santa Fe Province, grew explosively at the end of the nineteenth century in response to the growth of farming and grain exports. Still a major port city, it became the site of rapid industrial development after World War II. Mar del Plata was a small town in the late nineteenth century. Tourist promotions led to its expansion after the 1930s. Called "the Pearl of the Atlantic" by its boosters, Mar del Plata boasts beaches and casinos that attract visitors from other regions and neighboring countries.

Overall, the Pampa region contains 70 percent of the country's population. It also produces 80 percent of the country's agricultural output.

Eighty-five percent of Argentina's industrial enterprises are located there. It is the center of Argentina's economic, political, and cultural life.

ITS PEOPLE

An estimated 43 million people currently live in Argentina. Its population is concentrated rather than evenly spread across the country's different geographic regions. According to the most recent census, over 13.5 million live in Greater Buenos Aires. Over 10 million more live in the Pampa region. As a result, two out of three Argentines live in less than 30 percent of the country's geographic area. Ninety-two percent of the population resides in urban, rather than rural, areas. The largest cities are the Federal District, also known as the city of Buenos Aires (population 3 million), Córdoba (population 1.3 million), and Rosario (population 1.2). Mendoza, the capital of Mendoza Province, is the largest city outside the Pampa region. An estimated 917,000 people live within its city limits, and over 1 million live in the wider urban and suburban area. Despite government efforts since the 1980s to promote settlement in remote regions, Patagonia remains sparsely populated: An estimated 1.5 million people reside there.

Native American peoples lived throughout what became Argentina before the arrival of the first European settlers in the sixteenth century. In the north, Spanish settlers mixed with the locals. Warfare, the spread of European disease, the disruption of community life, and the recruitment of laborers for work in mines and haciendas beyond Argentina reduced the Native American population in other parts of Argentina. As a result, few descendants from the original Argentine population remain.

Immigration during the period 1860–1930 had a profound impact on the country. After military campaigns all but eliminated Native American settlements in the center and southern regions, Argentina began to grow rapidly as a result of immigration from Europe. Although more immigrants traveled to the United States during this period of rapid demographic growth, in Argentina immigration had a relatively greater impact. During the period 1860–1910, over 3 million European immigrants came to Argentina. According to the national census of 1914, 30 percent of the country's residents were born elsewhere.

Roughly 70 percent of the European immigrants who came to Argentina settled in the Federal Capital, in Greater Buenos Aires, or in the ranching and farming districts of the Pampa. Argentina attracted other immigrants from neighboring countries during the same period. Their presence was especially clear in the country's northern provinces: 70 percent of Formosa's population in 1914 was born in Paraguay; in the same year, Brazilians and Paraguayans accounted for 40 percent of the population of Misiones.

Despite waves of immigration from neighboring countries, Argentines overwhelmingly identify themselves as ethnically European. Most recent statistics report 97 percent of Argentines identifying themselves as "white." The remainder identify themselves as "Amerindian," "mestizo"—a mix of white and Amerindian—or nonwhite.

GOVERNMENT AND POLITICS

After officially declaring its independence in 1816, Argentina has shifted between periods of constitutional rule and dictatorship. Since the end of the most recent military dictatorship in 1983, the country has operated under a system of representative government. The current national constitution, which dates from 1853, underwent significant amendment in 1994. Under the reigning constitutional decrees, the national government is a mixture of European and American models. It has three branches: executive, legislative, and judicial. The president, who is elected directly by popular vote, controls the executive branch. Along with an elected vice president, the executive leadership serves for a term of four years. Presidents may stand for reelection. They may not serve more than two consecutive terms.

A bicameral legislature, modeled along European lines, shares authority with the president. The national Senate (*Cámara de Senadores*) has 72 members: Each of Argentina's 23 provinces and the Federal District control three seats. Two senators from each province or district represent the majority party. The third represents the party that captured the second-highest number of votes in the deciding election. Before the 1994 amendment to the constitution, senators were selected indirectly, by state and district legislatures. Under the revised constitution, they are now selected by popular vote. One-third of the Senate's seats are open for election every two years.

The Chamber of Deputies (*Cámara de Diputados*) has 257 seats, with each seat representing an equal number of citizens. The deputies represent districts of the whole from the different provinces or the Federal District. Seats are awarded in accordance with the percentage of the popular vote that each party captures. The deputies serve terms of four years.

The provincial governments operate independently from the national government. State constitutions regulate the operation of the representative bodies and executive branches of the provinces. Although Argentina has a variety of political parties, with coalitions that represent various ideological factions forming and disbanding after each election, in practice the political system has circled around a single, ruling party. The Justicialist Party, better known as the Peronist Party, has in recent decades been Argentina's dominant political force. Factions within Peronism range from ultraconservative blocs led by veteran politicians to left-wing activists who identify with the party's attempt to make workers and the poor an effective political force. Its origins date to the campaign that elected Juan Domingo Perón to the presidency in 1946.

With strong ties to organized labor and effective precinct and neighborhood committees that help maintain popular support, it survived decades of military repression. It has recovered its strength since Perón's death in 1973. Under the leadership of Carlos Saúl Menem, the Peronists captured the presidency and majority control of the Senate and the Chamber of Deputies in 1989.

Néstor Kirchner and his wife and ally Cristina Fernández de Kirchner established a new, more progressive wing of the party in the wake of his election to the presidency in 2003. In 2005, the pro-Kirchner *Frente para la* Victoria (Front for Victory or FPV) established itself as the dominant Peronist faction with its electoral success in that year's congressional elections. Néstor Kirchner's death in 2010 left President Fernández de Kirchner, reelected to a second term in 2011, in charge of the FPV.

The *Unión Cívica Radical* (Radical Party or UCR) made its first appearance as a protest group in 1890. By 1912, it developed into a mass-based national party. Although observers regard it as a moderate party, like Peronism it has important factions that range from the right to left in ideological terms. With the election of Raúl Alfonsín as president in 1983, the Radical Party led Argentina's most recent transition from military rule to representative government. While still a leading party in Córdoba and in the Federal District, factions within the Justicialist Party represent more formidable challenges to the Peronist FPV faction that currently controls the national government.

A number of other parties compete for support on the left and right wings of the political spectrum. Most are limited to effective provincial or urban bases and have little significant impact on national electoral contests. Alliances with or against Peronist candidates have allowed many to play important roles in both congressional and presidential elections.

Citizens 18 years and older are required to vote. Recent elections have been marked by a large percentage of blank ballots turned in by voters who voted for none of the listed candidates.

FOREIGN RELATIONS

Argentina's leaders first asserted an ambition to be regional leaders in 1806, when a citizen militia defeated a British force that hoped to separate the territory from Spanish authority. Four years later, the *cabildo* (city council) of Buenos Aires promoted moves toward independence.

In 1817, Argentine forces helped liberate Chile from Spanish occupation and then, in 1821, brought independence to Lima, the capital of Spain's South American colonies.

Argentina's international ambitions have led to tense relations with its neighbors. During the Independence era (1810–1825), the rebels in Buenos Aires fought wars with rivals in Paraguay, Uruguay, and Bolivia. Argentine defeats led to the separation of these territories into independent states after the war against Spain ended.

The War of the Triple Alliance (1865–1870) helped establish clear frontiers between the countries of South America's Southern Cone. From this point forward, efforts to extend Argentine territory at the expense of its neighbors ended.

In its place, Argentine diplomats pushed to make their country a respected leader in the Western Hemisphere. As early as 1823, in reaction to the declaration of the Monroe Doctrine in Washington, D.C., Argentina tried to organize Latin American resistance to the power and authority of the United States.

In 1912, Argentine leaders formed the ABC Bloc with Brazil and Chile. By combining the diplomatic resources of the three countries, the bloc served as an arbitrator of regional disputes through the 1930s.

Although the country was represented in the Pan-American Union and, intermittently, in the League of Nations, Argentina's Foreign Ministry continued to pursue goals of national and international interest independently. Along these lines, the efforts of diplomat Carlos Saavedra Lamas to negotiate an end to the Chaco War resulted in his winning the Nobel Peace Prize in 1936.

Argentina traditionally maintained neutrality during times of war. During World War I (1914–1918), Argentina refused to ally with Great Britain, which at the time was its key economic partner. During World War II, the government remained neutral until it joined the Allied Powers in 1945.

The failed attempt in 1982 to seize the Falkland Islands, which led to a disastrous war with Great Britain, forced a dramatic change in the country's foreign relations. In recent years, the Argentine government has altered its traditionally independent international stance. As the twentieth century ended, its government strengthened diplomatic and military ties with Europe and the United States. In 1991, Argentine naval vessels participated in the U.S.-led effort to force Iraq from Kuwait. Argentina has become more active in the United Nations, the Organization of American States, and other international bodies. It has signed a number of new bilateral and multilateral trade agreements: The 1995 creation of the *Mercado Común del Sur* (Common Market of the South, or MERCOSUR), which united the economies of Argentina, Uruguay, Paraguay, and Brazil, stands as the most important. MERCOSUR has served as the basis for further integration of South America's national economies. Side-agreements have promoted expanded trade with the Andean Bloc and Chile. In 2012, Venezuela became a full MERCOSUR member. Bolivia applied to join as well: As of July 2014, two of the five member states—Uruguay and Venezuela—have approved Bolivia's membership; the application remains in process in Argentina, Brazil, and Paraguay.

Argentine leaders will, however, evoke nationalist themes that run against the more open and multilateral trends when they wish to build popular support. Most recently, in 2011 and 2013, President Cristina Fernández de Kirchner has revived the country's claims over the Falkland—or Malvinas—Islands.

ECONOMIC CONDITIONS

Argentina has an estimated 17.32 million people in its active urban labor force. Agricultural operations, which employ approximately 5 percent of workforce, add thousands more to the total. Because many rural workers move seasonally from rural to urban jobs, the government does not include them in the official estimates.

The majority of Argentine workers, approximately 72 percent, are employed in service industries. Only 23 percent find employment in the country's industrial sector. While the country does have some elements of heavy industry, protected by government subsidies or price protections in decades past, most of the country's factories produce consumer products for the domestic or the South American market. Competition from Brazil has in recent years intensified the pressure on Argentine producers. In turn, economic conditions have worked against innovation and investment.

Farming and ranching remain leading industries in Argentina. The rural sector provides the majority of exports, in terms of volume and value, and, as a result, the majority of the foreign exchange that helps Argentina fund government operations. Rural activities also support major parts of the service sector. Consequently, what nineteenth-century policymakers labeled as the country's "mother industries" remain crucial.

Soybeans, sunflower seeds, corn, and wheat represent the country's most important crops. Ranching was one of the first activities to develop in colonial Argentina. During the nineteenth century, it became an important export industry when refrigerated ships made it possible to sell beef from the Pampas in the markets of Europe. After World War II, the country's expanding urban population consumed an increasing share of the country's annual meat production. In recent years, Argentine ranchers have modernized their operations and their production methods to keep them competitive with the world's best.

Other important agricultural industries include wineries, cotton, sugar, and tea. Mendoza Province is the center of the country's wine industry. With wineries that date from the colonial period, family operations and large-scale companies produce high-quality wine for the domestic and international markets.

Argentina's cotton and sugar production is concentrated in the northwest and northeast. The plantations that produce cotton and sugar first developed centuries ago in the one part of colonial Argentina that had a large labor force. These plantations serve as the economic foundation of powerful families. Their inefficient operations have continued in recent decades thanks to tariff protections. As import restrictions fall in the coming years, sugar and cotton production may decline.

In the northeast, tea plantations produce mainly for the domestic market. Fruit production for the domestic market developed along the Paraná River after World War I. Irrigation projects in northern Patagonia have also led to the expansion of orchards in Río Negro.

With the support of foreign investments, mining operations have expanded dramatically. Beginning in the 1990s, new legislation and policy changes encouraged local and international companies interested in the country's potential. Exploration for mineral deposits has expanded. While foreign investment in the sector slowed during the global recession of 2007, the number of companies, the amount invested, and mining output have expanded in recent years. Argentina is the world's third most important producer of boron, and the country also has significant deposits of tin, tungsten, and cement. It also produces small amounts of the iron ore, gold, silver, lead, uranium, and zinc within its borders.

Argentina has deposits of petroleum and natural gas, which are dedicated to meeting domestic energy needs. The government took charge of the petroleum industry after World War I, and for decades it monopolized oil and gas production and distribution. Government initiatives that led to the partial sale of the public-owned oil and gasoline company *Yacimientos Petrolíferos Fiscales* spurred investment, the search for new oil and gas fields, and the expansion of oil and gas production after 1993. Output peaked in 1998. The discovery of new shale oil fields may encourage a new period of expansion.

Since it gained independence and organized its first modern export industries in the late nineteenth century, the country has faced dramatic economic shifts driven largely by external factors.

In 1990, Argentina faced a massive foreign debt and currency instability. Monetary inflation soared: Peak inflation rates passed 200 percent per month. Investment capital abandoned the country. Falling tax and tariff revenues undermined the government's budget.

Drastic reforms took place beginning in 1991. The government issued a new currency and tied its value to the U.S. dollar. Privatization of government-owned or -controlled industries, utilities, and services followed. Liberalized trade policies opened the national market to imports and investments. Trade agreements with Latin American and European countries encouraged exports. Banking and additional monetary reforms promoted the expansion of domestic business and industries.

By 1996, the government's drastic actions reduced inflation. The cost, however, came in the form of high unemployment. Privatization led to factory closures and reduced payrolls. The positive effect of the policy changes dissipated as the decade closed. By 1999, Argentina faced another recession. In 2002, the crisis hit its lowest point. Official estimates reported over 60 percent of the population as living in poverty.

A change of governments brought a reversal of policies. Aided by improved economic conditions and the renegotiation of its foreign debt obligations, Argentine planners channeled public funds into a range of promotional programs. The economy rebounded and continued to grow rapidly for five years. Unemployment eased, exports—especially to Brazil and China—expanded, and the government moved to retake control of key businesses and industries that it identified as essential to the people's interests.

In 2009, Argentina appeared largely unaffected by the severe recession that then challenged Europe and the United States. As growth in China and Brazil slowed and demand for imports weakened, Argentina's economy again moved from boom to stagnation. Since the end of the nineteenth century, when wheat farming and cattle ranching funded a veneer of progress in and near Buenos Aires, its economic fortunes remain closely tied to its traditional foundation: agricultural exports.

CULTURE

Over 92 percent of Argentines are members of the Roman Catholic Church. The selection of Jorge Mario Bergoglio, the archbishop of metropolitan Buenos Aires and cardinal, as pope in 2013, has made the church even more popular. The Church's dominance is a product of the importance of Catholicism to the Spanish settlers of the colonial era and the decision by nineteenth-century leaders to preserve Catholicism as the official religion of the nation.

During the late nineteenth and early twentieth centuries immigration brought Jewish and Muslim settlers who formed small but notable communities throughout the country. Missionaries from Europe and the United States have in recent decades produced a small expansion of Protestant, Mormon, and Pentecostal faiths.

The stark division between urban and rural areas remains distinctive. Domingo Faustino Sarmiento (1811–1888) in his most influential essays defined Argentina as divided in two, with the civilized "city" at one pole and the "barbarous" wilderness of the interior at the other. Since Sarmiento's time the capital city of Buenos Aires has been Argentina's cultural center. Its neighborhoods and architecture reflect the changes that have taken place over the centuries.

Thousands gather at the Basilica of Luján during Pope John Paul II's visit to the Argentine city on June 11, 1982. (AP Photo/Mark Foley)

In its central plazas, the Town Hall and the *Casa Rosada* ("Pink House," which reflects a blend of the colors of political factions—white and red—from the Independence era) represent the generations of change from colony to republic. The neighborhood of *La Boca*, which once was home to the transient immigrant population of the nineteenth century that came to Buenos Aires in search of opportunity, retains houses and streets that reflect its distinctive past. The Teatro Colón, the city's opera house built in 1907, and the Avenida Nueve de Julio, built wider than the Champs Elysee in Paris, physically represent the era when the country's first export boom fueled expectations of great progress. Subways, commuter rail lines, and thousands of buses transport commuters between the city's center and outlying districts. The contrast between the modern office buildings and stores of the city's financial district with the *villas miserias* (shantytowns) of the poor symbolize the mixed impact of the political and economic turmoil of recent decades.

Before the rise of military dictatorships after 1955, Argentina played a leading role in Latin American arts and letters. Sarmiento, Estebán Echeverría (1805–1851), and other writers from the "Generation of 1837" brought international acclaim to Argentina. In the twentieth century, the complex and challenging fiction of Jorge Luis Borges (1899–1986) inspired generations of writers throughout the world. Argentina's strong public education system produced a population with one of the highest literacy rates in Latin America. Official estimates state that almost 98 percent of the population 10 years or older are literate. The country's newspapers and publishing houses were influential throughout the region. While public education at all levels suffered under the military dictatorships of the 1970s and 1980s, and recessions have made public funding less secure, Argentina still possesses one of the world's best educational systems. Enrollments and persistence rates have increased since 2003. In turn, the number of private schools, colleges, and universities has increased in recent decades.

People outside Argentina are most familiar with two cultural artifacts: the tango and the gaucho. The tango, a severe but strangely romantic dance, first appeared in the bars of Argentina's port cities during the closing decades of the nineteenth century. At first a dance for men, the tango changed significantly as the years passed. When it became stylish in Paris during the first decades of the twentieth century, it emerged as Argentina's national dance. Carlos Gardel, through radio broadcasts and motion pictures, helped popularize tango songs during the 1930s. Tango music and lyrics evolved to match the increasingly complex patterns of the dance. Traditional dance clubs, more popular with the old than the young, still maintain the tango's traditions.

The gaucho, Argentina's cowboy, appeared first in the colonial era to serve the labor demands of colonial ranches. As the country's towns grew into cities, the gauchos lived their lives on the plains. During the wars of Independence and national consolidation, gauchos served as mounted cavalry troops on all sides.

While scholars continue to debate their origins and influence, the gaucho symbolizes both the country's debt to ranching and a lost rural past. It is the gaucho of José Hernández's epic poem, *Martín Fierro* (1872), who laments the loss of valued traditions in the rapidly changing country.

If Argentines have a sole passion, it would be *fútbol* (soccer). Argentine soccer teams have been a major force in World Cup competitions. Individual players, including Diego Maradona and Lionel Messi, are among the world's best. The national team has won the World Cup twice, with their last championship claimed in Mexico City during the 1986 tournament. Most recently, the *selección* finished second to Germany in 2014. The matches involving teams of the First Division draw millions of spectators and dominate the weekends of many Argentines as the season progresses.

Cable television, the presence of foreign films, the appearance of multinational companies and enterprises, and the Internet have connected Argentina with an increasingly global culture. As a result, Argentine youth in particular have tastes in common with their American and European peers. Yet Argentina's past still lingers, especially in historic urban districts and in the towns of interior provinces.

2

The Colonial Era
(to 1800)

From its beginnings, Argentina's environmental and geographical diversity supported a wide range of human settlements. When the Spanish arrived there during the opening decades of the sixteenth century, existing conditions created significant challenges that the Spanish settlers struggled to overcome. Throughout most of the colonial era, Argentina survived as an appendage: Its small settlements depended upon support from core areas in the central Andes or from Spain itself. Shaped by international political and economic events, as well as through the initiatives of generations of settlers, the future of Argentina took shape. By the end of the colonial era, Buenos Aires emerged as the political and economic core of the territory.

AMERICAN ORIGINS

As occurred in the rest of South America, evidence suggests that the first human settlements appeared in what is today Argentina between 15,000 and 10,000 B.C.E. Sometime after 5,000 B.C.E., the first settlements that supported themselves through farming or herding appeared. The region's most densely populated communities were located in the northeast and the northwest. Although archeological research has added much information in recent years, the peoples about whom researchers know the most are those who had established themselves within 1,000 years of the arrival of the first Europeans. In the Mesopotamian region of northeastern Argentina, communities linked by a common language had established small agricultural communities over a broad area. Using *swidden,* or "slash and burn" farming techniques, Guaraní settlements lived a semi-sedentary existence: To clear an area for settlement and planting, Guaraní farmers would set fires that cleared the area of foliage. When the land showed signs of overuse, the community would move to another unoccupied site.

The Guaraní lived in villages made up of several large dwellings. These dwellings, called *malocas,* housed a number of families who followed the lead of a male chief. Each village had several houses. By the arrival of the first Europeans in the region, Guaraní settlements had spread from Paraguay and southern Brazil along the river basins south to the end of the Paraná River.

A number of distinct cultures had established sedentary communities in the northwest. Between 500 and 850 C.E., trade connected distinct societies that lived in the Andean highlands, the sub-Andean valleys and plains, the Chaco region, and southwest to the Cordoba hills. Around 1480, Inca armies conquered the Argentine northwest and integrated the residents there into their empire. Collectively called the Diaguitas, the conquered provided labor and resources for the Inca Empire.

To the south, in the Cuyo region, Huarpe villages developed from 500 C.E. Smaller in cale than the Diaguita communities, the population of Huarpe villages ranged from 50 to 100 residents. They supported themselves by growing corn, squash, beans, and quinoa, and they herded llamas. Although the Huarpes were not formally incorporated into the Inca Empire, the expansion of llama herding and the spread of the Quecha language after 1480 suggests that the Huarpe people were strongly influenced by the Inca presence to the north.

Nomadic peoples settled the remainder of Argentina. The Charrúa occupied Uruguay; the Querendí and the Serranos lived in eastern Buenos Aires; the Pampa roamed across the central plains; and the Tehuelche controlled the vast territory that stretched from Río Negro south across Patagonia.

Although these peoples were linguistically and culturally distinct, the characteristics of the regions in which they lived created similarities that spanned communities: They relied on hunting and gathering, as well as trade, to support their populations. Ongoing archeological investigations are finding linkages between these nomadic groups and other societies in cultural and material terms. For historians, the lack of written records imposes significant limitations. Knowledge of the political, social, and material history of these diverse peoples remains fragmented.

SPANISH EXPLORATION AND SETTLEMENT (1492–1596)

In the Pampa that would one day become the agricultural core of the country, nomadic peoples sparsely populated the vast plains. The patterns of human settlement would place important limits upon the efforts of Spanish explorers who visited Argentina for the first time in 1516.

More than two decades after Columbus's first expedition, Spain's rulers recognized that the American territories being charted and claimed by its agents were part of a new and unknown region. The motivations that drove Spaniards to risk expeditions across the Atlantic varied. The Crown was in the midst of two grand contests. It commanded a developing mercantile empire. The successful extension of Spanish authority over new territories would yield valuable assets: natural resources, such as minerals or commercial crops, and the labor necessary to extract and export such resources to Spain.

Spain was also interested in spreading its culture and, in particular, its religion to the peoples of the New World. These aims would grow in importance as the religious strife produced by competition with Islam and, later, through the Protestant Reformation grew in intensity during the sixteenth century.

For the individuals who carried into American territories the causes Spain defined and defended, material concerns mattered most, especially during the generation of initial contact, exploration, and subjugation of American lands and peoples between 1492 and 1525. In particular, the successful defeat of the Mexica and Inca Empires set precedents for all other expeditions. The communities and resources that these conquests added to the Spanish Empire impressed the Crown and earned titles and rewards for the surviving conquerors.

Because of the inherent risks and the expense of mounting expeditions to the Americas, the Crown put individuals in charge of separate expeditions. Although the royal government's authority and material investments helped start expeditions, each *adelantado*, as the commander of an expedition was known, had to recruit men and gather material largely on his own. This meant that new territories were often explored, claimed, and initially settled by a variety of expeditions with competing claims and ambitions.

The Spanish colonial enterprise also depended upon the labor of subjugated Americans. Few Spaniards traveled with each expedition. Successful settlement, colonial organization, and exploitation of a region required indigenous labor. As a consequence, until the 1700s, colonial settlers and administrators concentrated their efforts upon the most densely populated areas. The regions that had become the cores of pre-Columbian empires became the capitals of Spanish America. Areas that lacked large cities that provided the human capital to support Spain's ambitions languished.

The first Spanish expedition to Argentina came with grand ambitions. Under the leadership of Juan Díaz de Solís, an expedition of three ships left Spain in 1515 in search of a southern passage to the Pacific. After sailing along the coast of Portuguese Brazil, Solís diverted his ships into a large estuary on January 20, 1516. The explorers documented the find and established a Spanish claim to the region. In an attempt to treat with local leaders, however, Solís and a small band of his men died after being captured. The expedition ended in failure.

Rivalry with the Portuguese, who had claimed rights to Brazil, combined with the defeat of the Inca Empire in 1532, encouraged a second expedition. Pedro de Mendoza, who commanded a group of 1,500, arrived in Argentina in 1536. He founded a settlement on the southwestern bank of the estuary, which had been named "River of Silver" (*Río de la Plata,* or River Plate). The new town, which Spanish officials hoped to use as a base for the exploration of the region, was named Nuestra Señora Santa María del Buen Aire.

The Native Americans already established in the region aggressively resisted Spain's efforts to settle the region. Familiar with horses and Spanish battle tactics as a result of previous contacts, warriors of the Querandí people launched effective attacks against the settlement and any exploration parties that Governor Mendoza authorized. The settlers' failure to incorporate the locals into their colonial system reduced them to desperate conditions. Short of food and other essential supplies, Mendoza ordered the settlement abandoned in 1537. A group of survivors traveled north along the Paraná River. While the expedition's leaders, who believed greater glory awaited them, pushed to continue their explorations, many members of the expedition broke rank. They were relieved to find hospitality among Guaraní villages in the area that became Paraguay. These settlers, who intermingled with the Guaraní, founded the city of Asunción.

As knowledge of the Americas increased, areas such as the Río de la Plata offered little attraction for Spanish authorities. Further exploration and settlement efforts in Argentina developed from bases in the central Andes. Bands of Spanish *conquistadores* (literally "conquerors") moved south from the heart of the defeated Inca Empire or east from the Chilean frontier. They founded settlements that grew into Argentina's oldest cities: Santiago del Estero in 1553; Mendoza, 1561; San Juan, 1562; San Miguel de Tucumán, 1565; Córdoba, 1573; Salta, 1582; La Rioja, 1591; Jujuy, 1592; and San Luis, 1596.

FROM SETTLEMENTS TO COMMUNITIES (1540–1720)

Asunción in the years after its incorporation into the Spanish Empire differed dramatically from the desperate conditions that the men under the command of Pedro Mendoza found to the south. The first Spaniards to enter what would become Paraguay were treated well by the local Guaraní peoples. The village chiefs offered the newcomers ample food and gifts. By mixing with the locals, and in later years by marrying into the village elites, the Spaniards and their descendants took command of the communities and directed their operation in a manner that developed in a pattern distinct to that of the rest of Spanish America. Although far removed from the core of the Spanish Empire, and as a consequence of that distance soon isolated as mining operations led to a shift of attention toward Upper Perú, Asunción and the communities near it that were brought under Spanish control provided supplies that allowed the successful resettlement of Buenos Aires.

The communities that had become satellites of the Inca Empire in the Argentine northwest appeared to be suitable bases for the development of mercantile activities. Spanish authorities took charge of the labor resources of the communities that they conquered and directed the labor toward work that would benefit the goals of the Crown and of Crown officials. In Paraguay, the Spanish imposed the *encomienda* system, under which the Crown granted communities to individual Spaniards, who took them as their "charges." According to Spanish regulations, the individual granted the *encomienda*, known as the *encomendero*, became responsible for the protection of the communities granted. One of the *encomenderos*' main responsibilities was to supervise the religious training of the Americans. For taking on this and other responsibilities, the Crown granted the *encomenderos* the right to use the labor of the community for their own benefit.

The rapid decline of the American communities, which suffered catastrophic population losses as a result of Spanish exploitation and the exposure to new diseases that Europeans introduced into the Americas, led to the collapse of the *encomienda* system in most of Spanish America after 1550. In Paraguay, however, the small number of Spaniards, the manner in which the Spaniards were integrated into the Guaraní communities, and the relatively bountiful material conditions of the region allowed most communities to survive and adjust to the demands of the new order. Isolated from Spanish supervision and with ample labor resources to meet the needs of the Spanish elite, the *encomienda* system continued there for generations after it had disappeared elsewhere.

In Tucumán and in other districts surrounding it, the *encomienda* system developed, but in larger communities Spanish authorities relied on a different way of exploiting Native American labor. Viceroys in Lima had successfully undermined the efforts of *encomenderos* in Peru to make *encomiendas* inheritable properties. The viceroys also realized that the Inca system of labor organization, known as the *mita*, served the needs of the Crown well without overtaxing the labor resources of Andean communities. As a result, Spanish authorities exploited the communities under their charge using the *mita,* which in the Spanish colonial era operated as a turn-labor system similar to those that existed in parts of medieval Europe: Colonial authorities demanded from specified communities a set number of days of labor from a percentage of the adult male residents. The labor "turns" were rotated. In theory, this prevented any one community from being overworked and left without sufficient manpower to perform the agricultural and material tasks that guaranteed a community's survival.

Despite regulations, abuses occurred regularly. Although the number of Spaniards in all Argentina did not surpass 2,000 in 1570, the labor demands made by individual Spaniards disrupted most communities. Population registers, though not rigorously compiled, recorded a rapid population decline—90 percent or more in three or four generations—that in some areas led to the annihilation of entire villages. Consequently, by the end of the sixteenth and the start of the seventeenth centuries, both the *encomienda* system and the turn-labor practices similar to the *mita* went into decline in the northwestern Argentina.

The drop in population forced the Spaniards to try alternative labor schemes. Spaniards purchased slaves, both Native Americans, who were referred to as *yanaconas,* and Africans, the first of whom arrived in 1580. However, the relatively small scale of the mercantile operations and the meager markets that existed for their products discouraged widespread use of slaves. Cotton production, which had a promising beginning in the Tucumán and Salta, stagnated as a result of the lack of dyes and the competition presented by Andean communities to the north. The discovery of gold deposits in the Cuyo region produced few returns. By the 1600s, the Spanish settlements in Argentina's colonial west and northwest focused on the production of livestock and agricultural products for local use or for sale to neighboring colonies to the north.

The Spaniards regarded the diffusion and promotion of Roman Catholicism as one of their primary imperial tasks. With the Protestant Reformation in Europe and the military challenge of Islam threatening the Church's existence, the conversion of souls was a task that Crown officials took seriously.

Although the Spanish monarchs had received, by Papal decree in 1497, the right to supervise the operations of the lay and regular clergy in its realm, support of the Church's efforts to convert the Americas varied over time and place. In Argentina, Church officials arrived decades after the first explorers. Asunción became the territory's first bishopric in 1547. The town's first bishop did not arrive, however, until 1556. The sparse numbers of regular clergy left the promotion of Catholicism mainly to the lay clergy: the Dominicans, the Franciscans, and the Jesuits. The region's isolation made it difficult to fill clerical positions in the Spanish communities. As a consequence, well into the colonial era, the Church had less influence in Argentina than elsewhere.

The Jesuits, who arrived in the region in the 1580s, established missions in communities that were removed from the Spanish settlements. In their missions in the Mesopotamian and Andean regions of the colony, the Jesuits recruited labor, introduced their charges to Catholicism, and developed the production of merchandise for local and international sale.

Among the Guaraní, the Jesuits built their first mission in 1609. The Jesuits' aimed to make each mission not only self-supporting but also profitable: Ideally, each operation would generate revenue for the support of Jesuit operations in other parts of the world.

In their first decades of operation, slave-raiding expeditions from Portuguese Brazil posed a major threat. By 1630, attacks from Brazil had destroyed almost all the missions in operation. Jesuit leaders quickly rebuilt and expanded their missions, however, and funded a military defensive force to protect their sites from future attacks. Their operations were significant. Removed from most colonial restrictions and supervisions over their economic activities, especially before 1648, when for the first time Crown officials required the missionaries to pay tribute and other taxes, the Jesuits frequently violated colonial trading policies. They helped establish economic links between Argentina and Portuguese Brazil and also helped develop lucrative agricultural industries, such as tobacco production, that would provide a base for future expansion.

After 1620, conditions in Europe and in the core areas of Spanish South America created problems for the Spanish cities and settlements of Argentina. The costs of war and imperial ambition undermined the Spanish economy. As a result, the number of ships traveling from Spain to the American colonies declined. Within the colonies, the impact of the encounter between the worlds of Europe and the Americas reached its height. The disruption of indigenous communities and the disease-induced decline of the Native American population threatened the operations of Spanish mining and mercantile industries.

Although economic contraction appears to have been less dramatic in Argentina, problems in other parts of Spanish America had a negative effect on much of the country. In the northwest, demographic shifts and economic stagnation divided the small communities established there. Tensions led to warfare between Spaniards and Native Americans. The most serious encounter involved the Diaguitas in the Calchaquí Valley. Between 1630 and 1637, battles between the two communities intensified. The warfare ended when the Spaniards prevented the Diaguitas from sowing crops. Aimed at forcing the Diaguitas to accept Spanish authority, this action resulted in famine, disease, and the collapse of village after village as entire populations died off.

The conflicts with the Native Americans continued in Tucumán and Cuyo into the 1700s. The turmoil robbed the Spanish towns of their labor force. Although the local economies slowly found partial replacements for the loss of *encomienda* and *mita* labor pools by using slaves or wage workers, the tight labor supply limited the mercantile ambitions of the town leaders.

The strength of the Jesuit missions insulated the Mesopotamian region from a similar crisis, but the contraction of the colonial economy reduced the markets for local produce. Nevertheless, mission populations grew and the economic and cultural influence of the Jesuits increased. Yerba mate and tobacco produced on mission lands found markets in Brazil and Buenos Aires. Jesuit brothers became leading figures in the schools they helped establish in Córdoba and Buenos Aires. As confessors and as educators, Jesuits developed strong connections with the colony's elite.

The Jesuits' success generated resentment in the Spanish towns of Asunción and Corrientes. Beginning in the 1720s, the people who competed with the Jesuits for land, labor, and a share of the limited colonial markets engaged in violent protests. Labeled the *Comunero* Revolt (literally "Commoner," the rebels took the name of Spanish protesters who challenged royal authority in the early sixteenth century), the protests led to attacks against the Jesuit missions. Although the missions continued in operation, the revolts contributed to the mission's slow contraction in the decades that followed.

THE GROWTH OF BUENOS AIRES (1580–1760)

For strategic reasons connected with lingering concerns over Portuguese ambitions in the region, the Spanish Crown authorized a second attempt to create settlements in eastern Argentina. Expeditions from the town of Asunción traveled south along the Paraná River. Beginning in 1573, with the creation of Santa Fe, the Spanish established a series of new towns. Their efforts ended in 1580 with the construction of a fort near the site that Pedro Mendoza had selected decades before. Better supplied and defended, this site grew into the city of Buenos Aires.

The city's second founding did not begin in a promising fashion. The Europeans and the *criollos*—the American-born descendants of Europeans—found few Native Americans who they could organize into a labor force. Asunción, Santa Fe, and Córdoba provided essential supplies to support the settlement as it slowly grew, but hopes of developing local industries that would attract additional settlers and expanded support from Spain initially fell short.

Cattle ranching served as the settlement's first industry. The small number of cattle and the horses that the Mendoza expedition left behind when it abandoned the first site had multiplied into thousands. The animals thrived on the pampa: There were few predators, and the relatively mild climate and native grasses and plants supported large herds. Initially, the residence of Buenos Aires faced a number of difficulties in their efforts to turn the herds into profitable merchandise. Without sufficient Native American laborers, the *rodeos* (round-ups) of the cattle were difficult to organize with frequency. Lack of labor also slowed efforts to produce hides, tallow, and other products for sale within the colonial system. Equally important, the settlement's merchants found few takers of their produce within the Spanish colonial economy. Places where the cattle products would be in demand, such as Potosí or Lima, were far removed. Transportation costs, as well as competition from producers whose ranches were located closer to the colonial markets, limited opportunities.

Colonial regulations, established in the sixteenth century, required the settlers in Buenos Aires to export their goods through Lima, the vice

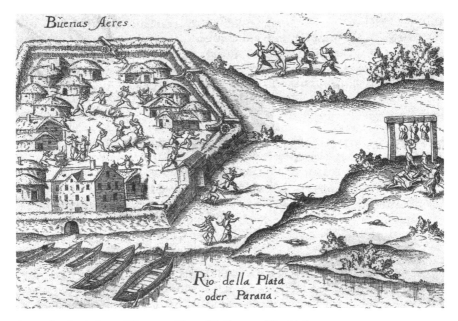

An early depiction of Buenos Aires. (Bettmann/Corbis)

regal capital. By limiting the sites where producers could market their goods, the Crown hoped to control the colonial economy, prevent the development of activities that would compete with Spanish industries, and draw out the maximum amount of taxes. The system benefited those at its core: the bureaucrats and merchants of Lima. It discouraged economic expansion in areas removed from the colonial capital.

Whereas legal mercantile promotions got off to a slow start, an illegal trade that sent silver from the mines of Upper Perú to Portuguese merchants operating in and near Buenos Aires expanded rapidly. The Portuguese merchants, a small but wealthy minority in Buenos Aires, focused on exchanging illegal imports of manufactured goods for silver. The ability of the Portuguese to supply Buenos Aires with the imports that were otherwise too expensive or simply not available through the legally sanctioned Spanish colonial system led the *porteños*, as the residents of Buenos Aires came to be known, to tolerate the foreign traders.

The port was not immune from the economic problems that plagued Spain and Spanish America during the seventeen century. Although it had developed in part independently from the legal trading system, Buenos Aires was affected by the general economic depression. During this era, fewer ships docked there, and less silver was available for trade. The settlement's strategic value, however, and the vice regal government's fears of foreign attack provided some stimulus: Soldiers stationed there during the 1600s bolstered the European population, and subsidies from Lima supported the city's administration. Further expansion through the promotion of new industries and trade links helped Buenos Aires grow. As Spain passed through generations of political ineptitude and economic crises, changes in the Río de la Plata region and in the wider Atlantic world encouraged the independent expansion of Buenos Aires.

A series of factors helped Buenos Aires. First, in contrast to the Spanish Crown, the Portuguese promoted the development of its Brazilian colony in the late 1600s. Portuguese interest in the products that merchants offered in Buenos Aires encouraged trade. In 1680, with the establishment of Colônia do Sacramento as their mercantile base in the *Banda Oriental* (East Bank), as Uruguay was then known, Portuguese activity in the area increased. In reaction, Spain reinforced Buenos Aires.

Fears of Portuguese competition in Buenos Aires, combined with Jesuit worries over a possible renewal of slave raids from Brazil, led to conflict. The Jesuits combined their forces with those of the governor of Buenos Aires to attack Colônia do Sacramento.

The forced closure of the new Portuguese town was only temporary. Threatened with war in Iberia, the Spanish Crown evacuated its forces from Uruguay. Portuguese colonists rebuilt the town, and by 1683 it continued to be an active center for contraband trade. Although Colônia and other port towns and cities on the Río de la Plata and the Paraná River provided some competition, the disruption of trade in the Banda Oriental helped Spanish and foreign merchants assert their control of foreign trade in the region.

In response to protests from merchants in Lima, and with the hope of regaining control of the regional economy, Spanish officials tried to eliminate the trading of silver through Buenos Aires: In 1622, the Crown created the *Aduana Seca* (literally "Dry Customs-House," a customs office that supervises overland trade and travel), which made the transport of silver to Buenos Aires illegal. This restriction on silver shipment and trade aimed at forcing the merchants of Córdoba and other interior cities to trade exclusively with Lima-based partners. Instead, foreign merchants ignored the Crown-imposed restrictions, and their success in selling their products in Buenos Aires encouraged Spanish colonists to violate the new regulations. Lacking a sufficient number of inspectors and unable to provide a competitive source of mercantile goods, the Crown's actions did little to stem illegal trade in the Río de la Plata region.

The significance of foreign trade and merchants in Buenos Aires grew in the eighteenth century. Slave ships brought increasing numbers of captured Africans to Buenos Aires. The slave trade soon grew into a major part of the region's mercantile economy. In 1702, the Spanish Crown granted the *asiento* (treaty) to Great Britain. This agreement made British merchants and ships the sole provider of slaves for the Spanish colonies in the Americas. Treaty regulations opened certain Spanish American ports, including Buenos Aires, to ships sailing under contract with the British. The city's merchants expanded their operations to accommodate the sale and transfer of slaves to the interior regions of Spanish South America. Most of the slaves brought to Argentina were shipped outside of the colony. Those who remained in the viceroyalty were usually put to work in the urban centers. By the closing decades of the colonial era, slaves and free blacks accounted for 25 to 30 percent of the population in Buenos Aires, Mendoza, Tucumán, and other cities.

The ships that traveled to Buenos Aires under the British *asiento* contract brought more than slaves: Using the excuse that they needed to carry supplies for their human cargo, British merchants smuggled manufactured goods into Buenos Aires free from Spanish interference. British and European merchandise arrived in increasing quantities as the years passed. British traders exchanged their illegal cargo for hides, tallow, and other products made in the countryside surrounding Buenos Aires, as well as for silver transported overland from the Andes. The British used this access to develop a lucrative trade that would continue to expand through the nineteenth and early twentieth centuries.

Trade, illegal as well as legal, enriched the city. Although silver would remain the most important export product until the end of the colonial era, the rising foreign demand for hides and tallow led to the rapid expansion of ranching. Through much of the 1600s, the cabildo, or city council, of Buenos Aires issued few licenses for cattle slaughters. The tight control on the right to gather cattle and take hides kept the supply under control and limited the number of people who could market the hides and tallow to a privileged few.

When foreign demand increased after 1700, the industry underwent a transformation. Investors moved to take control of the cattle in the countryside. They obtained the right to take cattle from designated areas. To guard their cattle, the investors and organizers hired a permanent workforce. From these beginnings, which assigned territory and market rights to a privileged elite, came Argentina's first cattle ranches, or *estancias*.

The expansion of ranching put the porteños into conflict with the Native Americans who dominated the Pampa. Expeditions to gather cattle, called *vaquerías*, had to travel farther into the interior as the years of *rodeos* and slaughtering reduced the herds in the areas near the port city.

Often, the expeditions were challenged by war parties. The battles were usually brief, but the conflicts antagonized the Native Americans. As the conflict developed, Native American leaders mounted raids against Spanish settlements and pushed back the frontier that separated the Spanish and Native American territories. When the attacks against ranching operations peaked in 1752, authorities in Buenos Aires organized a rural militia, the *blandengues,* to roll back the threat.

Ranching's expansion affected the rural society attached to the colonial city. By the end of the sixteenth century, a small number of people had retreated into the countryside. Their existence was independent but meager and often violent. To survive, these rural dwellers (who authorities referred to as a "lost people," or *vagos*) slaughtered cattle for food and traded hides for essential merchandise. In the eighteenth century, members of this marginal group emerged as gauchos: They provided labor for the *estancieros* during the *vaquerías* to earn cash. Although the authorities in Buenos Aires enacted a number of laws to regulate this group of outsiders, including vagrancy laws that threatened with imprisonment or militia service those who could not prove that they had steady employment, enforcement efforts were never successful.

Expansion of the rural population also encouraged the development of farming. In the area surrounding Buenos Aires, farming operations remained small in size and number and limited in terms of economic success. Although implements to grow crops were plentiful, costs of transportation limited farming to areas near towns and cities. Lacking active promotion from Crown officials, farming added little to the mercantile economy. The farms surrounding the city seldom produced enough grain to meet the needs of the urban population. Across the Río de la Plata, available evidence suggests that farming played a more significant role in the local economy. With the threat of attack by Native Americans reduced, more people engaged in farming near Colônia do Sacramento and Montevideo.

THE BOURBON REFORMS (1702–1800)

Until the eighteenth century, the region remained under the political and economic authority of the viceregal government in Lima.

To protect Lima's authority over the legal trading system that the Crown sanctioned, Spain had made silver exports through Buenos Aires illegal, and it put limitations on the kind and volume of trade in which Buenos Aires merchants could legally engage. These restrictions hardly affected Buenos Aires. Although the Crown wrote many laws, its Hapsburg rulers were unable to effectively enforce any of the limitations that affected either Spanish merchants or foreign traders.

After the Wars of Spanish Succession (1702–1713) placed a new ruling family—the Bourbons—on the Spanish throne, significant policy shifts occurred. During the initial years of Bourbon rule, the new royal family concentrated on asserting its authority over its European domain. By the 1750s, the Bourbon kings began a process of reform that invigorated the colonial bureaucracy and encouraged the expansion of economic activity throughout the Americas.

The policies of the Bourbons reflected the ideals of "enlightened despotism." Under this set of guiding principles and practices, the Spanish Crown pushed to accomplish three main things: First, it enacted bureaucratic reforms that brought its colonial territories under more effective control; second, it promoted the expansion of existing industries and the development of new activities to increase the economic and material benefits that the colonies provided for Spain; and third, it bolstered the military defense of the colonies and the mercantile trading system that connected Spain and its colonies in Africa, America, and Asia.

In the Río de la Plata basin, the first clear signal of the Bourbons' new ambitions was a series of military actions that began after 1720 in the Banda Oriental. Royal armies, backed by the militia of Buenos Aires, attacked the Portuguese settlements and port cities that represented a threat to Buenos Aires. Spanish raids disrupted ranching activities in an effort to undermine competition. Forts and settlements established in the region (Montevideo, founded in 1724, quickly became the most important) reinforced Spanish authority. The capture of Colônia do Sacramento in 1762, and again in 1777, guaranteed Spanish control of trade through the region.

In response to the threat of foreign invasion, which during times of war led Spain's imperial enemies to attack and seize colonial ports, the Crown modernized and expanded Buenos Aires' military defenses. Only a few hundred soldiers, poorly trained and equipped, were stationed in the city during the late 1600s. As the decades passed, the military forces expanded gradually. After the city became the viceregal capital, 3,000 soldiers led by Spanish officers protected the city. Their numbers increased even more during times of emergency.

The port's fortifications were rebuilt and reinforced with new cannon and supplies. Naval patrols from the city helped control smuggling but at the same time advertised Spain's increased presence.

The Bourbons also moved against the Jesuits. In general, the new rulers wished to maximize their control over their colonial territories, its industries, and its trade. Since the Jesuits operated largely outside of Spanish colonial authority, their mission operations represented a significant challenge to the Crown. The production and trade of tobacco, yerba mate, and ranching products on the missions, which were shielded from most taxes, represented lost revenue opportunities. Jesuit efforts to cultivate support among the colonial elite, through their schools and through their service as confessors, potentially weakened the loyalty of Spain's subjects.

For these reasons, the Spanish Crown stripped the Jesuits of their privileged status. As part of a broader trade agreement, Spain granted Portugal authority over the mission populations and properties east of the Uruguay River. The shift allowed Portuguese authorities to mount military raids against the missions in the 1750s. Although the Jesuits and their Native American charges resisted, eventually the raids destroyed the missions: Agricultural operations ceased, and much of the surviving mission populations was captured for sale as slaves. Spain completed the Jesuits' demise by expelling all members of the order from its colonial territories in 1768.

Buenos Aires became the chief beneficiary of these shifts, which are known as the "Bourbon reforms." The bureaucratic innovations began with the arrival of new royal officers, with the rank of *intendant* (administrative officer), in the region. Intendants were loyalists sent by the Crown to its American territories. Once there, intendants inspected the regions under their authority, made reports to Spanish councils on the conditions and operations of the colonies, and pushed established bureaucratic officers to fulfill their duties. The intendants were especially interested in ensuring that taxes due to the king were collected.

To speed the reorganization of colonial bureaucracy, Spain split the viceroyalty of Lima. A new viceroyalty in Nueva Granada separated the territories of Venezuela, Colombia, and Ecuador from Lima in 1739. In 1776, Buenos Aires became the capital of the viceroyalty of the Río de la Plata. As a result of this shift, Crown appointees in Buenos Aires took charge of Argentina, Uruguay, Paraguay, and Upper Perú. The grant of authority over Upper Perú meant that the silver produced in Potosí would pass to Spain through Buenos Aires, a practice common although illegal in previous years.

The new viceroyalty was to become, under Bourbon designs, a major center of mercantile expansion. The adoption in 1778 of the policy of *comercio libre* (free trade) spurred this shift. *Comercio libre* did not fully open commercial activity. Rather, the Bourbons ended the old system of controlled trade that required all merchandise legally offered for sale to move to and from Spain through the ports that serviced Mexico City and Lima. *Comercio libre* allowed approved colonial ports to trade directly with Spain. Eventually, trade among American ports developed as well. By allowing port merchants to trade independently of Lima and Mexico City, Bourbon authorities aimed at decreasing the volume of goods that traveled to and from Buenos Aires illegally. As legal trading increased, so too would the tax revenues that trading generated. Under the new system, the increased volume of trade encouraged the expansion of the region's population and the development of local industries.

Cattle ranching had been the main export industry of the Argentine plains even before the policy changes of the late 1700s. Once foreign trade became legal through Buenos Aires, the cattle industry expanded. Hides, tallow, and the raising of work animals had been the primary concerns of the region's *estancieros*. Exports of hides, one of the few products that merchants could legally ship from Buenos Aires before the Bourbon reforms, had surpassed 100,000 hides per year in the mid-1700s. After 1776, export volume increased rapidly, with over 700,000 hides exported during periods of open trade at the end of the century.

New industries connected with ranching appeared as a result of the more open trading policies. With hides plentiful, artisans in Buenos Aires began producing shoes for export. Of greater importance was the beginning of the beef industry. The sale of salted beef, treated and dried at *saladeros* (salting plants) in the rural lands around Montevideo, and the Paraná delta, provided cheap food for slaves in Brazil and Cuba. With mixed success, colonial authorities tried to open new land to the south for ranching, agriculture, and settlement. Military campaigns against Native Americans punished raiders. Additional forts along the Salado River created a more permanent military presence. Crown officials directed efforts to develop rural industries in Patagonia. Material limitations and continued Native American resistance limited the success of these ventures.

Overall, the promotions had a great effect on Buenos Aires and the area it controlled. The population grew: Approximately 12,000 lived there in 1750, which made it then the colony's largest city; by 1800, royal officials estimated that the city had 50,000 residents, or 10 percent of the colony's total non–Native American population. Cities in the interior grew as well, as the mercantile promotions encouraged their economic growth. Buenos Aires became an increasingly important market for local produce: Merchants shipped yerba mate and tobacco from the northwest, wine from Cuyo, and cotton from the northeast. New trade linkages developed as well: Mendoza by the end of the eighteenth century developed into an important supplier of foodstuffs, pack animals, and other products for Spanish settlements across the Andes in Chile.

But the interior cities' trade with Buenos Aires did not fully make up for other losses. The Bourbon reforms created new problems. Córdoba had been the region's intellectual and cultural center during the Hapsburg era. When Buenos Aires became the viceregal capital, Córdoba's prestige went into decline. Merchants who had benefited from the protected trade with Perú resented the competition that came with the creation of the new viceroyalty. The mining elite in Upper Perú complained bitterly about the controls that porteños enjoyed over their silver shipments.

The colonial innovations that the Bourbon reforms produced transformed Argentina from an isolated frontier into a promising colonial asset. The reforms also produced unexpected frustrations. The increased attention that the colony, in particular Buenos Aires, received did create new and expanded commercial opportunities for the porteños. With progress came increased supervision. Thousands of Spaniards assumed positions of authority over the colony. They often displaced locals. This, coupled with the more active enforcement of Spanish policies, emphasized the burdens of colonial administration.

More significant was the impact of international events. Just as Spain moved to bring the viceroyalty of the Río de la Plata under tighter control, wars in Europe disrupted the connections between the colony and the metropol. The war that created the United States also pitted Spain, as a French ally, against Great Britain. By enforcing restrictions on Atlantic trade, British ships interfered with Spain's mercantile trade. Even with the relatively open trading system of Comercio Libre, Buenos Aires and other colonial ports found it difficult to obtain manufactures from legal suppliers. The French Revolution and the Napoleonic Wars disrupted trade between Europe and the Americas to an even greater degree.

After 1800, the lack of legally approved merchant shipments from Spain pushed merchants in Buenos Aires to call openly for the end to all imperial trading restrictions. Spain's inability to meet the needs of its colonial populations in Argentina would play an important role in the fall of the colonial system and the coming of independence in the years after 1810.

3

Independence and the Construction of Argentina (1800–1880)

Buenos Aires had become an important port in Spanish South America. Its mercantile activities connected it with an increasingly dynamic trans-Atlantic economy. The series of wars between France and its European rivals isolated Spain from its American colonies. This set in motion a series of events that transformed Buenos Aires and the viceroyalty of the Río de la Plata.

THE COLLAPSE OF COLONIAL AUTHORITY (1800–1807)

The creation of a new viceroyalty based in Buenos Aires came as a result of the Spanish Crown's ambitious desires to promote the growth and development of its South American colonial possessions. Its establishment recognized the economic potential and strategic importance of the Río de la Plata region. Spain's concerns over the incursion of Portuguese officials and other Europeans into their colony made the elaboration of colonial authority in Buenos Aires essential.

The viceroyalty of the Río de la Plata developed, however, along lines that encouraged independent thinking and action. Having established a new viceregal capital and having moved to enforce its colonial policies in a more rigorous fashion, Spain became isolated from what would become Argentina. Unwillingly, Spain became involved in the dynastic and imperial struggle between Great Britain and France. The war that secured the independence of the United States, followed by the French Revolution and the Napoleonic Wars, blocked Spanish convoys from Buenos Aires and made the enforcement of Spanish regulations difficult. Even staffing the colonial bureaucracy with loyalists became difficult.

With British-enforced embargoes separating Spain from its colonies for much of the period 1776–1819, locals in Buenos Aires and in the interior of the viceroyalty increasingly pushed for a loosening of the ties with the Crown. Disagreements over trade regulations highlighted the limitations of the region's colonial status. The official policy of *comercio libre* had encouraged the expansion of domestic industries and the volume of trade through the ports of the region, especially Buenos Aires. However, the interruption of shipments to and from Spain made the Crown policy more of a burden than an aid. With legal merchandise from Spain scarce or nonexistent, illegal trade with non-Spanish merchants grew. Portuguese and other European representatives, based in the port of Colônia do Sacramento, expanded their operations. British ships, unaffected by the blockades, entered Buenos Aires and sailed up the Río de la Plata frequently. Local produce also flowed out of the viceroyalty to other ports in the Americas and beyond. Although this was illegal under colonial regulations, viceroys tolerated the lucrative practice.

Warfare in Europe, however, made Spanish ships rare. Lack of legal trading opportunities created a problem for the viceroys, whose government depended upon tariffs as a crucial revenue source. Pressed by ranchers and merchants to allow open trade, and facing the need for revenue to fund administrative and military expenses, viceroys first tolerated and eventually sanctioned trade outside the official system. The port of Buenos Aires, for example, welcomed a variety of traders. The city's merchants established relations with Portuguese traders, who sold Argentine beef and other goods in Brazil. Portuguese ships arrived filled with merchandise, such as sugar, slaves, and manufactures in high demand. Soon ships from the United States and the British colonies in the Caribbean arrived and helped the porteños expand their market connections.

Trade between Buenos Aires and other parts of Spanish America also developed. Trade restrictions and the reactions to them also increased tensions between Buenos Aires, the capital and favored port, and the interior. Merchants based in Potosi, which had once served Lima, resented the flow of its silver to Buenos Aires, where it supported the colonial bureaucracy and enriched porteño merchants who provided few benefits in return. Competing port cities, such as Montevideo or Santa Fe, resented the efforts of those in the capital to monopolize trade. Ranchers in the interior argued that colonial policies favored those whose grants were closer to the capital.

Policies and practices related to taxation worsened these tensions. Trade levies had traditionally provided the bulk of the revenue for colonial authorities. As European events interrupted trade, bureaucrats in Buenos Aires increasingly relied on taxes charged against silver shipments from Potosi or merchandise shipped from interior cities.

An increasing number of porteños pushed to make the open trading policy permanent. Manuel Belgrano, who was secretary of the *consulado* (merchant council) that controlled trade in the viceroyalty, became a leader for the advocates of true free trade. Influenced by the economic and political writings of European reformers, Belgrano and his allies asserted their challenges in articles that appeared in a growing number of journals and newspapers published in Buenos Aires and other cities. The critics often contrasted the rich potential of Argentina with economic problems that colonial rules and restrictions produced. They believed that unrestricted commerce would promote economic and political progress in and beyond Buenos Aires.

Not everyone supported such changes. Commercial houses tied to the official trading system aggressively pushed for the maintenance of the old policies that gave them control of all exports and imports, but increasing numbers viewed the colonial system as excessively burdensome. Its costs seemed to offer few benefits.

Even as the provider of military defense against foreign threats, the colonial government proved lacking. In 1806, a British force fresh from seizing control of the Malvinas Islands in the South Atlantic attacked Buenos Aires. The surprise attack overwhelmed the Spanish militia. In the face of the invasion, the Spanish viceroy, the Marquis de Sobremonte, abandoned the city.

Appearing to accept the British victory, the residents of Buenos Aires secretly prepared a response. After two months of careful planning, a rebellion recaptured the city. The weapons that the porteños captured from the occupation forces helped them defeat a second British invasion force in 1807.

The successful liberation of Buenos Aires had an enormous impact. The invasion had undermined support for Spanish authority in and beyond the city. It had also destroyed the bureaucracy and it discredited the authority of the viceroy. In turn, it demonstrated or at least hinted at the power of the Spanish king's subjects, who had defeated the British thanks to their own initiative.

In reaction, the city's audiencia stripped Sobremonte of his rank and authority. Santiago Liniers, who had led the effort to organize Buenos Aires against the British, became the interim viceroy in 1807. This made it clear that the porteños wanted more over their political fate.

THE END OF COLONIAL RULE (1807–1812)

In 1807, events in Buenos Aires and in Spain encouraged the porteños to challenge colonial policies and traditions. First, inspired by the absence of Spanish authorities, individuals of ambition in the capital city pushed for a loosening of colonial restrictions on commercial and political activity. Liniers, whose power as interim viceroy was limited, worked with the city's council, the cabildo, and the army to run the colony. In September, Napoleon invaded Spain. In March 1808, the French forced Charles IV to abdicate and then put Joseph Bonaparte on the Spanish throne. In resistance to the French, Spanish cities formed councils, with the most important being the *junta central* (central council) in Cádiz. The councils declared their loyalty to Charles's heir, Ferdinand VII. The ensuing rapid collapse of royal authority encouraged liberals and loyalists to push for power in much of Spanish America.

In Buenos Aires, Napoleon's invasion and the relatively autonomous operations of the viceregal government troubled local leaders. Conservatives, who hoped to preserve colonial authority, were the first to revolt. With Martin de Álzaga as their leader, the rebels tried to turn the colonial military against Liniers and his supporters. The citizen militia that had been formed in response to the British invasion remained loyal to Liniers. A brief battle left Liniers in command. His victory proved significant: The defeat of the loyalist rebels strengthened the position of the cabildo and its members, who quickly sought greater political liberties and a formal suspension of colonial trade restrictions.

In 1809, a new viceroy appointed by the junta central arrived in Buenos Aires. Viscount Balthasar de Cisneros inherited the problems that events had created. Of immediate concern was the government's lack of funds. Cisneros sought the cabildo's advice on commercial and tax policies. The request led the backers of open trade to call for an end to colonial restrictions. This assertion, most clearly stated in the text *Representación de los hacendados* by Mariano Moreno, demonstrated how far the citizens of Buenos Aires had moved from Spain in political terms. As Cisneros worked to frame a compromise between groups who wanted Spanish controls maintained and others who wanted local autonomy, events in Spain once again created a crisis in the capital.

The French Army completed its conquest of Spain's important cities between March and May 1810. The news inspired porteño leaders to pressure Cisneros. On May 22, the viceroy authorized a *cabildo abierto*. During this "open council," 200 leading citizens backed by the militia stripped Cisneros of his office. A new council, led by Saavedra and other liberals, took charge.

The new administrators did not declare the end of the colonial system. They hoped to maintain Buenos Aires's authority over the Río de la Plata region. The formation of a revolutionary junta, despite its leaders' declarations of their loyalty to the deposed heir and to Spain, led colonials living in the towns and cities of the interior to raise challenges. Three regions—Upper Perú, which had already fallen into rebellion against what remained of Bourbon authority in 1808; Asunción; and Montevideo, which resented the colonial restrictions that Buenos Aires had imposed upon them—did not recognize the revolution. As the viceroyalty split into regions loyal to or in opposition to the capital, a fourth challenge came from Córdoba. The move by the cabildo in Buenos Aires to name its own leaders angered Liniers. As the representative of Spanish authority, he turned to loyalists in the interior for help. He quickly organized a new military force to capture Buenos Aires.

The junta's army reacted quickly to the threat from Córdoba. The loyalist force evaporated when the militia arrived. Captured and transferred to the capital, Liniers was executed without a trial. Campaigns in Paraguay and Upper Perú, however, ended in disaster. Although a planned loyalist invasion from the *Banda Oriental* (Uruguay) collapsed, Buenos Aires soon lost control of this region as well. Rebels in the countryside north and west of Montevideo pushed for local autonomy. Hoping to prevent the spread of the revolt, Portuguese forces invaded the region. Although the intervention removed another part of the viceroyalty from its control, the Portuguese invasion ultimately saved Buenos Aires from a potential attack.

Coupled with the military disasters came political turmoil within Buenos Aires. Mariano Moreno, the junta's secretary, rallied support for a declaration of independence and political reforms that were more radical than those the junta had authorized. He focused his efforts on the militia and hoped to seize power militarily. The militia decided not to support his ambitions, and Moreno's challenge faded.

Military governors appointed by the junta in Buenos Aires tried to keep the remaining parts of the viceroyalty under the port city's control. Their interventions and the turmoil that developed in Buenos Aires encouraged regional movements against the centralizing ambitions of the junta. This division, between the port and the interior of the emerging country, became the defining theme of Argentina's first decades of independence.

UNITARIOS AND FEDERALISTS (1812–1829)

In the face of military disasters, the ruling authority in the capital city fell into a more rigid defensive posture. An executive council led by three individuals and known as the "Triumvirate" took charge. The secretary of the Triumvirate, Bernardino Rivadavia, emerged as the key player in the new order. More conservative and less flexible in political terms, Rivadavia pushed for a greater centralization of political and military authority. Regional concerns fell aside. Instead, the central government dictated its demands to the regions that it moved to control.

The continued division of revolutionary factions and a second loyalist revolt stalled the actions of the Triumvirate. An ambitious group of revolutionary supporters, under the leadership of José de San Martín, Carlos de Alvear, and Bernardo de Monteagudo, formed the *Sociedad Patriótica* (Patriotic Society). Capitalizing on the continued political instability and the stalled military situation, and building popular support by attacking Spanish merchants and Loyalists, the Patriotic Society forced the collapse of the first Triumvirate in October 1812.

The society pushed for the creation of a second Triumvirate. A new executive council led a reorganization of the military and formed a revolutionary Congress. The Congress approved the creation of a new government and named José Gervasio de Posadas as the territory's "supreme dictator."

From the beginning of 1814, campaigns against regional rebels and Spanish counterrevolutionaries took priority over all other matters. With concessions to British and foreign merchants providing tax revenue, the government first focused on defeating the Loyalist base of Montevideo. A siege of the city led to its capture in June 1814.

The defeat of the Loyalists, however, led to a confrontation with José de Artigas. Artigas was a brilliant, radical, and popular revolutionary who played an instrumental role in the 1812 rural revolt in Uruguay.

He had since built up a coalition of supporters from his base in Uruguay and his alliances with leaders from other interior regions. In January 1815, forces under Artigas's command captured Montevideo. A second force based in Santa Fe defeated an army sent from Buenos Aires. A brokered settlement avoided a subsequent attack against the capital.

These military events disrupted the political scene. First Posadas, then his successor Carlos de Alvear fell from power as the territory's supreme dictator in 1815. Factionalism within the city and challenges from beyond it made the assertion of authority almost impossible. As the situation in Buenos Aires remained unstable, a second revolutionary Congress met in San Miguel de Tucumán. It declared the end of slavery and, on July 9, 1816, formally announced the territory's independence from Spain.

To lead the United Provinces of the Río de la Plata, it named Juan Martín de Pueyrredón as director. Pueyrredón's rule began with good fortune. Portuguese forces, fearing that Artigas and his supporters might inspire a slave revolt in Brazil, again invaded Uruguay. After the Portuguese captured Montevideo in 1817, Artigas fought on against the invaders for the next three years.

With his attention focused on the Portuguese, Artigas no longer threatened Buenos Aires. At the same time, San Martín launched a successful invasion of Chile by crossing the Andes. This offensive effectively ended the counterrevolutionary threat to the United Provinces as forces loyal to Spain retreated north.

The improved military situation allowed Pueyrredón and his supporters to consolidate their position and assert the authority of Buenos Aires over its claimed territories in political, military, and commercial terms. By ordering tight controls on river traffic, which made Buenos Aires the sole port for imports in the new country, and by pushing forward a new constitution in 1819, Pueyrredón's government inspired fresh political protests and military challenges.

Trade restrictions angered merchants and producers in Santa Fe, Córdoba, Entre Ríos, and Salta. The constitution, which gave Buenos Aires broad powers over interior provinces, encouraged an even broader rebellion. Quickly, cabildos abiertos took place in many provincial cities. These councils moved to form militias and declared their objections against Pueyrredón's regulations.

The country now split between *Unitarios,* who supported the dominance of Buenos Aires, and Federalists, who preferred a more open and decentralized national government. A series of Federalist victories allowed a coalition of regional militias to capture Buenos Aires.

The Federalists abrogated the 1819 Constitution, organized new elections, and demanded free river navigation and commerce.

Almost immediately after the capture of Buenos Aires, the Federalist leaders split over various military, economic, and political issues. This allowed a revival of the Unitarios. Bernardino Rivadavia, who lost power in 1812, led the effort to rebuild Unitario military power and political authority. A renewed push for monopoly control over the import trade increased the city's revenues. While regional rebels fought among themselves, the Unitarios focused on campaigns against Native American peoples south of the city. The campaigns opened up new lands for ranching, which in turn increased tax revenues that brought economic benefits to ranch operators and investors.

Although many took up positions of authority in the reconstituted government, Rivadavia became the leading figure in the administration of the city and in the revival of the Unitario movement. He enforced trade and economic policies that reflected his faith in the liberal theories then gaining support in England and Europe. He streamlined the city's administration, again along European lines. He secured a new emancipation decree and established a government-backed university, which grew into the University of Buenos Aires. The new university was independent of the Catholic Church, in contrast to the older University of Córdoba, which had been the colony's intellectual and cultural center since its creation in 1618. The government underwrote the creation of a national museum and a public library to complete its cultural promotions.

In the countryside, two of Rivadavia's actions had lasting impact. First, he helped establish anti-vagrancy regulations that required rural residents who did not direct a farm or ranch to carry and produce on demand proof of employment. Those in violation of the law were sentenced to five years of service in the militia. The second was the Law of Emphyteusis, which borrowed its name from an ancient Roman law that promoted the colonization of open rural tracts. The act regulated the private use of public lands in the interior. In theory, the act imposed lease contracts on those who put the land to use. The contracts were put in place to create a new source of revenue that would allow the government to reduce tariffs and encourage an expansion of foreign trade. In practice, the law allowed those who acted quickly to gain exclusive control of the public lands. Since those who leased the land determined its value, and since the government did not set up a system to collect the rents, the law produced no public benefit. More significant, the act led to a rapid transfer of public land to private control. Within two years of the law's issue in 1826, 122 persons took charge of roughly 6.5 million acres of land.

Desperate for revenue, the Unitario government sought loans from abroad to pay for the development of the new country. Great Britain, which came to view the United Provinces as a potentially lucrative trading partner, obtained unique privileges. Culminating in 1824, with the granting of "most favored nation" status to Great Britain, the Unitarios assigned British merchants commercial and political privileges and freedoms that gave them a competitive advantage over other foreigners. The effort helped Rivadavia secure a loan from the Baring Brothers of London of £1 million.

Rivadavia also supervised the drafting of a new constitution, enacted in 1826. The constitution declared the formation of a republic, with powers divided between an elected president and a Congress. Although seen as a compromise by many Unitarios, the new constitution again asserted the power of Buenos Aires over the interior.

At this moment, Rivadavia's government mistakenly supported an attack against the Brazilian forces in Montevideo. The invasion's collapse led to a Brazilian blockade of Buenos Aires, which undermined the fiscal standing of Rivadavia's government.

As the newly constituted porteño government fell into crisis, a more serious Federalist challenge appeared. Claiming that the authorities in the capital city were neglecting their interests, ranchers in the surrounding countryside rose in challenge to Rivadavia. His resignation in 1827 did not quell the crisis. Continued factionalism and warfare quickly brought down the United Provinces. Federalists captured the capital in 1829. The defeat of the Unitarios set in motion the rise of Juan Manuel de Rosas, who became the dominant figure of Argentina's early national history.

THE ROSAS DICTATORSHIP (1829–1845)

Argentine historians have for generations argued over Rosas's significance. Nineteenth-century intellectuals who backed the efforts of the national state to promote the country's rapid economic modernization and political integration attacked Rosas as a barbaric tyrant who undermined the efforts of liberals and violated the rule of constitutions and laws. Nationalists, who read much into Rosas actions against political rivals and foreign powers, characterized Rosas as a hero who defended Argentina's overarching interests against those who wished to exploit the country and its people.

Juan Manuel de Rosas stands as a symbol of the emerging Argentina. Descended from a powerful colonial family, he became wealthy as a partner in a saladero. With his money, he moved from being a manager of ranches to a landowner. As a successful *estanciero,* he was a member of the country's new political and economic elite. As his economic fortunes developed, Rosas became increasingly active in the military and political events of the region. Before leading the capture of Buenos Aires, Rosas participated in military campaigns against native Argentines along the southern frontier and against enemies of Buenos Aires between 1820 and 1828.

Rosas emerged during a crucial period. As the political capital of the region, the city of Buenos Aires became the center of the independence struggle. As the city's transformation from viceregal to independent capital developed, the process its revolutionary armies set in motion produced unwelcome changes elsewhere. The breakdown of the colonial system created enormous problems for the territories removed from the Atlantic coast. In San Juan, Tucumán, and even Córdoba, the local economy and society developed around the colonial systems of production, trade, and governance. The splintering of the viceroyalty isolated the interior cities and provinces. Where they had once received supplies and support from Potosí and the silver mining industry, as well as instructions from Spanish officials whose authority came from the Crown, they now were forced to operate autonomously.

Their privileged access to colonial markets and protection from foreign competition vanished as well.

As political and economic authority shifted to the Independence movement in Buenos Aires, the cost of the new order became clear. Local industries lost their regional markets. The flow of silver was at first interrupted. After the defeat of the Loyalist resistance in 1823, merchants in Buenos Aires rebuilt an international trading system that favored foreign producers and porteño interests at the expense of all other ports, regions, and interests.

The fall of royal authority also led to the emergence of *caudillos*—military leaders who led the cavalry and militia forces that opposing sides had recruited from rural areas to fight for the cause. The ability to organize and command a force in battle automatically gave the leaders of these irregular forces political clout. As a result of the Independence wars, caudillos and their armies increased in importance. The splintering of authority in Buenos Aires allowed regional leaders to use their military power freely.

Rosas emerged as a defender of the interests of provincial Buenos Aires. For Rosas and his supporters, the establishment of a stable government was essential. Although he once supported the Unitario government, efforts to strip Rosas of his command of the provincial militia of Buenos Aires and disagreements over the Constitution of 1826 led him to challenge Rivadavia. While the economic, land, and trading policies of the Unitarios favored the ranchers of Buenos Aires Province, Rosas and his supporters believed that the capital had not done enough to protect the southern frontier and the estancias developing there against Native American attacks. Consequently, Rosas and his supporters found much in common with the caudillos of the interior who had rebelled against the Unitario government. Upon capturing the capital city in 1829, Rosas declared his allegiance with the Federalists.

He became governor of the province of Buenos Aires in 1829. The city of Buenos Aires remained at the center of Argentine politics,

Maligned by some as a bloody tyrant and praised by others as a nationalist hero, for 30 years during the mid-nineteenth century, Juan Manuel de Rosas dominated political and social affairs throughout the territory that became Argentina. (Pradere, Juan A. *Juan Manuel de Rosas: Su Iconografía*. Buenos Aires: Enrique L. Frigerio, 1914)

but now as a provincial capital. In reaction to the chaos the political wars of the 1820s had created, he instituted an authoritarian regime. He negotiated treaties with Native American peoples that helped pacify the frontier. Tribes that did not reach an agreement with Rosas's government faced war. The resulting campaigns cleared new territories for ranching and herding. He directed the construction of frontier forts to serve as bases for patrols that maintained an armed peace in the countryside.

Rosas grew notorious for his repression of political opponents. In the 1830s, he concentrated on political threats beyond his home province. Working with Federalist allies, military forces from Buenos Aires destroyed remaining Unitario strongholds in Córdoba, Entre Ríos, and Santa Fe. The military success of Federalists led to the formation of the *Confederación del Río de la Plata* (River Plate Confederation): Rosas, Estanislao López, and Juan Facundo Quiroga emerged from their provincial bases of Buenos Aires, Santa Fe, and La Rioja, respectively, as the key leaders of the new political order. Their military strength allowed them to control events in neighboring provinces as they worked to build up their local regimes.

After 1831, with all opposition forces routed, Rosas focused on the needs of Buenos Aires. Well aware of the economic possibilities of ranching, he used his power to promote its expansion and improvement in the province. His land policies allowed wealthy ranchers and investors to take possession of huge tracts. He instituted tariffs against ranching products produced outside the province, which in turn strengthened the economic standing of the estancieros.

His promotion of Buenos Aires province and its interests put his government at odds with other Federalists. Because Rosas controlled the port of Buenos Aires, his trade restrictions cut into the flow of goods into and out of interior provinces. As tariffs helped Rosas fund his military, Rosas's imposed restrictions threatened the fiscal health of other provincial governments.

Initially, Rosas limited any damage his actions caused by offering financial and military support to allies in other provinces. The tensions that separated Buenos Aires from the interior, which first appeared decades before as a product of the creation of the viceroyalty of the Río de la Plata, soon intensified as the Federalist era continued.

Having accomplished his immediate goals, Rosas briefly retired from government at the end of his term as governor in 1832. With Rosas out of power, the threat of renewed political turmoil, and even civil war, reappeared. Before any significant challenge appeared his supporters orchestrated his reelection as governor of Buenos Aires Province in 1835. With significant popular support, he built around him a dictatorial regime of unprecedented power.

The *Junta de Represent antes,* which was the province's legislature, granted Rosas broad authority. He conducted plebiscites to create a veneer of legitimacy as he dictated policy. Backed by the army and by the *mazorca,* a police force that Rosas used to keep order and repress enemies, he scheduled regular fixed elections that kept him as governor until 1852.

Under Rosas, Buenos Aires came to dominate the other provinces. Initially, Rosas negotiated treaties with caudillos who controlled the interior provinces. His government offered subsidies to combat complaints over the unfair trading policies that Rosas had imposed. After 1835, the dictator's relationships with rival caudillos shifted. Facundo Quiroga's death in 1835 eliminated a chief rival. López's hold on power in Santa Fe weakened as factions split his military base of support. López's death in 1838 left Rosas in a strong position.

In the place of negotiations, Rosas promoted factions within the interior provinces. Province after province fell into the control of Rosas's allies. With his allies ruling over the interior, Rosas could afford to ignore the interests of other provinces as he concentrated on the needs of Buenos Aires. The goal of making the port of Buenos Aires the dominant site for foreign trade remained central. To accomplish this, Rosas imposed tariffs on goods sold in Buenos Aires that had entered the territory first through other ports. Argentine opponents lacked the military force necessary to challenge Rosas. Foreign merchants, however, enlisted their governments' support.

The French in Buenos Aires were the first to rise. The lack of treaty protections made French citizens subject to whatever requirements the Rosas government imposed. A tariff law in 1836, which tried to block the importation of goods through the rival port of Montevideo, provoked the intervention of the French government in defense of local merchants. When Rosas refused to negotiate a settlement, the French Navy imposed a blockade on Buenos Aires in 1838.

The blockade created an economic emergency: Inflation plagued the economy; currency lost value quickly and created problems for merchants in Buenos Aires; even Rosas's strongest supporters, ranchers, lost access to the foreign markets for their hides and tallow.

The French worked to revive Rosas's Unitario enemies. Capitalizing on the crisis, Juan Lavalle led a Unitario army from Uruguay and captured Entre Ríos. The Uruguayan government, in support of the interests of Montevideo, declared war against Buenos Aires. As foreign and domestic enemies moved in unison against the dictatorship, a group of ranchers in northwestern Buenos Aires rebelled in protest over the economic hardship created by the blockade.

Rosas remained entrenched. He defeated the rebels and invaders in a series of wars between 1839 and 1841. Beginning in 1843, he sent armies that surrounded Montevideo and disrupted its port operations. The string of successes against a range of threats made Rosas and his allies more powerful.

Beginning in 1845, the dictatorship initiated naval patrols in the Río de la Plata and the Paraná River. The patrols enforced tight controls on river traffic and trade, with the central goal again being the promotion of Buenos Aires as the primary port in the region. As was the case before, Rosas's ambition angered foreign merchants. In response to the patrols, Great Britain joined France in a renewed blockade of Buenos Aires.

The dictatorship survived the second blockade as it had the first. Within Buenos Aires Province, political terror and propaganda checked all signs of resistance. Rosas's reinstitution of restrictions on trade beyond Buenos Aires in 1848, however, encouraged the regime's opponents.

Ranchers outside Buenos Aires who tried to sell their products through local ports resented the new trade restrictions. The Brazilian government, which found its access to its southwestern territories interrupted by Rosas's controls over transport on the Parana´ River, expressed its concerns. Montevideo, still under siege, became a center from which exiled opponents of the dictatorship prepared for the next confrontation.

THE RESISTANCE (1835–1852)

As Rosas successfully undermined his political and military opponents, his dictatorial actions inspired new challengers. Enemies of the Federalist regime that were connected with the defeated Unitario government had, by 1835, faded from the scene. In their place, young intellectuals voiced their concerns over the actions of the dictatorship first in literary journals. A circle of writers, who came to be known as the "Generation of 1837," took the lead. Their opposition developed first out of a collective effort to consider and frame what they argued the future of the country should be. The key figures in this group, Esteban Echeverría, Juan Bautista Alberdi, and Miguel Cané, advertised in *La Moda*, a weekly magazine that the group published, apparent support for the dictatorship. But in their stories, poems, and essays, the contributors who joined in support of the effort produced a body of work that called for the transformation of Argentina.

For the "Generation of 1837," the violence that Rosas used against his enemies reflected the barbaric nature of the dictatorship and its mass of supporters. As such, it was a product of the lack of a progressive, civilizing effort in the new country. The "Generation" authors asserted that the government had to pursue policies that would civilize and, as a result, modernize Argentina. The models that the group suggested were European and urban. As such, their model future offered a stark contrast to the important role that things rural played in the Rosas era.

The "Generation of 1837" had little influence over Buenos Aires while Rosas ruled. Its members ceased their literary and intellectual efforts in the city a little more than a year after they had begun. The dictatorship, recognizing the critical nature of the group's texts, forced the key leaders into exile. Beyond Buenos Aires, their literary protests gained supporters and allies. Domingo Faustino Sarmiento, who was an opponent of the caudillo rulers of San Juan before fleeing into exile in Chile, became an early supporter and participant in the movement. Although their writings did little to weaken the power of Rosas, their prominent place in the resistance guaranteed the "Generation of 1837" a role in future efforts to build a new Argentina.

The dictatorship's push to enhance the economic, political, and military power of Buenos Aires continued to anger competitors in other provinces. Justo José de Urquiza became the key player in building resistance to Rosas. Urquiza became a caudillo in Entre Ríos Province at first thanks to his allegiance to Rosas. In 1839, he led the effort to push out the Unitarios. For his service, Rosas helped Urquiza become governor. Once in power, Urquiza acquired enough land and cattle to become the region's wealthiest estanciero. The dictatorship's trade restrictions on the Paraná River made it difficult for Urquiza and other ranchers in Entre Ríos. In 1851, Urquiza challenged Rosas's reelection as governor of Buenos Aires. The challenge escalated into a military confrontation. The dictator's enemies united behind Urquiza. At the lead of an army of Uruguayan, Brazilian, and Argentine troops, the rebel general invaded Buenos Aires Province and moved toward the capital city.

Facing invasion, Rosas pushed to field an army in defense of his regime. Waning popular support, combined with the costs of the years of warfare and repression, undermined his efforts. The dictator could not raise an army of sufficient strength to meet the challenge. Rosas's defeat at the Battle of Caseros in 1852 ended his rule.

CONFEDERATION AND CONSTITUTION (1852–1862)

The enemies of Rosas were briefly united in a desire to forge a nation from the collection of provinces that emerged after independence. Emigré resistance leaders from the Rosas era became the intellectual framers of the new order. Following the lead of Domingo Faustino Sarmiento, Juan Bautista Alberdi, and others, the provinces sent delegations to San Nicolás, in northern Buenos Aires Province. The convention produced the *Acuerdo de San Nicolás* (San Nicolás Agreement), which endorsed liberal trade policies, public education, and the creation of a strong, centralized, constitutional government.

The city and the province of Buenos Aires refused to support the new order. The city's leaders clung to the advantages that Buenos Aires had obtained since independence. They asserted their port's commercial primacy and its autonomy from the Argentine Confederation established after the defeat of Rosas. They rejected the San Nicolás Agreement, refused to participate in the Constitutional Convention of 1853, and did not accept the newly drafted constitution despite its ratification by all the country's other provinces.

The Argentine Confederation carried on without Buenos Aires. Urquiza became the Confederation's president, and he made Concepción del Uruguay in Entre Ríos the new capital. Although Buenos Aires asserted its right to block all trade beyond its port, the city lacked the military power to enforce any blockades.

As Confederation president, Urquiza promoted the new country. In 1853, Great Britain was the first to recognize his government as the legitimate authority in Argentina. But without control of Buenos Aires, the Argentine Confederation was less attractive to British investors. Trade and ranching did expand in the interior, but foreign merchants continued to favor Buenos Aires. Threat of conflicts between Buenos Aires and the interior made it difficult to attract investment capital. Few ships sailed up the Paraná. Most docked at Buenos Aires, influenced by existing mercantile relations to the site where all the produce from any part of the Confederation could be obtained with the least amount of effort. In frustration, Urquiza directed another campaign against Buenos Aires. In 1859, Confederation armies defeated forces loyal to Buenos Aires at the Battle of Cepeda. The province agreed to provide financial support for the Confederation, but the province and the city did not endorse the constitution.

The autonomists of Buenos Aires rallied behind Valentín Alsina and Bartolomé Mitre. Following Alsina, Buenos Aires had managed to stalemate Urquiza and the Confederation, but little more. Mitre became the governor of Buenos Aires in 1860. Rather than resist the unification of the country, Mitre set about the task of making the Argentine Confederation serve the interests of Buenos Aires. He found supporters in the interior who organized rebellions against Urquiza. With the Confederation fractured, Urquiza led another attack against Buenos Aires. At the Battle of Pavón in 1861, a militia armed with modern rifles and cannon decimated Urquiza's cavalry and blocked the invasion. Rather than accept a continued stalemate, Urquiza withdrew his forces and eventually relinquished the presidency.

Mitre and his supporters continued to press for change on political and military fronts. Negotiations produced a number of important amendments to the Constitution of 1853. Following the ideals that Juan Bautista Alberdi established in his tract *Bases y puntos de partida para la organización política de la República Argentina* (*Bases and Starting Points for the Political Organization of the Argentine Republic,* 1852), the constitution reflected reigning liberal tenets and practices. It also put the national government behind a broad effort to develop the country through the extension, settlement, and exploitation of its western and southern territories. In 1862, Mitre became the Argentine Republic's first president.

MITRE AND THE ARGENTINE REPUBLIC (1862–1880)

As amended, the constitution gave enormous powers to the national government. Under Mitre's leadership, it first moved to revive the economic expansion of the country. Political conditions allowed a commercial recovery, which provided increased revenues for the government through tariffs. To help open up interior lands to investment and exploitation, the government began construction of a rail line between Rosario and Córdoba. It also initiated negotiations with British investors who set in motion the creation of new ranches and railroads.

The government's economic initiatives generated protests in the interior. The constitution did not fully settle the tensions between Buenos Aires and the rest of the country. The trading advantages that the city and the province had gained since the late colonial era guaranteed that a majority of revenues from foreign trade would go to Buenos Aires. Although the division of legislative powers made the national Senate into a body that represented privileged groups from the interior, there were no explicit checks on efforts to channel the benefits of commercial expansion to Buenos Aires.

When the Mitre government established national tariffs on exports and imports, Federalist echoes again appeared. Rebellions in La Rioja asserted the rights of provincial governments to protect their interests.

The military and financial power of the national government, however, proved irresistible.

The Argentine government's power increased with each year. The War of the Triple Alliance (1865–1870) cemented its supremacy. Argentina joined with Brazil and Uruguay against the dictatorship of Francisco Solano López in Paraguay. As the alliance armies slowly decimated the Paraguayan forces, the Argentine government used the war to modernize its army and develop the country's infrastructure. It also used the conflict as an excuse to militarily intervene in provinces that resisted the national government's authority.

The privileged status of Buenos Aires again became the primary concern in Argentine politics. As required by the constitution, Mitre stepped down from the presidency at the end of his term in 1868. His efforts to orchestrate the election of his successor failed in the face of provincial opposition to the power of Buenos Aires. Domingo Faustino Sarmiento, who as governor of San Juan had enhanced his national reputation, captured the presidency. Mitre's attempt to regain the presidency in 1874 failed as well. The opposition, unified in the *Partido Autonomista Nacional* (National Autonomist Party or PAN), secured the election of Nicolás Avellaneda of Tucumán. In protest of the defeat, Mitre led a brief but ineffective rebellion. The political supremacy of Buenos Aires suffered a third blow in 1880, when the governor of Buenos Aires, Carlos Tejedor, lost the election to Julio Roca. In the election's wake, the national army under Roca's command put down a violent rebellion that tried to block Roca's victory. Roca's administration federalized the city of Buenos Aires, which symbolically ended the dominance of Buenos Aires Province over the national government.

The collapse of Spanish authority posed the question of independence. What Argentina would become was not then determined. The push for independence produced instead decades of civil war and political turmoil. Finally, in 1853, a national government took shape. The rivalry between Buenos Aires and other provinces continued to divide Argentina.

Although the transformation of the city of Buenos Aires into a federal capital created a political solution to calm the rivalry, the events of the first half of the nineteenth century had done much to promote the ascendance of the most-favored province. Economic changes, in particular the rise of Argentina's "mother industries"—ranching and farming—would make Buenos Aires the country's economic center for generations to come. These mother industries would provide the foundation for an economic transformation that made Argentina into one of the world's wealthiest countries.

4

Argentina's "Golden Age" (1880–1910)

At the beginning of the twentieth century, foreign observers offered glowing reports about Argentina, its political and economic conditions, and its potential. Most regarded it as a land of great promise, and a few boldly predicted that its natural resources, its economic vigor, and its developing role in world trade would soon make Argentina one of the richest countries in the world. To many, it seemed destined to one day challenge the United States for hemispheric supremacy.

The foundations of such analyses and predictions lay in the plains that spread west and south from the capital. Although the development of ranching during the colonial era started the process, Argentina experienced a phenomenal expansion as a result of the development of more sophisticated and diversified rural industries. Ranching remained central, but hides and salted beef were no longer the rural sector's main product. Fundamental shifts within and beyond Argentina connected its estancias to a broad international market.

Foreign demand and domestic investments also transformed the Pampa into a major grain production zone for the world market. Farming and ranching became, by the late 1800s, Argentina's "mother industries."

With the wealth that rural industries and exports provided, Argentina entered a period of opulence and stability. Its economic and political progress, however, hid important problems. While immigrants toiled, a privileged few reaped most of the benefits. Its political system also appeared more stable and democratic than it was in practice: Violence, systematic fraud, and corruption left the concerns of the majority without representation.

MATERIAL FOUNDATIONS

Foreign trade had always been the key factor behind what progress Argentina had made after independence. International changes, which made travel and communications across oceans and continents easier and less expensive, helped make Argentina's land more inviting. Settlers and investors came to see Argentina as a land of opportunity. Its open spaces seemed rich with potential.

Steamships reduced the time needed to travel to Buenos Aires from foreign ports. The British government established a mail service in 1832 to aid its commercial interests in the region. The adoption of steam-powered ships in 1851 reduced sailing time from two months to 35 days.

Other governments and private companies soon joined the British in providing regular service to Argentina's Atlantic and interior port cities. Increased shipping traffic led to expanded trade. Steady growth occurred during the Rosas era. After the establishment of the Argentine Republic in 1853, a loosening of trade restrictions opened up interior provinces to direct foreign trade. Not surprisingly, improved access resulted in a more rapid expansion of foreign trade. In the 1850s, hundreds of ships entered Argentine ports to conduct trade and to disembark passengers. By the 1880s, foreign ships came in the thousands.

Although the warfare and strife that marked the country for decades after its break from Spain slowed the pace change, Argentina experienced rapid demographic growth, especially between 1853 and 1869. Its population more than tripled in the two generations that followed independence: Argentina's first census recorded 1,736,923 residents in 1869. The pace of this demographic explosion was most rapid in the Pampa region. The capital city, Buenos Aires, grew from roughly 50,000 to 90,000 between 1810 and 1854. Fifteen years later, its population had nearly doubled to 177,787.

By 1895, the year of Argentina's second national census, the country's population had increased to 3,956,060. In 1914, when the results of the third national census appeared, 7,885,237 people lived in Argentina.

Trends that made their appearance in the mid-nineteenth century became more pronounced. The provinces of the Pampa region had become dominant. Just under half the country's population lived in Buenos Aires, Santa Fe, Córdoba, and Entre Ríos in 1869; in 1914, the four provinces held 72 percent of the national total. The country had become more urbanized: Whereas 29 percent of Argentines lived in cities in 1869, by 1914 the total living in urban areas reached 53 percent. The Federal Capital had become even more important in demographic terms: By 1914, the city of Buenos Aires boasted 1,575,814 inhabitants.

Immigration, particularly from Europe, fueled Argentina's demographic transformation. In 1869, foreigners represented 12.1 percent of the country's total population. Between 1871 and 1914, nearly 6 million foreigners traveled to Argentina. Argentine government officials estimated that more than half, 3,194,875, stayed in the country to work and settle.

Changes within Argentina allowed the development of new, more intensive uses of land. The creation of a transportation system was an essential preliminary step. Rivers allowed transit in certain areas, but much of the country's interior was accessible only by travel over land. Consequently, Argentine leaders viewed railroads as a means of opening up the country to progress and development.

Efforts to build a network of railroads started slowly, however. Political tensions that separated Buenos Aires from the remaining provinces frightened investors. The national government's concessions to companies that agreed to build and operate the lines, though liberal, were not as substantial as those offered by other South American governments. Civil War in the United States and efforts to open up its western lands consumed capital and materials that might have otherwise met Argentina's needs. These factors made progress slow, but by the end of the 1860s Argentina's major lines had started their expansion: The Northern connected Buenos Aires to stations along the Río de la Plata delta; the Western aimed at crossing the Andes in order to connect Argentina and Chile; and the Southern opened its first line between the city of Buenos Aires and Chascomús in 1865.

Political stability came after 1880. This started an era of even more rapid railroad expansion. In that year, total rail mileage reached 1,570. In a decade, by 1889, 5,850 miles of track connected ports and provinces. By 1900, total mileage reached 10,300. In 1910, mileage increased to 17,350.

Argentine leaders anticipated the boom that railroads would bring. To prepare for the expanded trade, provincial and national governments funded major improvements in the country's ports. Dredging and the cutting of a canal made the docks at Rosario capable of handling oceangoing vessels. The improvements allowed the city to become one of the country's leading ports after 1880. Connected to the Southern Railroad network in 1884, Bahía Blanca became a major port for wool and grain shipments from the southern Pampa and Patagonia. In response to improvements made to other ports, Buenos Aires officials repaired the old docks and constructed new facilities. These innovations and its railroad connections with all points of the interior allowed the capital city to maintain its position as the country's leading port.

Modernization of the country's ports allowed a dramatic expansion of the country's international commerce. In 1880, foreign companies sent imports worth more than 45.3 million gold pesos to Argentina. Exports from the country, the bulk of which came from the Pampa region's farms and ranches, nearly reached 58.4 million gold pesos. Steady expansion continued through the end of the century. By 1900, imports approached 113.5 million and exports attained a value of 154.6 million gold pesos. From 1900 until the start of World War I, Argentina's foreign trade grew at a much faster rate. The year 1913 ended as a record year: Imports surpassed 496.2 million, and exports totaled just under 519.2 million gold pesos.

The newly unified national government was a significant promoter and beneficiary of expanded foreign trade. To promote fiscal coherence and increase the confidence of foreign governments and investors, the Roca government established Argentina's first national currency in 1881. Issued by the Banco Nacional, the peso had its value set at four pesos to one ounce of gold. A uniform currency ended the confusing system of rival currencies of uncertain values that provincial banks issued in previous decades. It also facilitated international trade by simplifying the conversion of foreign currencies and the calculation of commodities imported to and exported from the country.

The national government benefited directly from the expansion of trade. Tariffs provided the bulk of public revenues throughout the "Golden Age." In 1880, collections equaled 19.6 million gold pesos. By 1889, revenues had almost doubled to 38.2 million gold pesos. As revenues increased, the government's budget grew. In 1880, the national government's budgetary expenditures stood at 26.9 million pesos. By 1889, the budget doubled, to 55.8 million gold pesos. Anticipating a brighter future, government officials relied on foreign loans to fund their operating deficits and to underwrite ambitious public works projects. This led to a dramatic increase in the government's foreign debt, which reached 100 million pesos in 1885.

Argentina's growth took place during a distinct era. Industrial and technological advances not only made it easier to link Argentina to the wider world, but they also gave the country an opportunity to grow and develop. Meanwhile, Great Britain became an aggressive promoter of foreign trade, seeing its colonies and independent partners as providers of raw materials and as markets for British industrial goods. Although British merchants had established their presence early in Argentina's history, it was the development of Argentine agriculture that would make Argentina and Great Britain close partners. As other countries followed Great Britain, investing capital and encouraging trade, the dramatic opening of the world market in the late nineteenth century fostered a period of phenomenal economic expansion in Argentina.

CHANGES IN THE RANCHING INDUSTRY (1829–1870)

Juan de Garay unexpectedly established the foundations for ranching in Argentina when his expedition abandoned horses, cows, and other domesticated animals along with Buenos Aires in 1537. Facing few predators, the cattle quickly grew into large herds. The native grasses and relatively mild climate of the Pampa region sustained the wild cattle, called *cimarones,* as their numbers expanded. Royal promotions allowed the shipment of salted beef, hides, tallow, and other by-products to grow; but by the end of the colonial era, ranching remained a secondary activity overshadowed by other mercantile trades.

During the decades of political violence between independence and the consolidation of the Argentine Republic, a number of important developments set the stage for the creation of a modern, lucrative ranching industry. First, the land area open for ranch operations expanded. The national government's leasing of public lands during the 1820 encouraged ranchers to push their operations farther south and west than ever before.

When the United Provinces of the Río de la Plata collapsed in 1829, provincial governments turned to land sales as a revenue source. Ranchers took advantage of the sales and acquired large holdings. This rapid transfer of public lands into private hands had a major impact on Buenos Aires Province. During Juan Manuel de Rosas's dictatorship, political allies received land grants from the government. Soldiers were often paid with grants of land. Seizing an opportunity, speculators purchased the soldiers' lots in order to form large tracks for future use or sale. Lease holders who took charge of the province's most attractive land were given the opportunity to buy their tracks and acquire others.

Generations of historians have criticized the Rosas regime for its land policy. In less than two decades, the future nation's richest agricultural lands passed from public to private control. The large scale of the land transfer and the lack of markets, capital, and credit meant that a privileged few took control of most of the land. Some historians asserted that Rosas helped created a small, powerful elite of landowners who used their economic clout to dominate Argentina across generations.

Yet the rapid turnover of the properties during the nineteenth century challenges this assertion. Although a privileged few did benefit from initial sales and speculations, most of the first title-holders saw their properties subdivided and sold as the decades past. A vibrant land market through the nineteenth century allowed those with capital or credit to acquire the properties that they desired. Still, only a small percentage had the resources necessary to acquire rural land. The alienation of the public lands did have additional costs: Much to the frustration of leaders such as Domingo Faustino Sarmiento, after 1852 there was little land left for settlement, colonization, or alternative use.

Europeans, in particular British companies, moved to make the Argentine Pampa serve their needs. Industrialization and urbanization in the nineteenth century had increased the demand for raw materials dramatically. In particular, the production of woolens and carpets had grown dramatically. Companies searched for ample but cheap supplies of raw wool as consumer demand grew and as increasing numbers of factories entered into competition for shares of the world market.

British investors found Argentina, especially Buenos Aires during the Rosas dictatorship, inviting. The land and climate of the Pampa seemed ideal for the development of sheep ranches. Since the expansion of foreign trade increased government customs revenues, the Rosas government welcomed British and other foreign investors.

By the end of the 1840s, European companies had pioneered the expansion of sheep ranching in Argentina. The sheep *estancias* required little work during most of the year. A supervisor, often of Irish, Scottish, or Basque descent, worked the property with help from family or a few hired laborers. Contracts that allowed the ranch supervisor to work for a share of the wool yield and of the lambs born each year proved to be major inducements to the immigrants who ran the operations. Temporary workers, pulled in from the towns and cities, swelled the workforce during the shearing season, when the wool that the herds yielded was processed for export.

The wool trade quickly became lucrative for involved investors and provincial governments. In 1837, shipments of wool and other sheep-derived products were of minor importance. Such products represented just over 10 percent of Argentina's total exports. As the decades passed, wool destined for European factories grew into a major commodity. Wool exports set an annual average of 6,000 tons in the 1850s. Shipments in 1859 accounted for 33.7 percent of Argentina's exports.

Expansion continued dramatically in the decades that followed. Wool exports averaged 50,000 tons during the 1860s. By the 1880s, Argentine sheep ranches sent over 120,000 tons of wool overseas each year, and the stock held by Argentine ranchers surpassed 70,000 head. Sheep ranching brought about significant changes in the countryside. In search of higher profits, landowners shifted their properties away from the production of hides, tallow, and salted beef. These activities moved west and south toward the margins of the Pampa. A shift from range cattle to sheep herding allowed a more intensive use of the land.

Ranchers expanded the number of permanent and temporary workers as the wool trade developed. Continued success encouraged new investors to enter the industry, which expanded the numbers of landowners and ranches in operation.

Expansion of the sheep estancias also revealed important problems. Although these issues would become crucial at the end of the nineteenth century, the sheep ranches of the mid-nineteenth century did help landowners anticipate problems and find solutions. For example, the Pampa was a region of vast plains with few trees. As a result, herds roamed over enormous distances with few barriers. On a ranch that relied on wild cattle to produce hides, tallow, and salted beef, this mattered little.

Sheep ranchers, however, had to take firmer control of their stock. Certain breeds produced more desirable wool or provided a balance of meat and wool to suit the market better than others. Tailoring a herd for a particular market, especially when facing international competition, meant that ranchers had to isolate their stock, control their breeding, and limit their roaming.

As a consequence, the construction of natural barriers and fencing became a major task for the ranch hands throughout the year. The costs involved pushed ranch owners to find more cost-effective solutions. The importation of wood from other parts of Argentina helped, but barbed wire fencing, which made its appearance in 1854, proved to be the ultimate solution.

The success of the first sheep estancias led to a rapid increase in the land area devoted to sheep herding. This put the ranchers into conflict with the remaining Native American communities that lived in the Pampa region. Rosas had perfected his military leadership and tactical skills at the expense of the Native Americans during the 1820s. His campaigns to clear territories of Native American communities opened up land for ranching operations. By the 1840s, treaties and the presentation of tribute payments to Native American leaders established a truce in rural Buenos Aires Province, but the rapid expansion of sheep herding increased tensions in the countryside.

After Rosas's fall from power in 1852, tensions between Native Americans and settlers deteriorated into intermittent warfare. Argentine leaders moved to end this competition in the 1870s. First, the national government constructed a line of fortifications near the western boundary of Buenos Aires Province. A trench, designed to stall raiding parties and running 240 miles, connected military outposts. Although the static defensive line advertised a stronger resolve on the part of the government, it did not end the raids that threatened isolated towns and disrupted ranching operations.

The Argentine Army moved to conquer and annihilate the Native American peoples through its "Conquest of the Wilderness" campaign in 1879. Attacking along five columns that pushed from Buenos Aires Province into Patagonia, Argentine forces destroyed settlement after settlement. Within a year, the Native American population on the Pampa was eliminated.

Wool production would remain an important industry in Argentina. After 1880, the expansion of cattle-breeding and-fattening operations and the explosive growth of grain farming would push sheep herding out of the Pampa's core. Nevertheless, the sheep estancias had provided essential first steps: New land had been brought into production; property owners had taken charge of parcels and demonstrated their profitability; the industry cemented Argentina's economic connection with Europe, especially Great Britain; and initial success encouraged not only the development of new lands and economic partnerships but also fostered a new generation of immigrants from Europe whose capital and experience helped grow an industry.

THE REVIVAL OF CATTLE RANCHING

Having witnessed the success of the sheep estancias, cattle ranchers aggressively sought new markets for their product after 1860. The *Sociedad Rural Argentina* (Argentine Rural Society), founded in 1866, led this push. Domestic cattle, bred in the wild, had provided a supply of hides, tallow, and salted beef. More progressive ranchers hoped to find a European market for the meat that their cattle could provide, and this represented a major challenge because salted beef had limited appeal. While slaveholders in Brazil purchased it willingly as a cheap food source for their slaves, few in Europe considered purchasing it. The potential of the European consumer market became apparent in the 1860s, however, through the establishment of the meat extract industry. Operating in Entre Ríos Province and in neighboring Uruguay, the Liebig Company, using cattle from the area's domesticated herds, boiled mutton and beef to produce a paste that was easy to store and ship. High in protein, the company's meat extract won wide acceptance abroad.

Yet meat extract was a small component of the potential market that existed in Europe. Argentine ranchers hoped to market both live and slaughtered cattle abroad. Two problems blocked Argentine beef from Europe's markets. First, the condition of the cattle stock had to improve. The Argentine Rural Society embarked on an ambitious and perennial campaign to raise the quality and international reputation of Argentine cattle. It published and circulated a magazine that provided advice and communicated innovations to the country's ranchers on a monthly basis. It urged its members to replace domestic cattle with improved breeds that were familiar to European consumers and that produced more and consistently superior beef. It sponsored local and eventually an annual national cattle exposition. It also held contests and championed the pioneers who went the farthest toward perfecting beef production.

By the 1870s, the results of these promotions became evident. Argentina's stock was finally suitable for sale abroad. This brought to the forefront the second challenge: how to get Argentine beef to the overseas markets. The technology to slaughter and then can the beef already existed in Argentina. However, "tinned" beef had limited appeal and would produce slim profits for the country's ambitious estancieros. In the 1860s and again in the 1880s, shipments of live cattle for slaughter in Europe proved disappointing. The condition of the cattle that survived the ocean crossing lessened their appeal and hurt the reputation of Argentine beef exports. Fears that the imported cattle would infect domestic herds with "hoof and mouth" disease or other maladies led to a ban on the importation of live cattle from Argentina to Great Britain and other countries after 1900. Fortunately, technological innovations provided sound alternatives.

In 1876, promoters sent a shipment of chilled beef from Buenos Aires to France using a refrigerated cargo ship. Although the experiment produced mixed results, the first shipment encouraged additional trials.

The development of more reliable refrigeration systems quickly led to the establishment of a trade in frozen meat. The first packing plant to prepare meat for freezing and shipment abroad opened in the city of Buenos Aires in 1882. The plant initially concentrated on mutton and lamb exports, but as ships increased in size and speed, it and other plants initiated beef shipments within a year. Export volumes expanded dramatically: Frozen meat shipments averaged 34,016 metric tons between 1882 and 1889; between 1905 and 1909, shipments of frozen beef and mutton averaged 266,491 metric tons each year.

Meat that was slaughtered, frozen, and then exported made ranching more profitable than ever before. The leaders of the Argentine Rural Society and the owners of the packing plants were still not satisfied, however. The freezing process discolored the meat. This effectively limited Argentine producers to the lower, less profitable, tiers of the British and European market. In 1900, the modernization of the packing plants and ships made the shipment of chilled meat feasible. Unlike frozen shipments, chilled meat retained a fresher color and at market appeared comparable to local meat products. A fresh appearance, combined with low prices, helped Argentine beef capture a large market share. The first chilled shipments took place in 1908. Within 20 years, chilled meat shipments averaged 400,000 metric tons annually, nearly twice the volume of frozen shipments.

Able to sell quality cuts of beef to European consumers, Argentine ranchers continued to modernize their operations. Ranchers whose estancias were far removed from the packing plants shifted toward a specialization in breeding and raising calves. Ranchers whose properties were better situated purchased stock from the breeders and then fattened their herds on uniform, improved pasturage. Once the cattle reached the desired age and weight, the fatteners sent their cattle off to slaughter.

The technological and market developments that enabled Argentine beef to succeed in European markets ultimately secured the fortunes of Argentine ranchers, who channeled their ranching profits into other industries.

THE EXPANSION OF COMMERCIAL AGRICULTURE (1860–1910)

Cattle ranchers labeled their profession as Argentina's defining economic activity. Between 1880 and 1900, grain farming developed into the country's second "mother industry." As was the case with ranching, farmers first worked the fields of what would become Argentina during the colonial era. However, unlike cattle ranching or sheep herding, farming did not initially develop into an export industry. A lack of laborers and the relatively high wages commanded by those willing to work, combined with the expenses involved in packing and shipping grain over any significant distance, limited farming's potential.

Farms appeared near the towns and cities, where certain supplies of labor and a ready, accessible market existed. Many farmers worked independently on small plots. Others worked as hired hands on ranches that sowed wheat in tandem with their production of hides, tallow, and other products. No evidence exists of farm exports during the colonial or early independence periods.

In the 1850s, in a manner that paralleled initiatives in the United States, Canada, and elsewhere, private companies sponsored the immigration of European families to Argentina with the goal of establishing farming colonies. Ranching's dominance of the countryside left few areas open for such operations. These first colonization companies had to purchase land in the few areas where ranching had not yet developed.

In Santa Fe Province, land was available for the companies. Concerned about the area's distance from rivers and ports, about the climate, and about continuing Native American raids launched from the Chaco desert, ranchers judged Santa Fe as inappropriate for their industry. Colonization companies managed to attract settlers from Germany, Switzerland, and France with promises of certain success. The Central Railroad, which had received land along its right of way as part of its concession, worked with colonization companies and on its own to settle Argentines and foreigners along its line. For more than a decade, the colonies faced enormous challenges. They received little assistance from the Argentine government. Once railroad lines and port facilities developed closer to their settlements, however, the colonies managed to find markets for their grain in and beyond Argentina.

After 1880, ranchers in parts of the Pampa region helped farming spread. In the core areas of the ranching industry, such as northwestern Buenos Aires Province, landowners often used farmers to break the land. Two to four years of plowing, sowing, and harvesting prepared the land. After a final harvest, farmers who had signed on as hired hands, sharecroppers, or renters sowed alfalfa and then moved on to a new contract and a new parcel. Once established, alfalfa created a rich and durable pasture for fattening cattle. This process helped convince ranchers of farming's utility. At the same time, the success of grain farming as an export industry helped promote farming independently of ranching across a much wider area of the Pampa zone.

Independent farmers moved to expand their operations and take advantage of a growing international market for grains. Competing with other farmers in the Americas, Russia, and Australia, Argentines successfully captured increasing shares of the world market for wheat, corn, flaxseed, and other grains. New lands came into operation first near established port cities. As rail lines extended from Buenos Aires, Bahía Blanca, Rosario, Santa Fe, and other ports, additional areas became viable and farming operations increased dramatically.

The immigrants who came to Argentina seeking opportunity provided the human capital necessary for farming's expansion. Individuals, occasionally supported by members of their family, moved into the countryside and established crude homesteads. In relative terms, the newcomers worked large plots in an extensive fashion. Many foreign observers criticized the crude nature in which the *colonos,* as the farmers were often called, worked the land. They did little to prepare the land, they sowed their crop carelessly, and they selected seeds and farming methods that offered the cheapest costs and the greatest harvest volume in the short term, often at the expense of the land and the grain harvest's quality.

Additional waves of immigrants appeared in the countryside at the beginning of each harvest season. These *golondrina* (swallows), who purchased cheap passages on steamships, worked in the fields from December to May and then returned to their European or South American home countries when the harvest ended, provided cheap temporary labor that made harvesting the expanding farm regions possible.

An immigrant family at their homestead in the *campo.* (Library of Congress)

Farming's success spurred the expansion of Argentina's rural population. In 1869, an estimated 1,240,000 lived in the countryside. By 1895, the number living in rural areas increased to 2,475,000. By 1914, the total reached 3,728,000. The expansion of the rural population did not represent a settling of the interior, however. The Pampa remained largely uninhabited. Observers often characterized the rural population as vagrant or transitory. Many of the farmers lived on their farms temporarily. The majority did not own the land that they worked and shifted from parcel to parcel every two to four years. The shacks and hovels that they constructed did little more than protect them from the weather's extremes.

Despite the criticisms, farming developed into a fabulous economic success. Although the Pampa farms fell short of agricultural perfection, their low production costs and high productivity helped make the industry profitable. Landowners in much of the Pampa region shifted from ranching to farming as market conditions moved in favor of grains.

By the 1890s, farm exports consistently provided more than half of Argentina's export revenues. The farm industry's success made it a major employer. Its operations also supported the profitable operation of the railroads, the ports, millers, and the merchant houses that grew to be the dominant players in the national economy.

Other agricultural industries expanded during the "Golden Age." As railroads moved farther into the country's interior, a few local industries expanded their operations to capture a wider market. In the Andean provinces of Mendoza and San Juan, wine production developed during the early colonial era. Argentine policymakers in the nineteenth century judged grape and wine production as "natural industries" appropriate for support and development. As a consequence, and in response to the efforts of local politicians and landowners, the national government used tariffs to protect them from imported products after 1885. Railroads connected the grape and wine regions to the country's major cities in the same year. Protected and privileged with expanded markets, acreage devoted to grape production and the bottling of wine expanded rapidly. The change was most dramatic in Mendoza. In 1876, grapes grew on an estimated 250 acres in the province. The opportunities of the 1880s led landowners to import French vines and improve their wineries. By 1890, grape vineyards in the province increased to 16,000 acres; and by 1910, to 112,000 acres.

Sugar was another rural industry that expanded dramatically during the same period. The penetration of rail lines into Tucumán Province during the 1880s created market opportunities for landowners. With a climate suited for sugarcane, the land area devoted to the crop increased rapidly. Between 1875 and 1895, sugar acreage grew from 5,000 to over 135,000 acres in the province. Privileged families, who controlled the available supply of land, used their political and economic power to dominate the industry. As production increased, sugar hacienda owners hired migrant laborers from the neighboring provinces of Santiago del Estero, Salta, and Jujuy to meet the industry's seasonal needs. Influence in Buenos Aires led to the creation of high tariff barriers in 1890 that preserved the national market for this elite.

POLITICS IN THE "GOLDEN AGE"

The victory of Julio Argentino Roca and his supporters in 1880 led to the consolidation of an apparently stable political order. The constitution dictated a strong executive branch, with presidents serving single terms of six years. An independent judiciary and legislature shared powers with the executive branch in a manner that followed European precedents and practices.

The regional splintering of political power, where caudillos formed and shattered coalitions, had faded. Militias that fueled rebellions in support of unsuccessful candidates for national office were routed. New political parties, which developed from alliances that crossed provinces and regions, made their appearance. After 1880, the most important were the *Partido Autonomista Nacional* (National Autonomist Party, or the PAN), the *Unión Cívica Radical* (Radical Civic Union), and the *Partido Socialista* (Socialist Party). With all adult male citizens 18 years of age and older eligible to vote, the Argentine political scene seemed dynamic, open, and competitive.

In practice, a privileged few dominated politics during Argentina's "Golden Age." Historians have referred to the era as an oligarchy, where a wealthy, powerful, and small elite controlled the political system across the country. Although parties did compete for offices at the local, provincial, and national levels, the parties' leaders and organizations were more similar than distinct. The leaders were usually ambitious members of wealthy families. The dominant party, the PAN, was often referred to as the "Cattle Party" because of the prominence of ranchers in its ranks. Leaders of competing parties were usually just as wealthy and well connected.

In terms of the policies that the parties promoted, the similarities were stronger than any real or asserted differences. All accepted the reliance on agricultural exports to fund government operations and general prosperity. All called for the maintenance of a liberal, limited government that did little to interfere with the structure and operation of the economy and society.

Despite the constitutional privilege, only a small percentage of the eligible voters participated in most elections. Voting was not required. Those who decided to vote often had to publicly declare their preference to the electoral authorities, controlled by the ruling party. With no secret ballot, supporting a losing candidate often had significant costs. Parties did occasionally rig the balloting, but low voter turnout usually made systematic fraud unnecessary. Typically, between 10 and 20 percent of voters presented themselves at the polls. With the vote limited to adult male citizens, an increasing percentage of the population, immigrants and women, remained entirely outside the political scene. In this context, parties tailored their platforms and focused their attention on a politically active elite.

Competition for political office was fierce and often violent. This encouraged the national and regional parties to develop strong organizations that could produce votes on Election Day as well as muscle, in the form of armed supporters, in the face of postelection strife. Leaders used the power of government to reinforce their standing. Opposition governments in the provinces faced federal intervention, which stripped governors and legislatures of their powers. Opposition candidates faced harassment that grew from mild to harsh as their electoral chances grew.

The PAN's dominance was clear from 1880 to the eve of World War I. Although the party won most elections, rivalries between party leaders and the factions that they controlled often split the PAN. Julio Roca emerged as the country's central political actor after 1880. His successful leadership of the "Conquest of the Wilderness" made him a respected national figure with numerous supporters in the capital city, in Buenos Aires Province, and in Tucumán, the province of outgoing president Avellaneda. When violent confrontations developed over the push to federalize Buenos Aires in 1880, Roca's political strength and the support of the military allowed him to crush the rebels and maintain the PAN's control over the national government.

Roca then moved to create a national foundation for his regime. He built political alliances with governors in Argentina's most important provinces. In areas where opposition parties challenged the PAN, Roca used federal interventions and electoral fraud to thwart them. The expansion of trade increased tariff revenues and enriched the federal government. This allowed Roca to reward political supporters in the provinces as he maintained a fiscally responsible government in the capital.

At the end of his six-year term in office, most observers believed Roca would maintain his political power through his control of the PAN. Roca's successor, Miguel Juárez Celman, asserted his independence from Roca immediately. Beginning in 1886, Juárez Celman used the power of the presidency more aggressively than ever before. He not only moved against opposition parties. The new president and his supporters tried to push Roca loyalists from key positions with the PAN. His push to centralize his authority led his opponents to label his regime the *Unicato* (one-man rule).

Juárez Celman relied on the promise of economic development to broaden his popular support. His government encouraged foreign investment, which resulted in a dramatic expansion in foreign capital and in the number of foreign companies doing business in Argentina. At the same time, the Juárez Celman administration provided little regulation over the economy. In 1885, Argentina had abandoned the gold standard, which set the value of Argentina's national currency at a set level in relation to gold. Had the government limited the supply of money in circulation, the lack of a gold-backed currency would have had no significant impact on the Argentine economy. For reasons more political than economic, however, the government increased the money supply by printing more pesos. Private and provincial banks, which issued *cédulas* (mortgage bonds) to fund land purchases, effectively expanded the amount of currency in circulation.

Reforms passed by the Congress in 1887 set new restrictions and required banks to link their currency emissions to the gold reserves that they controlled. Enforcement of the new regulations proved haphazard and ultimately ineffectual.

As the economy overheated, President Juárez Celman remained focused on building his regime. He made his most aggressive moves against the supporters of Roca and other rivals within the PAN in 1889. The Federal Capital, with its commercial clout and its history of opposition to national governments, received the most attention. Juárez Celman and his allies hoped to completely replace established party and political officers with their loyalists. Before their plan succeeded, though, the government's irresponsible fiscal policy spawned a major economic crisis.

In 1889, the Baring Brothers, a British investment company that had been involved in commerce and finance in Argentina since the Independence era, offered for investment shares in a public works project in the city of Buenos Aires. Investor concerns over Argentina's financial condition left the offering without subscribers. The failure of this initiative created a panic in the financial market.

What became known as the "Baring crisis" shut off the flow of private investment funds from Great Britain. It also discouraged investment from other foreign sources. As a result of the financial contraction, the Argentine currency collapsed. In short order, export values fell along with the relative value of the peso. Imports, which became increasingly expensive as exchange rates grew, fell. By the end of the year, the financial panic had caused a serious recession in Argentina.

The crisis paralyzed the government. Sensing an opportunity, leaders of the opposition formed the *Unión Cívica* (Civic Union) and launched a rebellion centered in Buenos Aires. Their attacks, which attracted support from army units loyal to Bartolomé Mitre, challenged the government. However, the clashes never reached the scale of those that occurred in 1880. The PAN retained power, but not without cost. Hoping to undermine the opposition and to improve foreign opinion of Argentina in the short term, Juárez Celman resigned from office on August 6, 1890.

The rebels were unable to take full advantage of the situation. In secret, Mitre had made a pact with Julio Roca. Mitre agreed to preserve the government and support Vice President Carlos Pellegrini, who took charge after Juárez Celman's resignation. Roca agreed to support Mitre's candidacy for the presidency in 1892. With the pact sealed, the army turned against the rebels and ended the "Revolution of '90."

Juárez Celman's resignation, combined with the defeat of the rebels, fully revived the fortunes of the pro-Roca factions within the PAN. Vice President Carlos Pellegrini, an ally of Roca, assumed the presidency and ruled until 1892. Pellegrini used the power of the national government to strengthen the political position of the PAN in the 1892 elections.

Roca then broke his pact with Mitre. Working through presidents Luis Sáenz Peña (1892–1894) and José Evaristo Uriburu (1894–1898), Roca increased his political power. A measure of his strength came in 1898, when Roca was reelected president. Factional strife then returned. Conservative forces, which saw no reason to meddle with the practices that had brought and kept the PAN in power, rallied around Roca. There was dissent: Increasing numbers of PAN activists came to believe that mild to moderate electoral and policy reforms might weaken opposition parties. Roca rejected this argument. Instead, he sought out new allies in his efforts to maintain his power over the PAN.

In 1904, Roca promoted Manuel Quintana as the PAN's presidential nominee. Quintana was one of the dwindling supporters of Bartolomé Mitre's policies that favored Buenos Aires over interior provinces and ports. Roca's hold over the PAN's electoral machine ensured

Quintana's success. However, Quintana's death in 1906 left the presidency to José Figueroa Alcorta, who immediately moved to strip Roca of influence within the government and the PAN. He replaced Roca sympathizers and disbanded agreements that helped Roca and his allies control the balloting in interior provinces. When Figueroa Alcorta stepped down from the presidency, he left the PAN splintered and significantly weakened.

COSMOPOLITAN VENEER

The "Golden Age" produced significant and rapid changes in Argentina. Its population was transformed by immigration. The weight of the immigrant population in the country's urban centers made it seem more European than American in character. Because of the country's rapid demographic growth, the cities and the countryside were made over.

Few colonial buildings remained in older sections of the cities. Newer construction reflected more modern and more uniform design. Buenos Aires emerged as an important literary and cultural center. Visitors as well as locals began calling it the "Paris of South America." Its newspapers became models for the Americas. Most notably, *La Nación* and *La Prensa* gained international attention and prestige as they competed for a national audience. Literary reviews and political journals increased in number and quality. The city's theaters were numerous and vibrant. The revenue generated by foreign trade allowed public and private leaders to sponsor monuments to the nation's progress: The Teatro Colón opera house, opened in 1907, reflects this age of ambition and opulence.

The wealth was not, however, broadly shared. The interior, central to Argentina in the colonial period, became increasingly distant from Buenos Aires and the Pampa region in economic, social, and political terms. Economic expansion reinforced the status of the country's elite without bringing noticeable advancement to the urban or rural poor. Labor protests and political strife underscored these distinctions.

5

Democracy's Appearance
(1890–1943)

By 1910, Argentina had achieved a measure of political stability. Its rapid economic growth and success in the world's export markets made its leaders ambitious. Two world wars and two military interventions would fundamentally alter the country's historical trajectory.

CRISIS AND REFORM (1890–1912)

The stability of the Argentine Republic during the era of the National Autonomist Party's (PAN) dominance was achieved through fraud, corruption, and violence. Significant challenges to the network of alliances and agreements that cemented the PAN's hold on power began in 1890.

With a financial crisis paralyzing the national government, opposition parties organized major attacks. Violent confrontations occurred throughout the country. Although many groups participated, the *Uniôn Cívica Radical* (Radical Civic Union, or UCR) emerged as the primary threat to the regime in power.

The UCR began as a faction of the *Unión Cívica* (Civic Union, or UC), a political organization that sustained a collection of opposition forces, including the remaining followers of Bartolomé Mitre. A split occurred within the UC in 1891. When Juárez Celman resigned from the presidency, Vice President Carlos Pelligrini succeeded him in office. Hoping to gain favors by throwing support behind Pelligrini, many within the Civic Union ended their protests. This faction, led by Mitre and his supporters, adopted the label of the *Unión Cívica Nacional* (National Civic Union). A second faction remained in opposition to the new government and continued to push for reform. This faction became the UCR.

The Radicals, as they came to be known, coalesced behind the leadership of Leandro N. Alem. Born Leandro Alen in 1842, he changed his name in order to separate himself from his father, who was executed as a result of his service in Juan Manuel de Rosas's *Mazorca* (Rosas's political police force, literally, an ear of corn). After serving in the military, he became active in a series of political parties that tried to advance and defend the interests of Buenos Aires. Although he captured a seat in the provincial Chamber of Deputies in 1872, the Revolution of 1880 and the success of the PAN sealed his political ambitions. After resigning his seat in the Chamber, Alem stayed out of politics for nearly a decade. The events of 1890 led him to return as a leader of the Civic Union. When the crisis ended, as other leaders of the opposition made their peace with the government, Alem refused to compromise.

Although both the leaders and the supporters of the UCR differed little in aggregate from the activists in the PAN or in other political parties, Alem established clear distinctions for his party in terms of its program and its tactics. The corruption and centralized rule of the Juárez Celman regime led opposition parties to push for electoral and political reforms. Alem and the Radicals accused the regime of broader corruption, in moral and spiritual terms as well as in material and political ones. He advanced that free and fair elections, open to all and subject to influence from none, was the way to purify Argentina of the PAN and its crimes. He promised that the Radicals would create an honest government capable of administering the country in a fair and progressive manner.

To bring about change, Alem supervised the establishment of local party cells that spread the Radicals' message. Party locals brought voters to the polls during elections. In the face of government interference, the locals also organized armed resistance.

The change in governments did not affect the Radicals, who remained committed to reform. As the UCR grew in strength, Alem and its leaders launched a rebellion in 1893. Expecting a nationwide explosion of protests and attacks party locals in many districts undermined the rebellion from the start with their lack of commitment. Undeterred, Alem continued to push for change. Attracting new supporters through its resistance efforts, the Radicals presented a strong electoral challenge to the PAN in local and regional elections that took place between 1894 and 1896.

Despite the Radicals' growing presence, Alem and his supporters faced a nearly insurmountable challenge. The PAN, backed by the resources of the government, ensured its electoral victories by any means. Its ability to reward loyalists and to punish challengers, and the willingness of the PAN-controlled national government to use federal intervention against provinces where opposition leaders had won office, made partial victories futile. The lack of progress discouraged Alem. In the wake of government actions that set back Radical advances in Santa Fe and Buenos Aires provinces, Alem committed suicide in 1896.

After Alem's death, his nephew Hipólito Yrigoyen assumed leadership of the UCR. Yrigoyen had helped the Radicals to become a major force in La Plata, the capital of Buenos Aires Province. After the PAN had recovered from the 1890 crisis, however, all opposition parties faced enormous difficulties. Between 1896 and 1905, the defection of Radical activists to the PAN, official harassment, and divisions caused by a power struggle within the party leadership made the UCR ineffective.

Yrigoyen eventually consolidated his leadership. Slowly, he rebuilt the party's structure and hardened its opposition to the PAN. Under Yrigoyen, the UCR drew back from direct electoral competition. As long as the PAN could freely corrupt and, when necessary, overturn the electoral process, participation served no purpose. Instead of trying to capture a minority and usually temporary presence in the national government, the Radicals withdrew from the electoral process. At first, Radicals simply did not cast votes. Labeling elections fraudulent, Yrigoyen and the Radical leaders dismissed the contests as fraudulent and therefore invalid. In subsequent elections, UCR leaders urged their followers to vote "in blank": Rather than declare for a candidate or cast votes for a slate that had no chance of achieving victory, supporters submitted blank ballots. The strategy highlighted the Radicals' support of the electoral system as they condemned it at the same time. By focusing on the number of blank ballots cast and on the lack of participation common in the era, the Radicals created a sense of broad popular support for their cause.

In the face of police actions against their organization, the Radicals under Yrigoyen grew in strength as the years passed. The UCR organized another rebellion in 1905. Drawing fewer supporters than in 1893, the protest quickly collapsed.

For a brief period, the UCR was outlawed. After the Radicals received a grant of amnesty in 1906, Yrigoyen led the party along a different track. Party locals maintained the strategy of protest votes. To build popular support, party leaders advertised their "intransigence": They stated a firm refusal to compromise their goals of honest government and fair elections.

Yrigoyen presented himself as the sole redeemer of the country. A campaign focused on the Radical leader helped develop a following for Yrigoyen, whom Radical party propaganda depicted as incorruptible and resolute. In manifestos circulated by party members, he polarized the political landscape: He and the UCR advanced "the cause" that would liberate Argentina from the violent, unconstitutional, and corrupt "regime" that the PAN had imposed.

Pressure created by the sense that the opposition was gaining coherence and strength created problems within the PAN. Factions developed over the issue of electoral reform. "Modernists" and reformers used the issue to undermine support for the party's established leadership. President Figueroa Alcorta turned the power of the government toward the reform effort. Between 1906 and 1910, his administration intervened against provincial governments seven times. His government removed from power the allies of Julio Roca. The new administrations put in charge of the provinces helped ensure that reformers quickly gained a majority in the Congress.

With the party's traditional bosses pushed aside, PAN activists instituted reforms that they hoped would maintain their party's hold over the national government. Figueroa Alcorta guaranteed the success of the reform effort by ensuring Roque Sáenz Peña's election to the presidency.

Sáenz Peña had been an active and conservative member of the PAN for decades. As an elder and experienced politician, his personal relationships with opposition leaders insulated him from attack by the PAN's weakened conservative wing. He had become committed to the cause of electoral reform and made it the main focus of his administration. He believed that rising political tensions would make it impossible for the PAN to dominate coming elections without a change in tactics. He was convinced that the PAN, with its national presence and prestige, could transform itself into a popular party capable of winning elections without resorting to fraud. Sensing that the Radicals would rebel again and, potentially, bring about a serious political crisis, Sáenz Peña and his supporters viewed free elections as the ultimate solution to the Radical Party's challenge. In open competition, the reformers were convinced, the UCR would never defeat the PAN.

Electoral reform legislation passed the Argentine Congress in 1911. The reforms established a new set of electoral procedures. All males above the age of 18 remained eligible to vote. However, voter participation became mandatory. The national army gained the responsibility of supervising future elections. By taking the place of police forces, which reformers believed had participated in past electoral fraud, soldiers became the guarantee of effective reform. The ballot became secret, which limited the ability of parties and politicians to manipulate the balloting.

The reforms also changed the system of political representation. Party slates continued to compete for legislative positions. In subsequent elections, a percentage of the contested seats would go to the minority parties. Reformers hoped that by guaranteeing minority party representation in national and provincial legislatures, effective participation and authentic debate would develop.

A companion law cleared the voter roles of phantom voters and false names. The padded voter lists had in the past helped precinct bosses rig the vote when necessary. The new lists represented a final guarantee of clean elections.

The reformers believed that the changes adopted in 1911 would present no threat to their party's dominant status. Foreigners, who at the time represented roughly a third of the country's total population, had no voice in Argentine politics. Women remained disenfranchised. The PAN leaders, who viewed theirs as the country's only viable national party, anticipated continued electoral victories.

THE RADICALS TAKE POWER (1912–1916)

The reforms, generally known as the *Ley Sáenz Peña* (Sáenz Peña Law), took effect in 1912. Quickly, Radical Party leaders directed their organizational efforts toward the new round of elections. The party recruited local organizers, who helped the Radicals attract support from people who had not traditionally participated in past elections, such as the sons of immigrants. The local leaders took charge of party committees, which coordinated voter recruitment at election time. This effort created a massive national popular base for the UCR, which other parties, including the PAN, lacked.

The results became clear in 1916. In the first presidential election held under the new system, Hipólito Yrigoyen captured 340,802 of the 747,471 votes cast. Although the UCR did not receive a majority of the votes, the party's performance eclipsed that of all the other parties. The Progressive Democratic Party, whose leaders had once been part of the PAN, finished second with only 99,000 votes.

The electoral victory left the Radicals in control in the provinces of Córdoba, Entre Ríos, Mendoza, Santiago del Estero, and Tucumán. It also controlled the Federal Capital. Overall, it achieved a majority of the seats in the Chamber of Deputies. Turning the tactic of federal intervention against the conservatives, the Radicals soon took charge of other provinces, including Buenos Aires.

The national Senate, however, remained in the hands of the Radicals' opponents, who united to block new reforms. Although the executive branch sent a slate of proposals to Congress, the opposition block in the Senate stalled Yrigoyen's legislative agenda. Economic conditions then created additional challenges for the new administration.

WORLD WAR I AND ITS IMPACT (1912–1921)

The centennial of Argentina's independence was a year of celebration. Within two years, economic problems undermined any lingering sense of pride. One focal point of the crisis developed in Argentina's countryside. The success of the country's rural industries pushed land values to record levels. Farmers who once successfully worked the land found their chance at making a profit squeezed out by rising rents and level market prices for the grains they produced.

Conditions worsened the following year. A second source of trouble came into play. Conflicts over the Balkans tightened financial markets. Moves by Great Britain and other countries to shore up their finances rippled through the world economy. Higher interest rates put pressure on Argentina and other debtor nations. When weather and locust invasions combined to create a nearly total failure of the country's grain harvest, Argentina fell into depression.

The start of World War I in 1914 made matters significantly worse. The ranching sector benefited from the war, since the countries at war prized meat of any variety as rations for the soldiers: Canned and frozen beef and mutton found a rising demand throughout the war. Other rural industries fared poorly. Argentina's location presented a major problem. Argentina's wartime trading partners, essentially limited to Great Britain and France, did not risk sending ships on the long voyage to the South Atlantic for goods other than those judged crucial to the war effort. Meat shipments met this criterion. Grain shipments did not. Consequently, market prices for wheat and corn—the leading crops—plummeted. The lack of market possibilities left grain harvests lying in the fields. The crisis affected a variety of related activities: railroads, harvesting crews, farm implement producers and importers, and landowners who rented parcels to farmers, all felt the effects of the war-induced depression.

The Argentine government, its budgets broken by the wartime emergency, offered no remedies. When coordinated efforts by Great Britain and the United States managed to open up shipping channels to and from Argentina in 1917, foreign demand for Argentina's rural produce jumped. Laborers, who had been forced to deal with the depression on their own, pushed for improved wages and working conditions. To gain leverage, hired hands in the countryside organized a strike that threatened the 1917–1918 grain harvest. In the cities, laborers engaged in an unprecedented wave of strikes.

The Yrigoyen government dealt with each labor challenge in a fashion designed to maximize its political advantage. Rural strikes pitted laborers, many foreigners, against tenant farmers and landowners. The government sided with the employers in this instance. To quell rumored threats that "anarchists and agitators" would burn harvests and disrupt rail shipments, the government dispatched police forces into rural districts. Suspected organizers were arrested.

The UCR's rivalry with the Socialist Party, which viewed the city of Buenos Aires as its primary base, led the Radicals to side with labor, in part, when dealing with urban strife. Government intervention in a port strike in 1916 led to arbitration between workers and port managers. As a consequence, it allowed laborers to press British-owned railroad companies for higher wages and improved working conditions in 1917 and 1918.

The government's apparent pro-labor tilt angered its conservative opposition. Business groups, in concert with foreign companies and the Argentine Rural Society, accused the government of promoting alien ideas at the expense of Argentina's best interests. With the economic dislocations that the war produced still plaguing the country, the political scene became polarized.

At the start of 1919, the efforts of labor and the government collided violently. Workers at the Vasena Mills, a factory that produced steel for local industries, had organized a strike to win improved working conditions, higher wages, and union leverage. Exchanges between strikers and police in the city of Buenos Aires led to a mass mobilization of organized workers. On January 9, a mass demonstration in the Plaza del Congreso took place, involving over 150,000 protesters. Strikes shut down the city and port district. Conservatives blamed anarchists for the action, and they urged Yrigoyen to end the strikes.

Having lost control of the situation, Yrigoyen ordered army units to restore order. For a week, the army, along with vigilantes, ruthlessly attacked the protesters. By the end of the *Semana Trágica* (Tragic Week), the intervention had killed or wounded hundreds of workers and protesters.

The government's turn against the workers continued in the years that followed. It tolerated the actions of the *Liga Patriótica* (Patriotic League), which conducted terror campaigns against union leaders and their supporters. When field hands in Patagonia organized a strike against sheep estancieros in 1921, the government dispatched the cavalry to annihilate the so-called Bolshevik agitators.

PERSONALISTS AND ANTI-PERSONALISTS (1922–1930)

Yrigoyen faced the challenge of maintaining power within the party as his presidential term ended in 1922. Control of the government had been an essential part of his success as the leader of the Radical Party: From the presidency, Yrigoyen could dole out contracts and jobs to loyalists, who would then direct their energies toward advancing the interests of the UCR. In a surprising move, Yrigoyen arranged for Marcelo T. de Alvear to be the party's presidential candidate and his successor.

Alvear was from a wealthy family with a long history in Argentine politics. An early member of the Radical cause, Alvear was in Europe when news of his nomination broke. During the campaign, he remained abroad and allowed the party machinery to ensure his election. Other parties presented little opposition. Winning more votes in 1922 than Yrigoyen did in 1916, Alvear began his term with the Radicals in control of the Chamber of Deputies, the national Senate, and a majority of the country's provinces.

The still strong effects of the postwar economic turmoil directed Alvear's policy initiatives. Fiscal problems demanded that the government cut its budget. Alvear's ministers transformed the budget struggle into a campaign against corruption. Targeting graft and favoritism, the Alvear administration cut back unnecessary programs and cleared from its employment roles hundreds of workers who had received paychecks in exchange for their political service. Since these phantom employees were often Yrigoyen supporters, the actions of the Alvear government created a split in the Radical Party: The *Yrigoyenistas* (Yrigoyen loyalists) pledged loyalty to the party's leader, and the *Anti-personalistas* (Anti-Personalists) emerged as a growing faction in favor of change.

The collapse of the wartime meat export market quickly surpassed all other issues as the new government's primary concern. During the war, landowners diverted increasing amounts of their rural properties toward cattle ranching and sheep herding. New producers joined old in an attempt to take advantage of the artificial demand for meat. When purchases for the Grande Entente military forces ended, a shakeout occurred. Established ranchers, who had shifted out of the chilled beef trade, returned to their prewar practices. Others, including breeders who had dramatically increased the size of their herds, and speculators, who had started new ranches in the fringe areas of the Pampa, had no escape.

By 1921, marginal producers found no market for their herds. Alvear took office just as the call for government intervention in the crisis peaked. The Argentine Rural Society, working through its congressional allies, targeted the meat-packing plants. Society representatives accused the plants, which were owned by British and American companies, of fixing prices at levels that threatened the entire ranching industry with bankruptcy. They pushed the government to sanction the packing companies. They called for minimum prices and the creation of new, locally, controlled packing plants that would compete with the foreign companies.

As legislation that addressed these concerns appeared in the Chamber of Deputies, the packing plants reacted. A moratorium on meat purchases shut down cattle purchases and exports. This action sent the Argentine Rural Society, the Congress, and the Alvear administration into retreat. The ranching crisis ran its course.

By 1923, the Alvear government did present a set of proposals that supporters championed as progressive economic reforms and promotions. Affecting grain production and marketing, tariffs, rural colonization, and credit, the new legislative agenda fell short of true innovation. The promotions affecting grain farming, for example, aimed at making the harvests more marketable. The tariff reforms protected a few "natural" industries suited to Argentina and its role as an exporter of agricultural and mineral products. Rather than create new opportunities or fundamental change, the legislation brought forward between 1922 and 1924 reinforced standard practices.

The lack of ambition mattered little. Because of the split between the administration and Yrigoyen supporters, the Argentine Congress fractured. Debate and divisions between the two factions of the Radical Party prevented significant legislation from gaining sanction. At times Congress closed for lack of a quorum. From 1926, Radical Party leaders directed all their energies toward the competition for the presidency in 1928.

Alvear did little to help the Anti-Personalists. As a result, Yrigoyen supporters were able to take charge of the party machinery. By 1926, *yrigoyenistas* controlled almost all the precinct committees, and their representatives dominated the national and provincial legislatures. To build popular support, they made the issue of oil the focus of their push to reelect Yrigoyen.

Oil reserves had been discovered in Argentina's Andean and Patagonian regions. The discovery of a large oil field at the Patagonian site of Comodore Rivadavia in 1907 led to the creation of a national oil reserve. Pioneered by state initiatives and foreign companies, the industry developed slowly. Imported coal and petroleum remained Argentina's major energy sources through World War I. Despite wartime shortages and high market prices, domestic oil production accounted for less than 10 percent of the national demand. Yrigoyen had tried to build the oil industry into a larger public enterprise during his first term in office. The opposition-controlled Senate blocked his legislative efforts until 1922. In his final months in office, Yrigoyen secured the creation of the *Dirección Nacional de los Yacimientos Petrolíferos Fiscales* (National Oil Agency, or YPF). The YPF expanded its operations during the Alvear administration. In 1925, it opened a refinery in La Plata to provide gasoline, kerosene, and other products for sale through a network of fueling stations that it came to control.

As the YPF pushed to develop the industry, foreign companies had also secured mineral rights and developed wells. Their presence made them a target that Yrigoyen and his supporters used to focus their campaign. Playing on nationalist sentiments, Yrigoyen promised to nationalize oil production, refining, and distribution in Argentina once he achieved reelection. The Radicals transformed Standard Oil, an American corporation that had taken control of oil fields in Salta with the help of the province's conservative political leadership, into a symbolic enemy.

The nationalistic campaign against the capitalist invader rallied popular support behind Yrigoyen's candidacy. The campaign was enormously successful. Yrigoyen's faction of the Radical Party captured nearly 60 percent of the popular vote. Yrigoyen had firm control over the Chamber of Deputies in the election's wake, but the national Senate remained split: No party controlled a majority of votes in the upper Chamber.

Yrigoyen and his supporters worked to gain control of the Senate. In anticipation of the 1930 elections, administration allies initiated attacks against their rivals in the press. Confrontations between rival party loyalists became common. When Radical Party operatives assassinated Carlos Washington Lencinas in 1929, opposition to the Personalist faction in Mendoza Province crumbled. The executive branch also invalidated the Senate election results in San Juan the following year, which stripped two additional seats from Yrigoyen's rivals.

MILITARY INTERVENTION AND DICTATORSHIP (1930–1931)

Anticipating full control of the Senate, the Yrigoyen administration looked forward to 1931. Economic conditions had, however, already created major problems for the government. A large part of Yrigoyen's political strength came from the loyalty of the activists who supported him and his government. Many of these activists were rewarded for their loyalty with salaries that they received from the government. Hired as "inspectors" or administrative officers in one or more of the expanding departments of the executive branch, these paid loyalists earned paychecks for work that they did not perform. This system of rewards, as well as the administration's ambitious public works proposals, depended on a healthy budget. Revenues from duties on exports and imports were the government's primary support.

By the end of 1928, the effects of what would become the Great Depression were already present in Argentina. Excess supply in the world's grain markets sent wheat and corn prices to new lows just as the 1928–1929 harvest got underway. Dim prospects led farmers to cut back on their equipment purchases and use of hired labor. Reduced rail traffic and complaints about low wages signaled the beginning of hard times.

As operating costs outstripped revenues, government services were reduced. The harvest of 1929–1930 started in the midst of depressed market conditions abroad. By the harvest's end, in March 1930, Argentina's economic condition had become dire. The Yrigoyen government seemed paralyzed. The president's enemies suggested that he had grown senile.

Turmoil in Congress stalled any efforts to meet the emergency. In the midst of this crisis, right-wing opponents of the administration plotted a military coup. Within the plotters' ranks were extreme nationalists, who had broken from Yrigoyen during his first term in office. Labeling the president a demagogue and a promoter of policies "alien" to Argentina, this extreme faction pushed to bring down the government and replace it with a military-backed dictatorship. The nationalists united behind General José Felix Uriburu, who led a small detachment of troops into the Federal Capital on September 6,1930. The attack faced no significant opposition. Within hours, Uriburu and his followers controlled the Casa Rosada.

Uriburu became provisional president after the coup. As army units loyal to the movement arrested Radical Party leaders, Uriburu assembled a government from the ranks of his supporters. In the face of the economic crisis, the government's actions were mixed: in part, orthodox, in turn, pragmatic. As it struggled to balance its budget, the Ministry of Finance cut government spending. At the same time, concerns about mounting unemployment led to public works projects, including a national road construction program.

This blend of restraint and activism stemmed from the nationalists' desire to prevent any breakdown in Argentine society. The nationalists feared that the depression might lead to conflict between social groups. As a consequence, they planned to use the state as a tool to enforce social harmony.

One of the many demonstrations that occurred in the Federal Capital in the days that followed the *golpe* that removed President Yrigoyen from power on September 6, 1930. (Bettmann/Corbis)

Uriburu did not hold onto power long enough to launch any fundamental reform of Argentine society. Within the dictatorship, conservatives moved to isolate Uriburu and the nationalists and, in short order, displace them from the government. The regime's failure to check political challenges to the provisional government was telling. In April 1931, Uriburu allowed an election in Buenos Aires Province, believing it would demonstrate the popularity of the coup and his dictatorship. Contrary to Uriburu's expectations, the balloting turned into a condemnation of the regime. Candidates of the ousted Radical Party attained large majorities. Rather than accept popular will, Uriburu annulled the election and banned the Radical Party from any and all operations.

THE *DÉCADA INFAME* AND THE *CONCORDANICIA* (1932–1940)

Conservatives used the incident to build a case for a shift away from dictatorship. They successfully organized a second, national election in November 1931. With the Radicals blocked from the ballot, conservative supporters of coup took charge of the government. Agustín P. Justo, an army general and supporter of the Anti-Personalist faction of the Radical Party, became president. Three parties now shared power in Congress: The *Partido Democrático Nacional* (National Democratic Party, or PDN), the Anti-Personalist Radicals, and the Independent Socialists, a conservative faction of the Socialist Party.

The three parties formed a regime known as the *Concordancia*. Its critics referred to the Concordancia's reign as the *Década infame* (Infamous Decade). In control of the political system from 1932 until 1943, government leaders relied on fraud and force to rig elections and to maintain the appearance of a constitutional, representative form of government. Although the parties involved created a semblance of competition, the participants were largely in agreement over almost every policy until 1938.

In the face of the Great Depression, the coalition focused mainly on maintaining its hold over power and on defending the Argentine economy. The Justo administration's first reactions to the economic crisis were limited. Justo's ministers judged the depression to be a product of the collapse of the world market. From this assumption, the government moved in 1932 to protect its share of markets. British discussions with its colonies, which led to the Ottawa Pact of 1932, created a sensation: Under the pact, Great Britain gave trading preferences and protections to its colonies. Left standing, the policy of "Imperial Preference" established by the Ottawa Pact would have given Canada and Australia significant advantages over Argentina in the foreign market that government planners believed was most important.

The Justo administration dispatched a negotiating team to London. In 1933, negotiators signed the Roca-Runciman Treaty. This agreement guaranteed the British market for Argentine beef by setting 1932 import levels from Argentina as a minimum base. It also sanctioned the expansion of Argentine-owned meat-packing plants, which would help lessen the power of foreign-controlled companies over the beef trade.

In return, the British government won a number of concessions: Tariffs affecting British firms and merchandise were cut, British companies received priority treatment in the distribution of foreign exchange, loans owned to British interests had their service protected, importers were insulated from future exchange rate shifts, and British shippers gained preferential standing against all other carriers.

The pact came to symbolize the unequal relationship between Argentina and Great Britain. In the opinion of most government critics, the concessions made Argentina appear to be an economic colony of Britain. Government negotiators believed, however, that in the face of rising tariff barriers and trade ruled by treaty, the price of guaranteeing access to the country's most important partner was worthwhile.

In the following years, the Justo government negotiated trade treaties with other European and Latin American governments. It hoped to preserve Argentina's status as a leading exporter of agricultural goods in the face of rising tariffs and nationalist economic policies. By maintaining trade links, government officials also believed that the country's economic problems would eventually be relieved.

By 1933, worsening conditions in Argentina and abroad convinced the Justo administration that orthodox economic policies, which had served the country well during the previous century, could not withstand the pressure created by the Great Depression. Trade imbalances, falling export revenues, sluggish demand, and dwindling tax revenues threatened the government and the private sector with insolvency. The number of unemployed workers mounted in the capital and in the other large cities of the interior. Farmers, facing record low market prices, organized protests in Buenos Aires. Unable to meet mortgage or rent payments, they threatened to leave the coming harvest in the field.

Sensing an emergency, President Justo replaced his economic team. Federico Pinedo took over as the minister of economics. Working with the new agricultural minister, Luis Duhau, Pinedo unveiled the *Plan de Acción Económica* (Plan of Economic Action) in November 1933. The plan mainly addressed two pressing problems: falling commodity prices, which discouraged producers and threatened the industries connected with agricultural production and exports, and the collapse of the peso relative to other currencies, which disrupted foreign trade and hindered economic recovery.

The government had taken the peso off the gold standard in 1929 during the opening phase of the depression. With its value determined by the exchange market, the peso lost value in exchange for other currencies in the years that followed. During the Uriburu dictatorship, the government established a practice of buying and selling exchange for use in foreign trade. This placed limitations on currency flight, but it also frustrated importers and exporters.

The Plan of Economic Action put the currency exchange system under the control of a newly created exchange board, which granted traders permits that allowed them to conduct their business. Traders who lacked permits had to secure foreign currency for their transactions on a parallel market at much higher rates of exchange. The board's actions gave the government control over the companies that participated in foreign trade. The system also allowed the government to limit the amount of total imports allowed into Argentina as well as limit the number of countries from which imports came. This helped the government balance its foreign trade while it maintained more stable currency exchange rates.

The exchange controls generated sizable profits for the government. By 1940, after seven years of operations, the auctions and the permit sales had yielded over 1 billion pesos. These profits were directed toward solving the second grave problem produced by the Great Depression. Market prices for almost all of Argentina's agricultural goods had fallen to historic lows by 1933. With the stated goal of maintaining the existing structure of the rural economy, the Plan of Economic Action established a series of regulatory boards to set base prices for essential products, with wheat, corn, and meat products given the most attention.

The base prices were set at levels above estimated costs of production. Initially, all the prices were significantly higher than those found in the commodity markets. By purchasing the protected commodities at its base prices, the government guaranteed that producers could stay in operation as the depression continued. The funds created by the operations of the exchange commission enabled the government to cover the difference between its base prices and the lower market prices.

The government's intervention was timed perfectly. Harvest operations were completed on schedule with no disruptions. The use of exchange regulation revenues to maintain price supports might have created an enormous economic burden for the government had market conditions remained in depression. Fortunately for Argentina, conditions abroad brought needed relief. The "Dust Bowl" brought an unprecedented crisis to agricultural industries in the United States. Drought conditions in Canada and Australia, beginning in 1934, cut grain production in those countries at the same time. As a result, with falling production and reduced stocks in storage, prices for grain moved upward between 1934 and 1938. Within a year of its initial operations, Argentina's Grain Regulatory Board no longer needed to purchase wheat and corn at the minimum prices it had established. The Argentine government quickly directed its exchange board profits toward other necessities.

The government then put into place additional reforms that secured the national economy. In 1934, Minister Pinedo announced the creation of a central bank. Firmly in the state's hands, the *Banco Central* (Central Bank) gave the government control over its fiscal policy to a much greater degree than ever before: It controlled the supply of currency, credit rates, and the value of the peso in relation to other currencies.

Observers in Argentina and abroad hailed the 1933 interventions as major successes. Argentina's economy recovered, and its rural industries expanded. The interventions were, however, defensive. Pinedo, Duhau, and the Justo government hoped to keep rural industries, which served as the foundation for the country's service sector, transportation industries, and government revenues, in operation until the crisis passed. None of the proposals suggested reforms. Instead, the interventions aimed at keeping Argentina's "mother industries" as they were.

Of greater significance, the Great Depression set in motion significant social and economic shifts within Argentina. The economic crisis made rural producers change the way they operated. As a result, opportunities for work in the countryside fell. As this occurred, new industries appeared in Argentina's cities. The high cost of imported goods had created a market for locally produced substitutes, but a lack of capital and machinery limited the change. The new factories were small and focused on the production of simple goods like clothing or canned food. As new factories opened, they attracted laborers who settled in the country's expanding urban and suburban centers.

Argentina was already an "urban" country, with a majority of its population residing in cities by 1914. The Great Depression expanded the country's urban population and accelerated its urbanization rate.

The expansion of domestic industry increased the number of workers and the relative size of the industrial workforce in comparison to the smaller rural and larger service sectors. The lives and livelihood of industrial workers varied from those who worked in the traditional "mother industries" that had been responsible for Argentina's economic growth since independence. This shift would become a base for important social and political developments after World War II.

Its apparent success in managing the economy helped justify the Justo administration's aggressive moves against political opponents. Censorship made it difficult and dangerous for the press to report on political protests. Critical stories or suspected support of opposition causes led to numerous closures of local and national newspapers. Although the repression of activists connected with the Radical Party had ceased after 1934, many opposition leaders remained out of politics or in exile through most of the 1930s.

Within the Concordancia, critical voices emerged in reaction to particular policy actions. Lisandro de la Torre, a senator and the key leader of the *Partido Demócrata Progresista* (Progressive Democratic Party), based in Santa Fe, accused the government of corruption and favoritism in its handling of contract negotiations with foreign companies. In particular, de la Torre targeted pacts between the government and the foreign-owned meat-packing plants, which continued to process the majority of the country's meat exports. De la Torre's attacks continued until 1935, when one of his supporters, Senator Enzo Bordabehere of Santa Fe Province, was assassinated on the floor of the Senate.

Anti-Personalist Radicals became more than a "loyal" opposition after 1935. Within the Argentine Congress and, when allowed, in the national press, Radical leaders attacked the economic policies of the government and the lack of political freedoms. In reaction to growing protests, but also as an expression of confidence in the strength of the Concordancia and its hold over the political system, the Justo administration orchestrated the nomination of Roberto Ortiz as the favored candidate for the presidency in 1938. Ortiz had served as Justo's minister of public works. A member of the Anti-Personalist wing of the Radical Party, many believed that he would bring about political reforms that would soften the Concordancia and move Argentina back toward a more open political system.

Ortiz promised to run a fair campaign. Opposition candidates, however, had their efforts repressed by violence and fraud. Despite the rigged nature of his election, Ortiz committed himself to political reforms after assuming office. His administration accomplished little. Ortiz's health became a significant problem after 1939. A diabetic, his chronic illness soon left him blind. As the months passed, Ortiz's physical condition worsened. This left the government without direction as competing factions emerged.

Fractures in the national government occurred in the face of renewed economic crisis. The recovery of farming in North America saturated the world's grain markets and drove prices to new lows, and then the outbreak of World War II created a shipping shortage. Argentina faced a crisis that combined the effects of World War I and the Great Depression: scarce imports, reduced grain shipments, and low prices for Argentine grains.

Economics Minister Federico Pinedo proposed an ambitious plan to deal with the crisis in 1940. Setting aside the reliance on exports of agricultural goods and the importation of manufactures, Pinedo called for government investment in construction and industrial promotions that would make the country more self-sufficient.

The National Congress, still divided over the 1938 elections, refused to act on the Pinedo plan. In July 1940, Vice President Ramón S. Castillo assumed the presidency as a result of Ortiz's incapacity. Castillo, in political terms, differed from Ortiz in every respect. He represented the most conservative elements within the Concordancia. Having objected to Ortiz's more liberal economic and political policies, Castillo moved quickly to reverse them. The Pinedo plan died in Congress. Promises of future electoral reforms were replaced by police actions against political opponents and harsh censorship of the national press. These actions alienated reformers and lessened popular support for the administration.

THE FALL OF THE CONCORDANCIA (1940–1943)

The political opposition suffered major blows in 1942 and 1943. The few leaders who were capable of rallying the factions that might have challenged Castillo for control over the Concordancia, such as Marcelo T. de Alvear, Roberto Ortiz, or Agustín P. Justo, died. Opponents in the national government were pressured to resign and then replaced with hard-line conservatives. With his political position apparently secured, Castillo scheduled presidential elections in the fall of 1943.

Castillo's success against his political opponents did not stem a rising opposition to his government within the Argentine military. Castillo's government operated in isolation. Its political opponents, united in opposition to the regime, blocked congressional action. Limited in its ability to act, the executive branch focused on holding onto power and waiting for the war to end. Castillo and his allies anticipated that, after the war, trade would revive, economic conditions would improve, and the fiscal condition of the government would brighten. Peace would allow his government to end Argentina's political stalemate and take full charge of the Concordancia.

International conditions added to the country's isolation. Nazi victories in Europe denied Argentina free access to the continent. Submarine patrols reduced ocean traffic and interfered with exports to Britain. At the same time, the United States aggressively pushed for hemispheric solidarity against the fascist powers. For the Castillo administration, any move in support of the United States presented problems. American tariffs and quarantines had blocked Argentine goods from the U.S. market for decades. As a result, the Castillo government saw few advantages in any move to support the United States during the war. Up to 1943, it appeared likely that Europe would remain under Nazi domination for an extended period. Hoping to gain access to the continent as a trading partner in the future, the Castillo government maintained its neutrality and resisted U.S.-backed initiatives that would have compromised its status.

This led the U.S. government to challenge Argentina along a number of fronts. It offered no economic relief or trade promotions that might have helped Argentina absorb the problems created by the closure of trade with Europe. Military and economic aid to other Latin American countries, especially Brazil, created more serious problems. Argentine nationalists came to fear future military conflicts with neighboring countries.

These fears led nationalists to push for the creation of a domestic military arms industry. They believed that the ability to produce their own weapons represented the only guarantee of Argentina's sovereignty. Because of the government's lack of action, nationalists joined with Radicals in opposition to the regime.

Castillo's reliance on repression did nothing to stem the opposition. In the summer of 1943, election preparations got underway. Rumors that Castillo would orchestrate the election of Robustiano Patrón Costas to the presidency appeared. Patrón Costas, from Salta, was an aged but powerful leader of the most conservative faction of the Concordancia. The owner of sugar estancias, he had benefited from government price supports put in place in the 1930s. His economic power was matched by his political control over Salta. Having orchestrated Castillo's nomination as the official vice presidential candidate in 1938, he was rewarded with the opportunity to take control of the Concordancia.

Patrón Costas personified the extreme conservatism of the ruling regime. Observers were certain he would maintain the orthodox policies that Castillo had put into place. They also were confident that as president, Patrón Costas would continue to rely on corruption, fraud, and repression to hold onto political power. Although he had made no formal statements, nationalists were convinced that Patrón Costas would end Argentina's neutrality and join the Grand Alliance against the Axis powers. Combined, these fears set in motion a military coup that toppled the Castillo regime on June 6, 1943.

6

Perón and Argentina (1943–1955)

Many Argentines welcomed the coup that ended the Concordancia. The army officers involved faced no serious opposition, and they established a new government that promised to protect Argentina from all threats internal and external. Observers anticipated a moderate government that would return power to civilian hands in short order, but the military's intervention instead set in motion a fundamental shift in Argentine politics. Juan Domingo Perón, a junior army officer, emerged at the head of a political movement that remains a major force in Argentina.

THE MILITARY IN POWER (1943–1945)

General Arturo Rawson led the move against Castillo. He appeared to have strong support in the army and the navy. Assuming the powers of the presidency, he moved immediately to form a new government. In public statements, he promised that the government would bring stability back to the country. Rawson had helped unite the officer corps behind the coup. As the acting president, he quickly lost what support he had attained. Three days after pushing out the Castillo government, factions within the armed forces forced Rawson to step down. In his place, General Pedro Ramírez became president.

Ramírez had served as minister of war under Castillo. Despite this, he had been rumored to be plotting against the Concordancia in the weeks leading up to the coup. Upon assuming the presidency, he filled his cabinet with military officers who had helped push Castillo from power.

Outside of Argentina, the coup and Ramírez's consolidation of power signaled a shift in Argentine foreign policy. In Washington, D.C., U.S. State Department officials believed Argentina was moving toward joining their Pan-American initiatives. Within the new government, however, policy debates split open the cabinet. Moderates recognized that Argentina's neutrality led the United States to hold back economic and military aid while it rewarded neighboring Brazil. Holding little hope in U.S. assistance, nationalists believed the government should maintain its neutrality, which would serve it well once the war ended. Rather than look abroad for solutions, nationalists believed, the country had to become more self-sufficient in economic and military terms.

Within the Argentine armed forces, the nationalists were a minority faction. They were, however, well organized. Nationalist officers had formed a *logia*, or secret society, to create unity and coordinate a collective effort to shape military and political events in March 1943. Known as the GOU, an acronym believed to stand for *Grupo de Oficiales Unidos* (Group of United Officers), it had played a key role in the coup that toppled the Castillo government. As the military moved to consolidate its power, members of the GOU promoted the group's political views.

To hold their position, the moderates under Ramírez needed to win concessions from the United States. Lingering fears of Argentina's sympathies for Nazi Germany and Fascist Italy blocked such moves. When the United States refused to lift military sanctions against Argentina, moderates within the military government lost their credibility. Bending to nationalist demands, moderates resigned from the government in October 1943. Nationalist officers and ideologues then took their place. General Edelmiro Farrell, first appointed minister of war by Ramírez, became vice president. Gustavo Martínez Zuviría, a Catholic nationalist and literary figure commonly known by his pseudonym Hugo Wast, became the minister of justice and public instruction. Juan Domingo Perón, who had orchestrated the nationalist push against the moderates in the Castillo government, became the director of the National Labor Department.

International pressure against Argentina increased as 1944 began. The United States labeled Argentina's military government as fascist. It placed new financial and trade restrictions against Argentina and pressured Latin American governments to follow its lead. At the same time, the United States increased its military aid to its strategic partners in the region. The new shipments of arms to Brazil convinced many that Argentina would soon be attacked.

President Ramírez moved to steady the nationalists. The Argentine government signed reciprocal trade agreements with neighboring countries to partially offset its lack of European markets. It accelerated its efforts to develop a domestic military arms industry. It also increased its spending on military supplies and training, and it tried to find alternative sources for military aid and equipment.

With a world war raging, alternative sources of aid and equipment were scarce. Signaling its desperation, the Ramírez government sent a special envoy to negotiate with Nazi Germany. When British officials in the West Indies captured its agent, the Argentine government faced disaster.

Pressured by the British and the United States, Ramírez agreed to break all diplomatic relations with the Axis powers by the end of January 1944. This move alarmed the nationalists. Fearing Argentina would capitulate to U.S. pressure and end its neutrality, the nationalists forced Ramírez to resign from office. Vice President Farrell became president. Perón, who was then emerging as the government's most influential member, assumed Farrell's place as vice president and war minister while he retained his control over the expanded Secretariat of Labor and Social Welfare.

The cabinet shuffling assured the nationalists. Unfortunately, the U.S. government refused to end its sanctions against Argentina. As World War II moved toward its climax, the military government in Argentina remained isolated. Protests against its dictatorial rule mounted. Leaders of the Radical Party, which supported the coup in 1943, demanded a return to constitutional rule. Hoping to ensure its own survival, the military government moved to build popular support.

BUILDING A POPULAR BASE (1944–1945)

The government countered its enemies' protests by launching propaganda campaigns and relief programs. The government's economic promotions, which were aimed at stabilizing the economy and developing new, strategic industries, became symbolic acts. The military labeled itself as the champion of an independent and vibrant

Argentina in radio campaigns, public processions, and new publications that its ministries published.

Building on this rhetorical base, Farrell's ministers supervised the creation of new programs that aimed at linking the government to broader segments of society. In the countryside, the government hoped to gain support from the rural workforce through the introduction of regulations that would raise wages and improve working conditions. The regulations, grouped together as the *Estatuto del Peón* (Laborer's Statute), produced mixed results. Although they established clear improvements for rural workers, they angered farmers and ranchers, who vowed to resist their implementation.

Urban laborers became the government's main target. During the Concordancia, labor unions had grown in number and their membership had increased despite the antagonistic actions of the national government and employers. Communists and socialists channeled their energies into the union movement during this era. In the wake of the 1943 coup, the military came down hard on communist union organizers. To the dictatorship's liberals and ultranationalists, the communist influence over the workers represented a mortal danger. A key group of officers inside the military government took a more pragmatic stance. They believed that an alliance with the workers would provide a crucial base for their political ambitions.

Juan Perón, who had taken charge of the Labor Department in October 1943, supervised the effort to cultivate labor support. Born in 1895, he was the son of a farmer. Ambitious in his youth, he entered the *Colegio Militar* (National Military School) in 1911. By 1930, he had attained the rank of captain in the army. It was at this stage that he entered into political action: He participated in General José F. Uriburu's successful coup against Yrigoyen and then served as a messenger between the factions that formed around Uriburu, who became the provisional president, and Agustín P. Justo, who emerged as the leader of the Concordancia.

Perón's activism and loyalty allowed him to move up the ranks. He gained the opportunity to travel abroad between 1938 and 1940 as a representative of the Concordancia. This assignment allowed him to study Mussolini's Italy, where he served as Argentina's military attaché, and to visit Fascist Spain as Francisco Franco began his dictatorship. These experiences confirmed his nationalist ideals.

Although he was not yet well known by the Argentine public, Perón was highly respected within the armed forces. By 1943, the actions of the Castillo regime had led him to join in the formation of the

GOU and, soon after, the June Revolution that put the armed forces in power.

Perón had long argued within military circles that the army should lead an effort to reshape Argentina's economy and society. More than a decade before the 1943 coup, he called for the creation of a targeted industrialization program that would help the country move toward economic independence. With the armed forces in command of the government, Perón emerged as a key strategist. The industrialization program that he supported became official policy.

Perón supervised the push to build popular support for the new regime. In its first months in power, the military government had arrested strikers and harassed labor organizers in a fashion that varied little from the practices of the Concordancia. Declared enemies and suspected communists were purged from the unions. By the end of 1943, however, the government's labor policy changed. First, under Perón's direction, the Labor Department expanded. Redesignated as the *Secretaría de Trabajo y Bienestar Social* (Secretariat of Labor and Social Welfare), the division became a patron of organized labor.

The first signal of the shift came during a railroad workers' strike at the end of 1943. Perón intervened and settled the strike by rewarding the key *Unión Ferroviaria* (Railway Union) with major concessions: Its members received a pay raise and changes in work rules in exchange for ending their walkout. In 1944, unions in other industries launched or threatened additional strikes. In each case, Perón arbitrated a settlement that rewarded the unions. Within months, unions recognized their opportunity. In meetings, in publications, and through public demonstrations, the unions cheered Perón and his actions.

Behind the scenes, the union victories came with important stipulations. Perón did reward the unions, but with the clear understanding that the unions would accept government leadership over their affairs. The union movement lost much of its independence. Thanks to Perón's efforts, the military had turned labor from a political threat into an orderly and compliant source of support.

Not all were pleased with this shift. The owners of factories and businesses objected to the new pro-labor policies. As the secretary of labor and social welfare, Perón had decreed blanket improvements. Higher wages and better working conditions raised costs and created problems for employers. More important, their leverage over the workforce slipped. When Perón ordered all business to offer an extra month's wages and guaranteed vacations for urban workers, the employers labeled Perón and the military government as fascist.

With encouragement from the British and U.S. governments, who still regarded the dictatorship as suspicious, employers and the political opposition launched a campaign to roll back Perón's reforms and oust the Farrell government.

FROM DEFEAT TO VICTORY (1945–1946)

In late 1945, Perón faced more serious opposition within the dictatorship. Extremists viewed Perón's promotion of unions and workers as self-serving and dangerous. They preferred a ban on unions and a harder line on the government's political opposition. Consequently, the government again split into factions. At the same time, public protests against the dictatorship focused on Perón.

Surrendering to the pressure, President Farrell forced Perón to resign his positions within the government on October 9. Farrell then had him arrested on October 12 and ordered him held prisoner on Martín García Island. The political opposition, which had targeted Perón, believed Farrell's move signaled the imminent collapse of the dictatorship. The military leaders, however, refused to relinquish power.

Perón's arrest did not solve the dictatorship's mounting problems. With Perón in detention, public pressure turned back toward the government. Farrell and Perón's enemies within the military remained united against the suggestion that they surrender control of the government. The rival factions could not reach agreement over what the government should do next. During this period of confusion, Perón's arrest mobilized his supporters. Orchestrated by union leaders, allies within the military government, and his mistress, Eva María Duarte, columns of workers marched on the Casa Rosada on October 17. The demonstrators demanded Perón's return. His allies within the dictatorship had, in fact, already secured his position. As the protesters cheered, Perón stepped onto the balcony of the Casa Rosada. The crisis had turned: The mass demonstration shattered the opposition, and Farrell publicly reinstated Perón. To end the political deadlock that the dictatorship had fallen into, the president ordered the scheduling of a national election in February 1946.

Perón seized the opportunity. His supporters in the Federal Capital established the *Partido Laborista* (Labor Party), which then became the vehicle for Perón's ambitions. Nationalist organizations and a left-wing faction of the Radical Party—the *Unión Cívica Radical–Junta Renovadora*—endorsed his candidacy. Outside the capital, Perón made pacts with regional parties in an effort to broaden his support.

The opposition became energized with the announcement of elections. Leaders of traditional parties banded together to form the *Unión Democrática* (Democratic Union). José Tamborini, a congressional veteran and Anti-Personalist who had emerged as the leader of the Radical Party after the fall of the Concordancia, became the coalition's presidential candidate.

The election, distinctly competitive and free of fraud, turned on an unanticipated issue. The ambassador of the United States in Argentina, Spruille Braden, had done much to challenge the military government since his arrival in 1945. Just weeks before the election, a U.S. State Department study surfaced that labeled the leaders of the military government Axis sympathizers and singled out Perón as a suspected fascist. Braden had the "Blue Book," as the study became known, widely distributed in Argentina.

The ambassador had hoped the accusations in the "Blue Book" would weaken Perón as a candidate. Instead, Perón turned Braden's actions against the Democratic Union. Proclaiming his patriotism and advancing that his opponents were following the ambassador's lead, he characterized the election as a simple choice between the agents of Braden or the interests of the Argentine nation.

The slogan "Braden o Perón" (Braden or Perón) galvanized Perón's campaign. Perón won 54 percent of the votes cast. The alliance supporting Perón won majorities in 10 provinces and in the Federal District. His electoral margins were largest in the Pampa region and in the large cities, where the votes of laborers went solidly against the Democratic Union. His victory launched a new era in Argentine politics.

PERÓN'S POPULIST INITIATIVES (1946–1949)

In some respects, Perón's first government was an extension of the military dictatorship. Nonetheless, it appeared to be a fundamentally different kind of political machine. Freed from the need to respect rival factions within the dictatorship, Perón and his supporters expanded the political, economic, and social policies that first appeared in 1944. He shifted the focus from the reactionary and secretive concerns of the military officers toward a new era of state-directed reform and development. He maneuvered groups that were once ignored or repressed to the center of a movement he defined as revolutionary. In the wake of his election in June 1946, Perón created a party and a state of near hegemonic power.

Perón and his supporters constructed their regime on old and new bases. The armed forces served as the foundation for his regime.

His nationalist policies and promises isolated potential rivals and rewarded both officers and soldiers. New programs and increased military spending during the government's first year in office expanded the authority, ambition, and power of the army, the navy, and the newly created air force. The number of officers in the ranks increased, and many were given command of industries and government agencies rather than soldiers and units.

As the officers loyal to the state received their rewards, Perón cautiously reduced the overall size of the armed forces. Full conscription ended and the number of soldiers in uniform declined between 1945 and 1949.

Perón aggressively took up the cause of the working class. Workers in every setting gained unprecedented protections: The government set minimum wages, limited the length of the work day, restricted employers' rights over the dismissal of employees, and mandated workplace standards in key industries. It dictated new benefits: pension plans, vacations, medical services, limitations on Sunday work hours, and housing programs. Trade unions, sanctioned by the government to represent workers in distinct industries and economic sectors, gained new freedoms and powers. The number of workers organized in unions exploded: Thanks to the government's support, union membership grew from 522,088 in 1945 to almost 2 million by 1949.

Perón ensured the unions' loyalty by forcing out leaders who appeared to have political ambitions separate from his own. Shop, local, and national elections put in place loyalists who committed their unions to Perón and his government. At the same time, Perón turned his attention toward the political machine that had carried him into power. Independents and activists, including many who had helped form the Labor Party, fell out of favor. Within a year, Perón dissolved the Labor Party and replaced it with the *Partido Único de la Revolución Nacional* (Sole Party of the National Revolution). Perón emerged as the party's unquestioned leader. Loyalists and cronies filled the new party's staff positions.

In the wake of the election, a wave of strikes ripped through Argentina. The national government intervened in favor of strikes organized by unions loyal to Perón. Backed by the government, striking unions in industry after industry won wage and workplace concessions. The victories strengthened the unions and, at the same time, enhanced the reputation of Perón as a defender of the workers.

Independent unions continued in operation, but the government effectively undermined their power. Working through the Labor Secretariat, the regime stripped independent unions of their right to represent workers in negotiations. Strikes by unrecognized unions attracted state intervention. Workers who remained loyal to their independent unions lost out on the wage increases and other benefits that the government imposed upon employers. As a result, independent unions quickly withered.

Union members were the popular foundation of Perón's government. To expand his political base, Perón also reached out to the urban poor. Migration from the provinces to Buenos Aires and its suburbs had increased since the Great Depression. Two broad economic shifts had fueled this demographic shift. First, farming and other rural industries changed profoundly since World War I. Machinery and the need to reduce production costs, especially during the 1930s, cut the demand for seasonal and permanent laborers in the countryside. Second, international and domestic economic conditions had spurred the development of industries within Argentina. Pushed out by the stagnant rural economy, migrants moved into Argentina's urban centers in search of jobs and a better life. Most found work, but many struggled to support themselves and their families.

Perón's political opponents shunned the migrants, referring to them collectively as part of a "zoological flood" that had inundated the Federal Capital. In contrast, Perón advertised himself as their champion. He promised the *descamisados* (literally "shirtless" ones) opportunities for regular work, decent housing, adequate food, and education.

Eva María Duarte de Perón played a key role in connecting the urban poor to the state. She had married Perón after his liberation from Martín García Island in October 1945. As Perón began his political career, she became an important advisor and a crucial asset. Cultivating allies in the army and in the unions, "Evita" became a leading figure within the building Peronist movement. After the 1946 election, Evita took charge of the newly created *Fundación de Ayuda Social* (Social Aid Foundation). Funds from the state and the CGT allowed Evita to become a patron of the descamisados. The foundation funded hospitals and charities, food programs, and disaster relief. Hundreds of unfortunates lined up at the foundation's office door, where they received direct assistance. Propaganda and well-orchestrated promotions helped Evita build a popular following of her own. She used her growing popularity effectively.

Spearheading the campaign to give women the right to vote in 1947, she added another layer to the foundation of Perón's regime. With the support of women, Perón again reconstituted his party under the name *Partido Peronista* (Peronist Party).

Although her official role was never defined and she held no post within the government, Evita's importance to Perón, his party, and

Juan and María Eva Duarte de Perón: the political movement
that they created in 1946 remains the dominant political force
in Argentina today. (Hulton Archive/Getty Images)

the state increased rapidly. Through radio broadcasts and public
appearances, she became a celebrity. Behind the scenes, she grew
increasingly involved in the union movement. She led the fight against
the independent union leaders in 1946, and she participated in the negotiations between the new leaders and their local organizations in the
years that followed. In charge of the Women's Branch of the Peronist
Party, created in 1949, she played an indispensable role in generating
popular support for Perón and his policies.

The military ensured Perón's position. The unions and Evita represented his party's rank and file. To cement his political base, the Peronist
government reached out to industrialists. As a result of economic disruptions dating back to World War I, local industries had grown in number.
They employed a small but increasing percentage of the workforce in
the years following World War I. When World War II isolated Argentina

from foreign markets, new industries appeared and established firms expanded in an effort to make up for the lack of imported goods.

Most industrialists objected to Perón's actions in support of strikers during World War II. The *Unión Industrial Argentina* (Argentine Industrial Union, or UIA), an organization of Argentine business owners, became a leading opponent of the military dictatorship in 1943. Beginning in 1945, the UIA strongly supported the Democratic Union in its efforts to block Perón's rise to power. Seeing Perón as a demagogue, UIA representatives labeled him a mortal enemy.

Perón, however, hoped to gain the support of the business community. The expansion of industries would bring with it new jobs. The new workers, as members of state-controlled unions, would augment the base of the Peronist Party. In his arbitration efforts, Perón cultivated the support of many industrialists by promising to use the power of the government on their behalf. The benefits granted to workers came with important controls and restrictions that Perón characterized as advantageous for employers and employees alike. He promised government promotions of industrial expansion. Recognizing the value of government support, a small number broke ranks and offered their support to Perón after he had declared his candidacy. Upon gaining the presidency, Perón rewarded his supporters. The most fortunate received near monopoly control over key markets and lucrative contracts from the national government. The effort to cultivate and maintain this base of potentially antagonistic groups depended on the successful implementation of a new economic strategy. The military government, when it turned to managing the economy, tried to preserve Argentina's "natural" industries, such as grain farming and ranching, as it developed new industries of strategic importance, such as an aircraft industry.

In the months leading up to the election, the outgoing Farrell administration expanded the government's power over the economy. Price and production boards became increasingly active. In turn, the dictatorship took firm control of the Central Bank by eliminating the institution's board of directors and replacing them with appointed officers of the state. Along with new currency and deposit regulations, these executive actions gave the Argentine government complete independence in the charting of fiscal policy.

As president, Perón expanded the government promotion of industrial development to unprecedented levels. In theory, by creating jobs, the growth of urban industries would expand the ranks of the new government's most loyal supporters and thus ensure Perón's political future. Programs supporting industrial investment and expansion would please the factory owners who had joined in support of the new regime. By making the development of steel production and arms manufacturing key priorities, industrial promotion maintained the support of the military. Perón and his advisors believed that an aggressive promotion of local industries was economically as well as politically sound. The rise of the United States as the dominant economic power created problems, however.

The United States competed against Argentina for shares of the world market for agricultural goods. Unlike Argentina's traditional trading relationship with European countries, the Argentine arrangement with the United States meant Argentina could not exchange its exports for U.S. imports, since tariffs and subsidies effectively blocked Argentine grain and beef from the U.S. market. Since the country could not maintain a balanced trade with the United States, the expansion of industry would allow Argentina to meet domestic demand for manufactures.

The expansion of industry would also isolate Argentina from any postwar economic crisis. Given the condition of Europe, Argentina's traditional trading partner, after World War II and the actions of the United States, which continued to use its economic and diplomatic resources to punish the Argentine government, the effort to make Argentina economically more self-sufficient made sense to those in command.

Paying for industrial development represented a major challenge. To fund the creation of new industries, the government took charge of its "mother industries," farming and ranching, and the revenues they generated. A new bureaucracy, the *Instituto Argentino de Promoción del Intercambio* (Argentine Institute for the Promotion of Trade) took control of the country's export industries. IAPI became the sole purchaser of rural produce. As the sole purchaser, the institute had the power to set prices. By setting base prices below what its agents obtained for grains, meat, wool, and other products sold abroad, IAPI generated a surplus by inserting itself between producers and the export markets. Between 1946, when IAPI began its operations, and 1956, when its last fund transfers were completed, the institute produced over 8 billion pesos m$n.

IAPI profits funded the government's ambitious economic and social welfare programs. Peronist economic goals were made clear in the official five-year plan, labeled the *Plan de Gobierno* (Government Plan), which the Economics Ministry released in 1946. Perón called it a plan for economic independence. At the plan's core was the targeted creation and expansion of favored industries. The plan's designers projected more than 43 percent growth in the country's industrial sector by 1953. As the economy grew, Perón's ministers would also "liberate" transportation and utility companies by purchasing railroads, communication companies, docks, grain elevators, warehouses, and power companies from the foreign interests that controlled them.

In actions and in public performances, Perón built himself into the champion of Argentina's sovereignty and national interests. Beginning with his use of the trade surplus funds to purchase British-owned assets, Perón defined his government as anti-imperialist. As the state became more active in economic affairs, he characterized his state and its programs as unique: The centralized, planned development of Argentina's economy represented a "third way" between capitalism and communism.

As numerous policy actions built up state power and the regime's political base, the Peronists simultaneously attacked their political enemies. Supporters of the Democratic Union that had opposed Perón in 1946 faced harassment. Universities and public schools fell under tight restrictions. Professors and administrators identified as political enemies lost their jobs. Opposition parties in the Congress, already limited by their minority status, faced censure if they voiced protests against state actions. Judges, including those on the Supreme Court, were impeached and replaced with loyalists. Newspapers and periodicals that challenged Perón were closed.

Perón, Evita, and their supporters proclaimed the regime as a political movement that went beyond the structures of the party and the state. Under the banner of *Justicialismo* (Justicialism), they declared themselves as the leaders of a revolution. The nature of Peronism as an ideology or a political movement, however, defies simple definition. Its efforts to organize and control social groups, to direct the economy, to shape culture, and to dominate politics led opponents to label it totalitarian. U.S. officials called it fascist and frequently compared Perón to Mussolini or Hitler.

Judged by its leader's action, Peronism was about the consolidation of power. In 1949, Peronists moved to amend the Argentine constitution. They deleted the ban on presidential reelection. Given the strength of the Peronist Party, this guaranteed a second term for Perón. With a new constitution in place, the Peronists believed that they would remain in charge for decades. The power and authority of their regime had reached its peak.

ECONOMIC AND POLITICAL CRISES (1949–1952)

For those who had joined in support of Perón, the first two years of his presidency were worthy of celebration. Wages and living standards for workers and their families increased. Expectations for even greater improvements in the years ahead built public confidence in the government and the president. By 1949, the march of the "Peronist Revolution" ended.

Changes in the world market started the reversal of Argentina's fortunes. In 1948, the United States launched the Marshall Plan. Designed to save Europe from communism, the Marshall Plan provided loans and credits for European countries. Recipient countries could use the cash and credits to buy U.S. and Canadian products. The plan helped Europe recover from the damage that World War II had wrought. It provided food for European consumers and manufactures that helped stock stores. It also helped European factories and businesses rebuild.

For the United States, the Marshall Plan bolstered its allies in Europe during the opening phase of the Cold War. It also helped the United States avoid any postwar recession as war industries retooled. For Argentina, however, the Marshall Plan was a disaster. It channeled North American grains and meats to European consumers. In doing so, it shut Argentine products out of their traditional markets. By supporting record production in the United States and Canada, the plan also helped hold down international market prices for grains. Contracting markets and stable prices made the government's intervention into grain marketing, via IAPI, increasingly unpopular. Argentine farmers were well aware of the prices that foreign producers received for their harvests. Frustrated over the government's policies, which taxed their industry to support policies that served the workers and the state, many shifted their acreage away from crops that were under government control. Corn production experienced the most significant change. More labor-intensive than wheat, corn production was viewed by farmers as especially burdened by government interference. Rather than follow the labor codes and pricing guidelines that the Peronist regime had put into place, farmers increasingly shifted to alternatives such as oats, which could be cut and sold as feed independent from IAPI. Others planted alfalfa, which served as pasture for cattle. Coinciding with these shifts by farmers, bad weather in the 1948–1949 agricultural year reduced the crop yields. The resulting harvest cut the volume and value of grain exports significantly from the levels attained in preceding years.

Urbanization, combined with higher wages and changing consumption patterns, added a new and unanticipated problem. An increasing amount of the country's rural production never made it to the export markets as a result of rising domestic consumption. With each year, a greater percentage of the harvest stayed in Argentina to feed the growing urban population. Whereas before World War II, almost half of the grain harvest was sold abroad, in the years 1945–1949 the volume of grain exported fell to under a quarter of total output.

A similar problem affected the beef market. Beef and meat products were the main exports from Argentina during World War II. In the years following the war's end, domestic consumption rose while production remained largely unchanged. Meat exports had in decades past provided some insurance: When grain production fell, the value of meat exports helped Argentina balance its foreign trade accounts. But as was the case with grains, the rising domestic demand for beef cut into meat exports.

The Peronist government had counted on farm and ranch exports. The revenues generated by government controls on grain marketing and by taxes on foreign trade supported the investments in industry and public services that had helped it build and reward its political base. The combined effects of bad weather, increased consumption, and production shifts threatened the Argentine government with a major economic crisis.

Argentine economic strategists hoped that international conditions would rescue their government. Negotiators hoped to receive assistance from the United States, either directly through loans or indirectly through a change in the Marshall Plan that would allow European governments to purchase Argentine products with U.S. funds. Secretly, they believed that the mounting conflict between the Soviet Union and the United States would be their ultimate salvation. Many believed that a third world war, pitting communists against Western democracies, would send commodity prices up to record levels. This would then relieve Argentina from the impact of shrinking export volumes.

When the Korean War stopped short of sparking a superpower confrontation, these hopes dimmed. Export prices increased in 1950, but the release of grain stockpiles in 1951 pushed international market prices back down the following year. A more severe drought then cut into grain production across most of the Pampa. The resulting harvest was Argentina's lowest in 50 years. Wheat production dropped so low that the government had to import grain for the first time since 1898.

The collapse of the "mother industries" undermined the government's economic strategy. Within the urban sector, additional problems exacerbated the growing crisis. The growing urban population and the expansion of industry significantly raised Argentine consumption of petroleum, natural gas, electricity, and other sources of energy. The government had tried to increase domestic production of oil and coal, but existing deposits did not come close to meeting the growing demand for fuel. As a result, Argentina had to import increasing volumes of oil and coal. Shortages of electricity became increasingly common when shortfalls in foreign exchange made it impossible to fund imports from the United States.

Between 1949 and 1952, this conjuncture of problems slowed economic growth. Shortages of key materials produced price increases. When the prices for food, utilities, and rent rose, workers pressed the government for wage hikes to cover their increased cost of living. Quickly, the Peronists found themselves caught between the need to take charge of the economy and the desires of their political supporters.

With economic resources dwindling, Perón mobilized popular support in defense of his government. Union leaders discouraged strikes. Peronists organized mass demonstrations that targeted enemies of the state and its programs. Declaring a state of war against internal enemies, the president sent police and security forces into action against political rivals. The tactics energized the political sphere. In the election of 1952, the Peronist machine dominated the shattered Radical Party and other, smaller rivals. It took control of every provincial government, captured all the national Senate seats up for election, and obtained a commanding majority in the Chamber of Deputies. Allowed to seek reelection as a result of the constitutional revision in 1949, Perón captured over 64 percent of the national vote.

THE REGIME CRUMBLES (1952–1955)

In 1952, the Peronists appeared to be thoroughly in command of Argentina. The government had stifled the opposition. Periodic censorship, police raids, mob attacks, and harassment of reporters undermined the freedom of the national press. In one dramatic episode, the government censured, expropriated, and then turned over to the CGT the most active opposition paper, *La Prensa,* in 1951. Perón had successfully built the unions into a loyalist force. Union leaders, who gained their positions as a result of their willingness to follow the president's commands, held labor in check. Perón and his supporters believed that the government needed to create new organizations that could help in the coordination of important social and economic sectors. The state sponsored the formation of the *Confederacón General Económica* (General Economic Federation) for managers of important businesses. In turn, it created the *Confederación General de Profesionales* (General Federation of Professionals) in an attempt to create links between the state and white-collar workers. Finally, it formed the *Unión de Estudiantes Secundarios* (Union of Secondary School Students) and the *Confederación General Universitaria* (General University Federation) in the hopes of taking command of students in the public schools and the universities. Critics of Perón again charged him with fascism. Their accusations appeared on target.

Although the president declared these efforts great victories, they did little to effectively broaden the regime's political support. The promotion of rhetoric over substance took its clearest form in the universities. New professors, Peronist partisans who made the party's ideological line the core subject matter in their classes, took over from independent ones. Party and ideological loyalty brought rewards to students. The curriculum shifted: New courses on Justicialist philosophy and even on Evita as a historical and political force became requirements.

The military remained a key foundation of the regime, but the officer corps grew estranged from the increasingly ambitious Peronistas. Remaining ultranationalist officers, who disliked the regime's championing of the common people, saw the Justicialist Party as potentially upsetting the balance and norms of society. Harsh treatment of senior, retiring officers alienated many others. Promotion of favorites added additional tensions. As a consequence, although the regime seemed to be in command, a military rebellion was brewing.

In 1952, the Peronist movement suffered a severe blow. Evita Perón, who had become a major part of the state and the party, died of cancer just weeks after the reelection of Juan Perón. Just months before, her husband tried to have her stand for election as vice president. This effort, which the CGT strongly supported, led the army to unite in protest behind the scenes. Army discontent was strong enough to block the move. As the election approached, her illness limited her energy and her schedule. Through great effort, she managed to hide the fact from the public.

Evita's death on July 26, 1952, sent the Peronist faithful into mourning. For Perón, it represented a terrible political as well as a personal loss. Evita had become a symbol of the regime's concern for the poor and unfortunate. She was also a close and valued advisor, as well as a capable organizer. Her supervision of the party's women's auxiliary organizations, her manipulation of union leaders and army officers, and her skill as a spokesperson for the government and the president had helped maintain Perón's control over the country. Many observers at the time suggested that her death played a key role in the regime's disintegration. This is an exaggeration. The collapse of Perón's government came as a result of the state's inability to deliver on the promises that it had made.

The fall from power was rapid. The collapse of Perón's economic program initiated the crisis. Inflation was the main signal of economic imbalance: By 1952, the inflation rate reached 30 percent annually. Reduced export revenues, a product of continued problems in the country's agricultural sector, made it impossible for the government to maintain its social programs and its economic promotions.

In 1953, the government embarked on its second five-year plan. Stepping back from its industrial promotions, government planners instead promised to reduce inflation and revive agriculture. The government tried to attract foreign investment, especially in the automobile industry.

The plan's architects hoped that foreign companies would finance the development of heavy industry and improve Argentina's ability to import the components necessary to produce sophisticated industrial goods. As factories grew in size and number, the government would try to find foreign markets for the new industrial output.

The plan did reduce inflation, which fell to 4 percent in 1953. But both industrial and agricultural production stalled. In reaction to the economic plan's lack of success, Perón turned again to rhetoric and mass actions. The Evita Perón Foundation continued its programs and promotions, but its charitable acts on behalf of a select few individuals and families did not make up for the lack of broader wage increases or social welfare reforms.

The president urged union and party members to attack the groups that had undermined the government efforts. Perón accused the landed oligarchy and their political allies of blocking reforms that would have helped the government achieve its promised reforms. His supporters responded in April 1953 by attacking the Jockey Club, a private retreat associated with elite rural landowners and cattle ranchers, in the Federal Capital. In succession, mobs attacked and destroyed the offices of the Radical and the Socialist Parties.

The attacks distracted Perón's most loyal supporters from the government's failures, but only for a short time. Within a year, unions lost patience with the restrictions that the government had imposed. Led by the metallurgical workers, a new round of strikes began in April 1954. A wage hike ended the challenge from the unions. By granting concessions to the workers, Perón angered their employers.

A more serious challenge came from the Catholic Church. Perón had managed to neutralize the Church during his campaign for the presidency by promising to build a stronger society and to promote harmony among the different social groups. In 1947, he approved the return of religious instruction in the country's primary schools.

As the years passed, however, the regime's social policies and programs created new concerns. Church officials came to view the government as a competitor in many respects. The charity work of the Evita Perón Foundation received the strongest criticism. After Evita's death, Perón authorized a campaign to canonize her. The Church, which regarded the campaign as propaganda, refused to support it.

Perón moved toward confrontation with Church officials. The Church, in turn, became a symbol and a catalyst of resistance against Peronism. Efforts to restrict the Church's organizing efforts in 1954 and 1955 backfired. Religious processions in celebration of traditional holidays became political rallies. In retaliation, Perón promised legislation that would create a firm separation between Church and State. He ended religious instruction in public schools. He cut government support for parochial schools, and had his congressional supporters draft laws that would have legalized divorce and prostitution.

To counter the growing popular protests that rallied around the Church, the Peronists sponsored their own mass demonstrations. Although the government's censorship of the press and radio reports hid the fact, the political scene had become polarized. On August 31, 1955, Perón spoke before a large public gathering outside the Casa Rosada. He publicly offered his resignation, which the crowd on cue refused. In response to their support, he threatened civil war, and urged Peronists to kill five enemies of the movement for every supporter that might fall in the coming conflict.

The armed forces' support for Perón collapsed in the wake of the speech. Although a previous attempt to spark a coup in June had failed, a more coordinated effort, supported by large army units based in Córdoba and Bahía Blanca, began on September 16. Forces loyal to Perón at first appeared to have ended the rebellion. When the navy intervened, blockading Buenos Aires and threatening to shell the Federal Capital, military support for the government evaporated. General Eduardo Lonardi, forced into retirement in 1951, took command of the rebellion. As opponents of the regime moved in support of the rebels, Perón accepted his fate. On September 19, he resigned from office.

Lonardi declared his rebellion the *"Revolución Libertadora"* (Liberating Revolution). Many hoped that coup would solve the country's problems. Instead, Perón's fall from power plunged Argentina deeper into political and economic chaos.

7

Under Perón's Shadow (1955–1972)

In the wake of his government's collapse, Juan Domingo Perón continued to be a central figure in Argentine politics. The coalition of competing forces that he had forged into the foundation of his regime had splintered. The political scene polarized. Governments both elected and imposed rose and fell in quick succession. Under the banner of nationalism and order, the armed forces dictated the series of governmental shifts. With each change, their control over society weakened while their commitment to an increasingly rigid and reactionary set of ambitions hardened.

Organized labor emerged as the main political adversary of the armed forces. The movement's organizational structure and the loyalty of its membership allowed union leaders to coordinate political action. After Perón's fall and flight into exile, unions squared off against anti-Peronist forces in an effort to preserve the gains that they had made before 1955.

The battle up to 1972 ended in a draw. Efforts to crush labor and purge it from the political process were costly. The resilience of the union organization and the commitment of its leadership to the Peronist cause remained strong. Through strikes that paralyzed the country, the unions worked with political activists in an effort to make the country ungovernable.

The political battle between the armed forces and labor occurred during a period of economic disintegration. The country's rural industries were no longer the powerful motors that pushed Argentina's rapid economic growth as they had a century before. Urbanization and foreign competition limited the volume and value of agricultural exports. Lacking domestic capital resources and the ability to finance imports of raw materials, machinery, and innovations, the country's industrial sector sputtered. Cycles of expansion and collapse created fiscal challenges that undermined all efforts to plan a return to stability.

Decades of struggle and failure hardened the resolve of extremists and undermined the efforts of moderates. By the end of the 1960s, violence added a dangerous new dimension to Argentina's political scene. The era ended with the apparent victory of the Peronists. Having failed in an attempt to force social peace, the military allowed Perón to return from exile and stand once again for election as president. Perón's return did not bring peace. Instead, it inaugurated Argentina's worst period of state-sponsored political violence.

THE RESTORATION OF A LIBERAL STATE (1955–1958)

The final months of Perón's presidency had created a sense of unity within much of the armed forces. Perón's mobilization of his supporters, their attacks against the Catholic Church and symbols of the "oligarchy," and the threat of continued violence against the regime's enemies angered and mobilized conservative officers. The armed forces split between liberals, who preferred civilian rule, and nationalists, who put their faith in putting the military in charge. For the moment, the liberals held sway.

When General Eduardo Lonardi took command of the coup in September 1955, the Revolución Libertadora quickly forced Perón into exile. Lonardi's political ambitions were limited. He aimed at ending Peronist attacks against the new government's enemies, the establishment of political stability, and the creation of a coalition government that included representatives from military and civilian groups. He promised that the new regime would coordinate a rapid transition toward legitimate constitutional rule.

While Lonardi objected to Perón's political excesses, he did not move against the past regime's tight control over the economy. His desire to continue economic nationalism and industrial promotions, along with his acceptance of Peronist participation in politics, undermined political support for the coup leader within and beyond the armed forces.

At the same time, Lonardi's policies did little to close the gap between the Peronists and their opponents. To emphasize both the legitimacy and the limited ambitions of his dictatorship, Lonardi had adopted General Urquiza's slogan from 1853 after Urquiza had pushed Juan Manuel de Rosas from power: "Neither victors nor vanquished" (*Ni vencedores ni vencidos*). However, Peronist supporters in the unions and the local party commissions remained loyal to the deposed president and refused to support the new government.

Within two months, Lonardi fell from power. Liberal officers, who wanted to purge Peronism and its influence from the country, seized power and fell in behind General Pedro E. Aramburu. Acting as president, Aramburu moved to placate liberal demands. The government froze wages despite the onset of inflation in the wake of the coup. It decommissioned many of the Peronist programs and promotions that had favored industrial development and the urban sector at the expense of agriculture. It allowed the creation of new unions and associations in an attempt to dilute the authority of Peronists within organized labor. It also sacked real and suspected Perón supporters from the armed forces.

Having consolidated his position, Aramburu then directed a more aggressive campaign against the Peronists. The newspaper *La Prensa* was taken back from the control of the General Labor Confederation and returned to private hands. It became a rabid anti-Peronist organ as the campaign against the deposed president and his supporters took shape.

Thousands of union leaders were arrested and then banned from political and union participation. Many fled into exile after their release from detention. Those who stayed in Argentina faced continued harassment in the years that followed.

The government banned the Peronist Party from future elections. Its organization was shut down, its properties were seized, and its local, provincial, and national leaders were blocked from the political process. The display of Peronist propaganda, the publication of slogans, and even the singing of party songs became illegal. In May 1956, the constitutional reforms put into place by the Perónists seven years before were struck down. Under Aramburu, Perón's rivals hoped to sweep all hints of the past regime from view.

The anti-Peronist campaign spurred protests. General Juan José Valle led the most notorious. Based in Corrientes Province, Valle launched a rebellion against Aramburu in June 1956. The liberal officers who supported Aramburu quickly ended the uprising. Hoping to discourage future actions, Aramburu ordered the execution of 27 officers connected with the rebellion. Those outside the military who had aligned themselves with Aramburu's dictatorship applauded the action. The purging of disloyal, politically suspect, and neutral officers from the ranks in the months that followed gave Aramburu tighter control over the armed forces. But the executions, which observers compared to the political violence of the previous century, hardened the resolve of Peronist activists.

Working within the unions and other organizations, they began planning a campaign against the military government. Aramburu had promised a "de-Peronization" of the unions and a total ban of Peronists from the political process. In 1956, workers successfully fought efforts to put anti-Peronist officers in charge of their unions. Arrests of union officers and a ban against their participation in union activities backfired against the government. Peronist activists who remained after the attempted purge took the place of the arrested leaders. They collectively formed the "62 Organizations" in August 1957, which then coordinated future actions against the regime.

On the political front, Peronists continued to show strength. On October 16, 1956, the government issued its "Statute of the Political Parties." The decree banned all parties that used personal names in their titles and demanded annual budget inspections and the presentation of lists of supporters from approved organizations. These requirements were aimed at the Peronists alone. The Aramburu regime hoped to create a "democratic" political process that limited participation to true "democrats" while it blocked supporters of "totalitarianism." The Peronists, working through neighborhood commissions, the unions, and personal contacts, orchestrated an effective reply to the ban. When elections to select a constitutional assembly took place in July 1956, Peronist supporters turned in blank ballots, which accounted for a majority of the votes cast.

As its attacks against the political legacy of Peronism intensified, the dictatorship began the dismantling of the toppled regime's economic structure. Aramburu directed a return to the orthodoxy of the pre-Perón years. Aramburu and his advisors hoped that this move would end Argentina's economic problems: The recovery of farming and ranching, and the resulting revival of export-led economic growth, became the central goals of the government's economic planners. It named Raúl Prebisch, who had helped frame the Concordancia's economic policies during the Great Depression, as the architect of its economic recovery program.

Under Prebisch, strict planning and intervention in the country's financial and export sectors ended. The government shut down IAPI. Price controls and forced sales to the government ended. Currency devaluations helped make Argentine agricultural products more competitive in overseas markets. Trade regulations that controlled the flow of goods into and out of the country ceased. In part, the dismantling of the Peronist economic program was aimed at the United States and the International Monetary Fund (IMF). The restrictions that the United States had place on Argentine exports, along with trade and financial sanctions, had created enormous problems for the Peronist governments. The return to orthodoxy helped Argentina normalize its relationship with the United States and enabled it to qualify for IMF assistance.

Currency devaluations helped cut imports, expand exports, and produce a balance of payments surplus in the economy's trade. Hopes that fiscal shocks would establish a floor on which the dictatorship could rebuild the country's economy quickly evaporated. The large export volumes and revenues of 1957 appeared promising, but contractions in cattle and grain production the following year led to new trade deficits and falling tariff revenues.

The legacy of decades of economic policies shaped mainly by populist political ambitions finally became clear. To return to the export-led economic growth program that had worked in the years before the Great Depression, Argentina had to modernize its rural industries. Lacking domestic sources of agricultural implements, fertilizers, chemicals, and other inputs, the directors of rural operations had to import the technological improvements that would allow them to compete in the world market. Imports were expensive, and continued trade and currency imbalances made it difficult for Argentina to obtain the tools and materials that its rural industries needed.

To succeed, the Aramburu regime needed to make up for two decades of economic neglect and interference. Since the 1930s, capital had flowed out of the countryside. A quick return to the practices of the "Golden Age" was not possible. The promotion of industries had created new demands for resources and capital. Argentina's urban population was much larger, and it consumed more of the country's rural output than it had in previous decades. Conditions within Argentina and abroad made the marketing and sale of grain and meat more complicated.

Circumstances made it impossible for the Aramburu government to wait for success. Having dedicated themselves to resistance, the Peronists applied pressure on the government through the unions.

First, individual factories, services, or businesses faced work slowdowns. Then, in fall 1957, the General Confederation of Labor launched two general strikes that stalled all activity in the country's major cities.

By the end of 1957, the dictatorship had achieved little. It had promised to eradicate Peronism. Instead, its actions—which achieved little—mobilized an active and massive popular resistance against the regime. It had promised to create a strong and stable economy. Its policy changes left the country stagnant. Although it had cleared Peronist sympathizers from the military, its actions and bans did not satisfy radical nationalists within the armed forces who wanted a stronger reaction against real and suspected enemies. The elections that the government scheduled for February 1958 appeared to be more of an escape for the dictatorship than a triumph.

FRONDIZI AND "THE RESISTANCE" (1958–1962)

The Peronists remained barred from politics. In response to the government's regulations against their participation, Peronist leaders urged the people again to turn in blank ballots as a form of protest. The remaining parties, eager to compete for power in an election free from Perón's dominance, campaigned actively for popular support. The Radical Party (UCR) emerged as the leading force, but in the preparations for the elections, it split into two major factions. Ricardo Balbín, who had led the party in its opposition against Perón before 1955, pushed his party to accept the process. He hoped that the Radicals could take advantage of the electoral ban against the Peronists and once again become Argentina's dominant party. Rivals within the UCR objected to both Balbín and his populist strategy. Balbín's active support of the 1955 coup angered many. Others believed that the ban against the Peronists made the coming elections illegitimate. They argued that participation in them with Balbín as their leader would damage the party in the years ahead.

The opponents of Balbín rallied behind Arturo Frondizi, who had run as the party's vice presidential candidate in 1952. Frondizi felt that efforts to court Peronists would broaden the Radical Party's popular base and give their efforts to govern greater support. Delegates supporting the two candidates split during the party's national convention in November 1956. Unable to form a compromise ticket, Balbín and other regional party leaders moved to reconstitute their party during a series of meetings that began in February 1957. Eventually, the group declared Balbín as the candidate of the *Unión Cívica Radical del Pueblo* (Radical Civic Union of the People). Frondizi's supporters had urged him to break from the Radical Party's political bosses to form his own movement in the wake of the national convention. In reaction to Balbín's announcement, Frondizi distanced himself from his rivals. He defined the Liberating Revolution as a move not against totalitarianism but, rather, as an action in defense of an oligarchy against the interests of the people. Beginning in March 1957, Frondizi and his supporters constituted the *Unión Cívica Radical Intransigente* (Intransigent Radical Civic Union, or UCRI).

Frondizi hoped to create a new political movement that included Peronist supporters. He took popular stands in support of union activism, the expansion of government investments in industries and economic development, and public assistance programs for the poor. He also made broad attacks against the United States and its "imperialism" in Latin America, and he called for an end to the electoral ban against Peronists.

In his campaigning, Frondizi targeted those who had come to support *Peronismo sin Perón* (Peronism without Perón). With the deposed president living in exile, leaders in this emerging faction hoped to continue the efforts to advance the goals of the banned Peronist Party through alternative and independent actions. Frondizi, at least in his rhetoric, appeared to be a suitable candidate for their support. Frondizi's attraction of Peronist supporters worried Perón. Operating through intermediaries, Perón communicated his political goals. Initially, Perón hoped to maintain the political presence of his party, as well as his leadership, through a boycott of the 1958 elections. Electoral law, however, imposed significant sanctions upon anyone who refused to vote in an election. Since the penalties would most likely force Peronist participation, Perón shifted toward the tactic of filing blank ballots. As it had in 1956, the millions of blank ballots would undermine the election's legitimacy and, at the same time, demonstrate continued popular support for the exiled leader.

Frondizi's growing support among Peronists as the election approached forced Perón to change his position. With the central aim of maintaining his authority over the Peronists, the ex-president began secret negotiations with Frondizi. After a round of discussions carried out through intermediaries, Perón agreed to support Frondizi in the elections in exchange for the legalization of the Peronist Party in the future. The effect of the agreement became clear during the voting on February 23, 1958. Frondizi and the UCRI captured over 4 million votes; Balbín and the UCRP ran a distant second. Blank ballots totaled only 800,000. The alliance with the Peronists allowed Frondizi to overcome the Radical Party machinery that Balbín still controlled.

Victorious, Frondizi promised to put the interests of the Argentine people first. His government embarked on a new economic strategy labeled *desarrollismo* (developmentalism). Defined as a campaign to secure the victories of the Argentine people against the interests of "oligarchic forces," Frondizi's new policy centered on an aggressive coordination and promotion of economic development. Tight controls on trade and finance returned. The government again tried to direct revenues from trade toward the development of new industries. Frondizi believed that these policies, labeled as being in defense of the nation's interests, would generate economic expansion and improve conditions for Argentine workers. In anticipation of future success, and in the hopes of demonstrating his commitment to his Peronist supporters, Frondizi authorized massive wage increases and a price freeze on consumer goods.

The efforts to tighten government controls while it rewarded the working class created significant problems in the Argentine economy. Inflation increased rapidly. More important, industrial and rural production stagnated. To avoid economic collapse, the government entered into negotiations with the IMF. It recommended a reversal of the government's economic policies and the introduction of new programs that would force stability. Recognizing the need for investment capital, Frondizi and his advisors agreed to end the price freeze, end trade and exchange controls, cut government employment and spending, and increase revenues by raising utility and transit rates. In return, the IMF granted a short-term $328 million loan.

The policy reversal had little effect on the economy. Exports did not increase enough in volume or in value. Government revenues fell short of expenditures. Continued inflation discouraged industrialists and angered consumers.

One part of his policy reversal had a major political effect. Frondizi criticized Perón in 1952 for allowing U.S. companies to participate in the search for and exploitation of oil reserves in Patagonia. He promised in 1958 to preserve national control over the oil industry as a key part of his "developmentalist" strategy. The potential value of Argentina's oil reserves, combined with the lack of domestic capital needed to find and pump out petroleum deposits, made the reserves an attractive enticement for foreign investors. In secret, Frondizi had approved contracts with Standard Oil that allowed the company to develop potential oil deposits. He revealed the agreements in July 1958. Although he argued that Y.P.F., the government-owned oil company, controlled the operations and limited Standard Oil's interests, the agreements made the president's promises to protect and advance the nation's interests seem false.

By the end of 1958, Peronists had lost patience with the new government. Launching an attack through the unions, they orchestrated a new round of strikes in protest of the government's abandonment of its election promises. Perón undermined Frondizi's standing by making their 1958 agreement public. Having alienated much of his popular support, the revelation of his negotiations with Perón led the armed forces to reassert their authority.

Military officers first challenged Frondizi's advisors. Those tainted with any association with the Peronists became targets. Facing threats from the armed forces, Frondizi thinned the ranks of his cabinet. The military next moved to shape the government's supervision of the economy.

Anti-Peronist officers demanded a shift toward more conservative fiscal and trade policies. They also pushed for a crackdown against union activists who tried to organize protests against the government. As the new policies took effect, popular support for Frondizi dropped. Peronists continued to push their program of resistance. They worked to make Argentina ungovernable until their movement regained its legal standing and their leader was allowed to return from exile. With no popular base to counter the Peronists, Frondizi became a captive of the military. Its support helped keep the government in operation as it forced Argentina to adjust to the effects of its economic program.

By 1960, the "developmentalist" strategy had produced few gains. Foreign investments had funded the expansion of old industries and the creation of new ones, but the contradictions of the government's forced industrial promotions created more problems than benefits. For example, foreign loans and government promotions helped expand steel production within Argentina. Frondizi and his advisors viewed this as a great victory. They hoped that as steel production grew, the country could reduce imports of the strategic metal. However, since Argentina lacked sufficient supplies of iron ore, the forging of steel created the need to import more raw materials than before. In the end, rather than liberate Argentina from a dependence on foreign supplies, the foreign loans taken to fund the project and new imports needed to produce steel put additional burdens on the already fragile economy.

Having abandoned their alliance with the UCRI, Peronists expanded their resistance activities. Unions called for more strikes in 1960 and 1961. In local and provincial elections, activists organized blank vote actions or sanctioned support for candidates in opposition parties.

Frondizi countered the Peronists by moving in two directions. Within Argentina, the UCRI abandoned any efforts to win support from the Peronists. Instead, they presented their party as the only one strong enough to block a return of Peronism. Abroad, Frondizi courted the United States. Its influence in the world market, its role in the IMF, and its funding of new political and economic development programs as part of its "Alliance for Progress" helped the government maintain its fiscal solvency.

Victories in provincial elections in 1961 convinced Frondizi that the UCRI could defeat the Peronists in future contests. He opened the 1962 national elections to the Peronists. They were allowed to organize and present candidates, so long as Juan Perón remained banned from participation.

The move involved enormous risks. Within the armed forces, many officers wanted the Peronists permanently banned from the political scene. Legalizing the party of Perón might have led to a coup before the elections could take place. Frondizi ignored the risks and moved ahead with the open elections.

When the votes were counted in March 1962, ten Peronist candidates won election as governors. Party leaders gained control over most of the country's provincial assemblies. Although the UCRI ran well in the Federal Capital, in Entre Ríos, and in other interior provinces and territories, the election shattered the notion that it was Argentina's leading party.

Frondizi ordered federal interventions in Buenos Aires, Chaco, Río Negro, Santiago del Estero, and Tucumán. The Peronists promised to resist the move. Quickly, the political situation overwhelmed the Frondizi government. Within the armed forces, calls for the president's removal came forward. On March 29, after failing in an attempt to create a unity government involving all the parties, the military arrested Frondizi and once again took charge of the national government.

BETWEEN THE MILITARY AND THE PERONISTS (1963–1966)

Although the military took control of the government in 1962, it continued to work through a puppet government that leading officers assembled after Frondizi's arrest. In an effort to create the illusion of constitutional rule, the military had José María Guido, president pro tempore of the national Senate, named as the country's provisional president.

Guido stepped into a chaotic situation. Politically, the fall of Frondizi encouraged the Peronists to put more pressure on the government and the political system. Although the Peronist Party remained banned from active participation in public affairs, party members continued to engage in strikes and protests that maintained their status as a major force. The Guido government hoped gradually to lift the ban, but each step necessary to bring the Peronists back into the political process created major problems.

Any action that favored the Peronists angered many within the armed forces. Whereas a majority of officers continued to favor civilian governments so long as they did not include Peronists, hard-line factions within the army, the navy, and the air force pushed behind the scenes for a different approach. The most conservative officers had come to see the political process as dangerous and politicians as unworthy of trust.

International conditions checked the conservatives. The military and economic aid that the United States and other nations provided would end if dictators tried to rule directly. Nevertheless, in the months following the coup against Frondizi, a series of military rebellions took place.

Every cabinet nomination and each policy shift put military factions into competition and confrontation. The most serious crisis occurred in August 1962. After President Guido nominated as his secretary of war an army officer who supported constitutional rule, the army split into two. Officers who wanted to end civilian rule rallied behind General Federico Toranzo Montero and demanded the nomination of a different candidate from their faction.

Their challenge led to the stationing of army units in the capital. The supporters of constitutional rule, who later labeled themselves *Los Azules* (The Blues), refused to back down. The challengers, who became known as *Los Colorados* (The Reds), lacked broad support within the army. As the days passed, the Colorados held their positions. The crisis cooled temporarily when President Guido offered a compromise over the nomination of cabinet officials.

Guido's intervention, however, angered the Azules. Following the lead of General Juan Carlos Onganía, they launched a propaganda campaign by radio. They called on the rebels to promise their support for the government and for continued civilian rule in the future. Believing that the rebels would not compromise, army units under the Azules' command attacked the rebel positions in the capital. The navy remained neutral, but the air force backed the Azules. The confrontation ended on September 23. Onganía's troops forced the Colorados to surrender. In the days that followed, the army demoted and forced into retirement 140 officers who sided with the rebellion.

The fragile political situation, coupled with continuing economic problems, pushed the Guido government toward the scheduling of new elections. Government officials believed that elections would allow a new government, backed by a popular mandate, to set policy and settle Argentina's pressing political and economic challenges.

The scheduling of elections for July 7, 1963, brought to the fore the question of the Peronists: What role would they play? The Radicals and other opposition groups continued to see the Peronists as dangerous. President Guido determined matters by appointing General Osiris Villegas as minister of the interior in May 1963. From this position, Villegas controlled the electoral process. His first key action relating to the elections was a total ban on Peronist participation. In short order, Villegas announced that all persons suspected of being an agent or representative of Peronism would not be allowed to stand for office.

Villegas's ban challenged both the Peronists and Frondizi's supporters, who found themselves labeled Peronist sympathizers and thus blocked from participation. Perón and Frondizi ordered their supporters to vote in blank. The candidacy of Pedro Aramburu, who formed the party *Unión del Pueblo Argentino* (Union of the Argentine People), presented a new danger, however. Aramburu hoped to attract the anti-Perón vote. Having led the Liberating Revolution, he hoped to attract enough votes to become president and then continue his crusade against the Peronists. Aramburu's presence encouraged many Peronists to support the candidates they felt would do the least damage to their cause. When the balloting ended, the UCRP candidate Arturo Illia finished with a plurality.

An obscure figure but generally respected as honest and trustworthy, Illia faced the task of bringing peace and stability to the country. The new government focused on solving the economic and political problems that had lingered since the overthrow of the Frondizi administration.

First came the economy. The 1962 recession continued on into 1963. Unemployment approached 10 percent of the active workforce, foreign and domestic investment dropped, and industrial production was sluggish. The Illia administration also faced political pressure from two directions: Nationalists wanted the new government to lessen the influence of foreign companies and investors, especially in the oil industry; and the unions, still loyal to the banned Peronist movement, launched a campaign of strikes and protests in defense of the working class.

Illia directed a series of limited actions that addressed these challenges. The new government cancelled the concessions that Frondizi had signed with foreign oil companies. This shut off foreign investment in the sector and temporarily stalled the expansion of oil production in the country.

By acting in the name of national interests, Illia connected his government with the popular policies of past Radical Party leaders stretching back to Yrigoyen. Illia's economic advisors hoped that increased consumer spending within Argentina would help end the recession. In the face of strong protests from the business community, the government raised the minimum wage. The government also promoted an expansion of credit for businesses and for consumer loans.

The government's economic policy benefited from unrelated shifts. Since the 1950s, policymakers had tried to encourage a recovery in the country's farming sector. International conditions, however, made it difficult for farmers to acquire the machines, fertilizers, seeds, and other inputs—most of which had to be imported—that they needed to compete with producers in North America for a share of the world market.

Beginning in 1963, conditions changed. The break in inflation that the recession forced allowed farmers to fund imported capital goods. Government programs that made it easier to obtain loans and service debts encouraged higher levels of investment. As new technologies entered the rural sector, production became more efficient. At the same time, favorable exchange rates made Argentine farm and ranch products more competitive in overseas markets.

These changes led to a rapid expansion of farm production. Between 1963 and 1966, Argentine farmers increased their output by nearly 50 percent. Although farm acreage lagged behind the peak levels set more than 30 years before, the increased productivity of the farming sector led to near record harvests of export goods. Increased agricultural exports helped Argentina maintain its balance of payments. They also ensured a ready supply of foreign exchange. As a result, the Illia administration operated free of the foreign economic restraints that undermined the economic promotions of past governments.

Despite its apparent success in economic matters, the Illia administration faced mounting political opposition. Unions emerged as its most powerful opponent. The unions had remained independent despite the efforts of military and civilian governments to limit their power. With their actions coordinated by Augusto Vandor, the president of the General Confederation of Labor (CGT) and head of the "62 Organizations"—a coalition of key industrial labor unions—the unions remained committed to the destruction of a government that they viewed as illegitimate.

Even before Illia took office, Vandor and the CGT began a push for the legalization of the Peronist Party and the eventual return of Juan Perón as president. In May 1964, the CGT mobilized its members.

For three weeks, a series of factory occupations, strikes, marches, and protests demonstrated the popular strength of the unions and challenged the government's authority.

Vandor and his loyalists pushed for the creation of new social and economic programs that targeted the poor and the workers. The strikes and negotiations put the unions at the center of Argentine politics. The military developed into a second challenger. Publicly, the military appeared to have accepted Illia's electoral victor as a mandate for the return to popular rule. The split between officers who supported constitutional rule with the military removed from politics versus those who wanted the military in charge remained. General Juan Carlos Onganía replaced Pedro Aramburu as the armed forces' key spokesperson. In 1964, he emerged at the head of a new movement to make the military the protector of the nation.

The public actions of the unions and of the armed forces isolated the Illia administration and chipped away at its public support. Behind the scenes, additional problems mounted. The armed forces became increasingly factionalized but also more ambitious. The officers who followed Onganía pushed for greater involvement and a harder line against elements within Argentine society that they viewed as threats to the nation and to their interests. Increasingly, this faction became intolerant of civilian leadership. Their fear of Peronism and their anger over the actions of the unions made them favor a rapid return to military rule.

The unions continued to demonstrate their power and used increasingly large and effective strikes to gain leverage in negotiations with the government and with business leaders and factory owners. This wave of union activism hid growing divisions. Perón's most loyal union supporters lined up behind Augusto Vandor. With Perón still in exile, however, loyalists split into two camps. Many remained committed to Perón's authority and worked for his return. Others used the name of Perón to chart the creation of "Peronism without Perón." This represented an attempt to carry on the political mission of Peronism but under new, younger leadership.

Congressional elections in March 1965 brought this division within the Peronist movement to the fore. The Illia government allowed Peronist parties to form and participate in the process despite strong objections from the military and conservative opposition leaders. The combined vote of the Peronist Parties in the various provinces was 20 percent more than that of the Radicals. The electoral success made many Peronist leaders, including Augusto Vandor, impatient. They pushed for the creation of a movement independent from Perón, who remained banned from the political process.

Recognizing the threat, Perón rallied the remaining loyalists within the movement. Working through his third wife, María Estela Martínez de Perón, he orchestrated the creation of a second General Confederation of Labor to challenge Vandor. In the struggle for control of the movement, Perón encouraged his followers to seize control of unions and harass those they regarded as traitors to the cause. This competition would continue for years.

The growing challenges presented by the military and the Peronists coincided with a collapse of the Illia government's economic program. The policy shifts that had helped lift Argentina from recession lost their force after 1964. By 1965, inflation grew into a major problem. Prices for consumer goods, according to government estimates, increased at a rate of 30 percent per year. The wage concessions granted in 1964 did not keep pace. Workers found their living expenses rising. The government, however, shifted away from policies that favored consumers and toward actions that fought inflation. Its new economic program did not receive congressional approval. Consequently, as economic conditions again moved toward recession, political conditions checked the Illia administration's reactions.

Popular support for the national government dived as the months past. Elements within the military plotted another coup. Beginning in May 1966, Onganía's supporters moved to provoke a crisis. After weeks of tense public and private challenges, the final confrontation came when General Pascual Pistarini arrested a member of the dwindling faction within the armed forces that supported civilian rule. When the president ordered Pistarini to resign, Onganía's supporters moved against Illia. On June 28, 1966, the ranking officers of the armed forces formed a new ruling junta. The junta dissolved Congress, suspended the constitution, banned all political parties, forced all sitting politicians in the capital and the provinces to resign, and closed the Supreme Court.

Through a public announcement, labeled the *"Acta de la Revolución Argentina"* (Act of the Argentine Revolution), the junta declared an end to civilian rule. A new era, during which the country would be placed on what many in the military viewed as a proper and sound path, had begun.

ONGANÍA'S "REVOLUTION" (1966–1970)

The junta remained in control of Argentina for one day. It then named Juan Carlos Onganía the country's new president. The pronouncements that constituted his regime gave Onganía an unprecedented degree of independence. Politicians were banned from participation when the new regime defined them as a corrupting influence. The military was also separated from the actions of the state. Although the military put Onganía into power and formed the basis of his authority, the documents released to the press announced that the military would not participate in the operation of the new state. The Argentine Revolution of 1966 made Onganía the sole authority.

Onganía had become known as a result of his public statements concerning the military and its role in society. Chief of the armed forces when Illia gained the presidency, he resigned after challenging the secretary of war over government supervision of military affairs in November 1965. He had championed the military as a preserver of civilization and of Christian values. None questioned his loyalty to the military. However, he lacked political skills. Ideologically rigid, he viewed Francisco Franco's Fascist dictatorship as a model. With no institutional checks on his whims, Onganía set about saving Argentina from the political and cultural excesses he so feared.

Onganía started his campaign against liberal and Marxist influences with a move against the country's public universities. In 1919, the Universidad de Buenos Aires led a national campaign for independence and autonomy from state supervision. The reformers' success led to the development of a strong and critical university system. Perón ended the university system's independence in 1946. After he was pushed from office in 1955, the national universities again gained autonomy from state supervision.

Onganía announced his government's intervention in university operations in August 1966. Police moved onto university grounds in the capital and elsewhere as the governing councils of the schools were shut down. In the wake of the intervention, faculty members who prized their academic freedom resigned their posts. Many moved abroad. Government appointees then took charge of revising the curriculum and restricting political activism.

Under the banner of modernization, Onganía next attacked the government-controlled port and railroad network. Unions connected with the facilities organized protests, but military and police actions limited their impact.

The economy remained a major challenge. Sluggish growth in the non-agricultural sectors of the economy, combined with continuing high rates of inflation, had helped undermine the Illia administration. In the wake of the coup, economic conditions gradually worsened. Onganía promised aggressive action, but his administrators failed to put into place any clear and effective policy. As 1966 came to an end, the dictatorship had few supporters outside of military circles.

Opposition to Onganía's "Revolution" soon mounted. The unions again took the lead. In December 1966, the CGT launched a new series of strikes, factory occupations, and demonstrations. In the face of active and firm repression, with blanket arrests of union officers and harassment of members and activists, the protests mounted in size and frequency. Signaling clear defiance against the regime and underscoring the unions' strength and resolve, the CGT coordinated a national strike that effectively shut down the country's major cities and transportation links.

In reaction to the workers' challenge, Onganía took a harder line. He announced that the Argentine Revolution would continue. First, the dictatorship would bring stability to the economy and then direct a thorough modernization program that would make the country more competitive in the world market. Then, it would promote a reordering of society under which the advances made from his regime's economic successes would be shared with all social sectors. With these phases of the revolution complete, Onganía promised a political revolution that would put the government in the hands of authentic representatives of the popular will.

Onganía named Adalbert Krieger Vasena his new economics minister. He quickly introduced the regime's revised economic program. Krieger Vasena believed the economy needed a series of controlled shocks. To deal with stagnation and mounting government deficits, he announced a schedule of currency devaluations. At the same time, he introduced taxes on export-producing industries, such as grain farming, to increase government revenues. Hoping to break the cycle of inflation that devaluations had spurred in the past, he ordered a combination of wage freezes and industrial promotions that would hold the line on production costs. He sought international investment and financial support from the IMF.

In sum, Krieger Vasena moved to increase the fiscal resources of the state, improve the economic standing of the country's agricultural and industrial sectors, and promote economic growth while freezing wages and operating costs. In theory, the policy initiatives would provide the time and the resources needed to break free from the vise of stagnation combined with inflation that had choked off economic growth in past years.

The new economic program gained the endorsement of the business community. The unions, however, objected. In the wake of the program's implementation in March 1967, the CGT again called for worker protests and strikes. As the CGT leaders met to plan their campaign, the dictatorship retaliated. Union operating funds were frozen. The government stripped a number of unions of official recognition, which made it illegal for them to represent the workers. Following these actions, a new round of arrests pulled union leaders and activists from the streets.

The ferocity of the repression cracked union resistance effort. Facing a government threat to ban the CGT, union leaders called off their planned strikes. To underscore its victory, the government announced that unions no longer had the right to negotiate wage agreements and that wages would remain frozen for two years.

Through 1968, the government's economic reforms and promotions appeared to be working. Inflation had become a key measure of economic performance. Having peaked at 30 percent in 1966, it had fallen to an annual rate of 10 percent in two years. Farm exports continued to generate foreign exchange and tax revenues. Tariff protections helped spawn new businesses that increased employment and domestic industrial production.

The appearance of economic progress did little to hide growing problems. Farmers became more resentful of the taxes placed upon them. The government's scheduled devaluations, in turn, made the cost of imported machinery and other goods essential for their operations more expensive as the months passed. With their wages frozen, workers increasingly believed they were paying the most for the government's reforms and gaining the least from them.

Of greater significance, the military's support for Onganía's "Revolution" had begun to fade. The Azules grew impatient with Onganía's autocratic and authoritarian regime. They wanted the regime to move more quickly toward a return to civilian rule. Their rivals within the armed forces, the Colorados, were also disappointed. They believed that the dictatorship had not gone far enough to clear from Argentina dangerous ideological influences that threatened society. They wanted a more authoritarian regime, with the military firmly in command.

Conflicts over military policy, which pitted the dictatorship against the military's chief of staff and its senior officers, further reduced the regime's credibility and support. Consequently, when a new round of popular protests rocked the country in 1969, Onganía found little support within the one group that had proven crucial in his rise to power.

The series of events that would push Onganía from power began in Corrientes. In March 1969, student protests against state intervention in the university system became violent. By March 15, student protests appeared in Rosario and other cities. Rounds of police attacks

and student demonstrations mobilized increasing numbers of protesters, and their cause broadened into a general attack against the dictatorship. Meetings between union and student leaders in Córdoba
culminated in the *cordobazo*.

On May 29, a mass of students and workers filled the streets of central Córdoba. Caught unprepared for the size and intensity of the action, police units withdrew and left the provincial capital in the hands
of the protesters for two days. Unchecked by authorities, the rebels
occupied and sacked offices and buildings connected to the government and to foreign conglomerates. Army troops finally pushed the
rebels from the city.

Onganía remained president, but his ability to rule had suffered a
mortal blow. As the months passed, the regime's promise of economic
development faded. Popular protests continued and forced the dictatorship to increasingly rely on force. The military, lacking confidence
in Onganía's abilities, demanded increasing control over state operations. On June 10, 1970, a new military junta announced that it had
forced Onganía from power.

WAITING FOR PERÓN (1970–1972)

Although divided into factions, the Argentine armed forces still believed in 1970 that the country was not ready to return to civilian rule.
Political parties and civilian governments had failed to meet the challenges that faced the country. More important, the threat of Peronism's
revival represented one of the few issues that united almost all in the
officer corps.

In Onganía's wake, generals tried to dictate solutions to a country
that had become increasingly unwilling to follow their lead. Armed
resistance groups launched military campaigns in the hopes that they
would win control and be able to impose a different kind of revolution. As political strife became increasingly common and more violent, Argentina's economy slid further into chaos. A new generation of
more militant leaders had taken control of the union movement. These
leaders worked to revitalize the unions and reclaim their place at the
center of Argentine politics.

Argentina had splintered by 1971 into a collection of warring groups.
Having failed to achieve basic agreements over a proper course of
action, the military accepted the eventual return of civilian rule. Out
of options, the generals who directed the military's exit from power
determined that Juan Domingo Perón, their chief enemy, stood as the
only figure who could bring order to the country.

8

A Society at War
(1970–1983)

Between 1955 and 1972, Argentina had become divided over the challenge and the legacy of Juan Domingo Perón. The armed forces, with distinct factions angered by the actions and broken promises of the Peronist movement, effectively banned the deposed president from the political process. Politicians alternated between efforts to incorporate or to isolate Perón's followers from power.

The exiled president's reputation as the champion of the masses created a deep connection with a majority of Argentines. Perón's promotion of state-led industrialization as the basis of a "third way" toward economic progress between capitalist and communist roads invigorated workers who remained loyal to their leader as the decades passed. Their support for the leader and the movement did not seem to be affected by the failure of his economic program.

As governments came and went, efforts to push Argentina out of its downward spiral crashed. Politically, the country became increasingly polarized. Political parties lost credibility. Perón's supporters, denied the right to create and back any organization connected to their leader, found strength in the union movement. Through the unions, Peronists could paralyze the political system that blocked them from participation.

Juan Carlos Onganía had promised to save Argentina from the Peronist political and cultural excesses that he blamed for the country's disastrous condition. Yet his "Revolution" fell far short of its promised goals. The brief reassertion of military rule that followed Onganía's dismissal in 1970 left many convinced that Perón was the only person who could bring stability back to Argentina.

In 1973, Argentina came full circle: Perón once again captured the presidency. When even he proved incapable of halting the country's fall into political violence and economic anarchy, the most extreme wing of the armed forces asserted its authority. Their program, the *Proceso de Reorganización Nacional* (Process of National Reorganization), unleashed upon the country a military campaign of repression, torture, assassination, and intimidation.

PERÓN'S RETURN (1972–1974)

In 1970, General Roberto Levingston replaced Onganía as Argentina's president. Levingston represented a group of army commanders who had resented Onganía's incompetence and his refusal to allow a greater role for the military in government.

Initially, the new government focused on the country's economic problems. An industrial recession coupled with monetary inflation and declining investment had put the country in a desperate condition. When conservative measures failed, the government shifted toward incentives and tariff protections aimed at the encouragement of domestic industries.

It also unveiled a promotional campaign that targeted consumers: Through leaflets, advertisements, and new purchasing regulations, it encouraged businesses and consumers to buy Argentine products instead of imports.

The promotions had little impact. Sensing the government's weak standing, political activists pushed for a return to constitutional rule. In November 1970 a coalition of leaders from the country's political parties, led by the Radicals and Peronists, declared *"La Hora del Pueblo"* (The Hour of the People). Levingston had hoped to build up popular support for the dictatorship by gradually incorporating civilians into the policymaking process. The national parties countered his move and mobilized their organizations against the government. Working in unison, they demanded an end to military rule.

In March 1971, rioting in Córdoba led to a second occupation of the city. Named the *"viborazo"* by the press, a phrase coined from the military's labeling of the city as a "pit of vipers," the action underscored the rise of "guerrilla" groups that moved to challenge the regime through the use of violence. The mounting crisis led to a change of command.

On March 22, the military junta forced Levingston to resign. General Alejandro Lanusse, who as the army's chief of staff had played a leading role in the coup against Onganía and had operated as the power behind the scenes in the Levingston administration, became the new president.

Lanusse set in motion plans to turn the government over to civilian rule. He set aside the military's ban against the Peronist movement and signaled that Perón and his supporters would be allowed to participate in the coming elections. After having struggled for decades against Perón and his supporters, Lanusse and other military leaders accepted the necessity of Peronist participation in future years. As a result of the escalating political violence and the lack of viable options, the armed forces negotiated a settlement. Perón was allowed to return to Argentina. Although he would not be allowed to run for president, his party would be allowed to compete in the elections. To ensure the ban against Perón's reelection, the junta imposed a residency requirement for all potential candidates.

Perón and his supporters agreed to the residency requirement. In the months leading up to the election, which the government scheduled for March 11, 1973, the Peronists rebuilt their political machine.

Operating from abroad through intermediaries, Perón reasserted his authority over the unions and the Peronist movement. The *Frente Justicialista de Liberación* (Justicialist Front of Liberation, or FREJULI) united provincial and splinter parties behind Perón's approved candidate, Hector Cámpora. He had been a minor figure in Peronist politics. He was one of Perón's representatives and negotiators during the period of transition and had no independent political experience before his nomination.

The elections gave the Peronists a sweeping victory. Cámpora captured just under half of the national vote. The Radicals finished a distant second, with just 29 percent of the votes cast. The elections gave FREJULI control of Congress. Its candidates also captured all the provincial governorships and took control of almost all the provincial legislatures. Although the election had put him at the head of the Peronist movement and the state, political challenges from the unions, popular organizations, and rivals within the party made it clear that he was no match for the demands of office.

Labor, which had sustained the Peronist movement during the decades of military repression, splintered. Union officials had lost command of many local organizations. Alliances between groups of unions weakened the unity and structure of the CGT. Independent unions organized strikes that challenged both the union leaders and the Cámpora government.

Groups within Peronism, split along ideological, social, and occasionally regional lines, worked to claim the movement as their own. Fighting between the factions produced violent confrontations. The economy remained in dismal shape, and the political turmoil undermined efforts to construct a clear policy. When Perón announced his intentions to return to Argentina, many believed that he alone possessed the authority necessary to unite the country and move Argentina forward.

On June 20, hundreds of thousands of supporters gathered near Ezeiza International Airport to greet Juan Perón when he arrived from Spain. All the factions of the revived Peronist movement were represented there. As the crowd waited, a scuffle involving members of the *Montoneros* (name taken from *montonera,* the mounted troops of the Independence era)—a guerrilla organization that had become active in the *Juventud Peronista* (Peronist Youth)—and armed guards hired by union leaders exploded into a running gun battle. The crossfire killed and injured hundreds of spectators.

Cámpora resigned the presidency on July 13. The resignation of Vice President Vicente Solano Lima on the same day mandated a new election, one that would return Perón to the presidency for the third time.

Perón's brief campaign surprised many. He called on union and youth activists to end their protests. He promised stability and national recovery. Behind the scenes, he worked with union and party leaders to shore up their control over the movement. Although he captured a resounding victory in the election—capturing 62 percent of the votes cast—his move to the right ideologically alienated those who hoped his return would bring about a new era in Argentina.

A surge in agricultural exports and the ensuing improvement of the economy took place during the opening months of the new administration. This gave Perón resources to fund economic reforms, modest social welfare programs, and efforts to stabilize the national currency at the same time. The brief holiday from economic problems gave his government an appearance of credibility and success.

Echoing the actions of the original Peronist administration, the new government announced the formation of a "Social Pact." This initiative established bureaucratic links between the government and the distinct elements of society that Perón hoped to rally in support of his regime. As designed, the pact would bring industrialists and workers, agriculturalists and exporters, bankers and business leaders together under the authority of the government, which would then supervise the framing of economic policy. Along with the effort to group social actors into corporations, Perón authorized the creation of regulatory boards and controls that once again put his government at the center of the economy.

These efforts to organize Argentina signaled Perón's intentions to pick up where he had left off in 1955. In contrast, the president's plans relating to the political direction and future of the Peronist movement were not as clear. During the months between his return and his election, the different branches of Peronism—the CGT, the Peronist Youth, and the *Partido Justicialista* (Justicialist Party, or the PJ)—put forward contradictory visions of the movement's goals and future. The union leaders of the CGT, who had helped Perón maintain his authority during his exile, hoped to become the muscle of the movement by tightening their control over the workers and urban groups that delivered votes to Perón and his candidates. They pushed for greater authority over the party's political infrastructure.

The Peronist Youth, radicalized by the involvement of guerrilla sympathizers and activists, held onto the belief that Peronism could serve as a vehicle for revolutionary change. The party leaders, who focused on the need to rebuild the country's political system, hoped to transform the movement into a traditional party that used its popular base to dominate the political system.

Perón's ambiguous position on Peronism's future led leftists, moderates, and conservatives to compete for position within the government and in the Peronist unions and organizations. In 1974, Perón led the government's move toward the right. The Congress passed new laws against political violence. Using his broad support in the unions, he reinforced the authority of CGT officers and filled every post with loyalists.

Working through the Ministry of Social Welfare, headed by José López Rega, the government stepped up its funding of right-wing pressure groups whose members attacked "bolsheviks" and other enemies of the movement within the unions, the universities, and the party.

On May 1, Perón used the annual Labor Day parade and demonstration as an opportunity to clarify and strengthen his position. Before a crowd of thousands in the Plaza de Mayo, Perón criticized the leftist leaders of the Peronist Youth and the Montoneros. Followers anticipated that the president would purge the leftists from the movement in the weeks that followed. As tensions mounted, Juan Perón died of a heart attack on July 1.

THE DESCENT (1969–1975)

In the wake of Perón's death, Argentina fell into a period of escalating political violence. The battle between terrorist groups, which came to involve the armed forces, the police, and state agencies, dated from the

1950s. In reaction to the military coup that pushed Perón from power in 1955, his staunchest supporters committed themselves to resistance. The unions had emerged as the key force in maintaining the Peronists' political ambitions.

They were not the only organizations involved in the fight to preserve the Peronist legacy. The ban placed against groups allied with or connected even loosely to Perón and Peronism encouraged the formation of a variety of organizations that worked outside of the political system to defend the movement and effect change. Important precursors to these resistance groups were connected with the Catholic Church and its efforts to reach out to Argentine youth during the late 1950s. *Acción Católica* (Catholic Action), which organized secondary school students in urban Argentina and directed them toward community work, was the most important of such groups. It instilled doctrines of social justice, protest, and activism, and it created a sense of rebellion against established political practice.

Priests working at the margins of the official church activities had a direct impact on the individuals who would emerge as the leaders of resistance groups on the left and the right of the political spectrum. Carlos Mugica, a member of the Jesuit Order and of the Movement of Third World Priests, personified this generation of religious activists. Mugica helped create community groups in Tucumán, Salta, Cuyo and in the *villas miserias* ("shanty towns," or squatter communities) that appeared in or near the country's major cities that directed young reformers toward efforts to improve the life of Argentina's poor.

By the mid-1960s, international events helped radicalize the activists. The Cuban Revolution and, in particular, Argentine-born Ernesto "Che" Guevara provided models for promoting change through struggle and collective action. Guevara's theories, popularized by his writings, asserted that small groups of armed and committed activists could galvanize revolutionary change within communities, even in the face of active repression from government forces.

As the political scene in Argentina polarized, a new generation of leaders appeared. Fernando Abal Medina, Carlos Gustavo Ramus, and Mario Eduardo Firmenich, who founded the Montoneros, all had worked with Carlos Mugica and other activist priests as part of Church-sponsored reform programs. According to Firmenich, Mugica argued that one could not be Christian without having love for the poor and without being willing to struggle against poverty and the exploitation of the poor, to obtain justice.

Perón, during his years in exile, encouraged leftist activism and confrontation: For example, he approved the formation of the *Movimiento*

Revolucionario Peronista (Revolutionary Peronist Movement) in 1964. He did this partly to destabilize his political opponents in the governments that banned him and his party, and partly to divide the Peronista movement and block the rise of potential rivals who would make Perón's return to Argentina and to power unnecessary.

By the end of the 1960s, a number of Peronist and independent groups pushing for revolutionary change through armed resistance had taken shape on the left wing of Argentina's political scene. Finding recruits among middle- and upper-middle-class young adults, these groups became active in almost every part of the country, especially in the larger cities. The most important were the Montoneros and the *Ejército Revolucionario del Pueblo* (Revolutionary Army of the People, or ERP).

The Montoneros and the ERP became more active and brazen in the wake of the cordobazo. The Montoneros focused on developing an armed movement of resistance in Argentina's cities. To get cash and to develop a popular following, the Montoneros embarked on a campaign of bank robberies and political kidnappings. Leaders in the business community, conservative union bosses, and officers of foreign corporations, whom the guerrillas labeled enemies of the people, became the group's main targets. The group's most notorious action came in 1971, when it kidnapped and killed Pedro Aramburu, who had helped lead the coup that displaced Perón in 1955.

The ERP was also active in urban districts, but its main goal was the creation of a revolutionary center in Argentina's rural northwest. The ERP leaders hoped to emulate the example of the Cuban Revolution and build a political base among the country's peasantry and rural poor.

With Tucumán Province serving as a focal point, the ERP launched attacks against army posts and ambushed military and police sites. Its partisans also attacked police officers and military personnel. Both groups tried to develop support within the Peronist movement by taking charge of Peronist Youth groups in the country's larger cities and public universities. When the military accepted a return to civilian rule, leaders of the ERP and Montoneros hoped to make Peronism into a vehicle for revolution.

Forces on the right had also armed themselves and adopted violence in support of their ambitions. Initially, enforcers recruited from the military or police forces or the unions and party organizations challenged rivals for control of the movement's offices and organizations. Paralleling the growing tide of leftist violence, counterattacks from the right grew. The targets of the guerrilla forces formed "death squads" to get revenge for family members and friends killed by the attacks.

Union leaders formed the *Juventud Sindical Peronista* (Peronist Syndical Youth, or JSP) to challenge the Montoneros' recruiting efforts within the unions and the JP. The mobilization on the right dramatically escalated the level of violence in the country.

The events of 1973, beginning with the battle at Ezeiza and ending with Perón's public condemnation of the guerrilla movement, isolated the leftists. Even before taking office, Perón had ordered actions against the left. Governors and mayors that Perón's advisors judged to be sympathetic to the guerrilla organizations were pushed from office. The Peronist Youth, which had served as a bridge between Peronism and the guerrilla movement, had its offices raided by the police. Seeing Perón's pronouncements and actions as attacks against their organizations and their goals, leaders of the main guerrilla organizations decided to break from Peronism.

Perón's death ended any attempt by the government to create consensus. Pacts with rival parties and compromise agreements with employers and workers ended. María Estela Martínez de Perón, better known as Isabel Perón, whose first political campaign was as her husband's running mate in 1973, followed the advice of her most loyal allies: the leaders of the country's largest unions and José López Rega, the minister of social welfare and the new president's private secretary.

In the place of conciliation, Isabel Perón led a push to face down all challenges to her government. Union discipline, enforced from the CGT, would bring the workers into line. Rival parties were given no active role in setting policy. FREJULI leaders took charge of the legislative branch. To keep the military in line, the government approved a campaign of counterterrorism. Once the political threat from the left faded, the government would then bring discipline to the economy. In the wake of Juan Perón's death, the Peronist government became an authoritarian regime.

López Rega took charge of the most sinister aspects of this effort. Beginning in 1974, in concert with the government's move to the right, he directed the *Alianza Argentina Anticomunista* (Argentine Anticommunist Alliance, or AAA) against the "subversives" who challenged the government and its policies. Political activists were the first targets. Soon union activists who challenged the authority of their leaders came under attack. By the end of 1975, AAA leaders widened their campaign to include leftist sympathizers within the university system and the media.

The AAA benefited from state support, employing police and military veterans and using police and military equipment, stripped of official markings, during their operations. Once AAA identified its suspects, the group conducted kidnappings or assassinations in an effort to exterminate any opposition to the government.

The government's support actions dramatically increased the level of political violence. The guerrillas countered the state's attacks with counterstrikes of their own. Having broken with the Peronist government in 1973, the ERP intensified its military campaign in Tucumán. Its immediate goal was the establishment of a revolutionary state in the province, from which it would then push to take control of other northern provinces.

Meanwhile, the Montoneros publicly declared their return to violent action in September 1974. Its cells moved independently against sites connected with the government, the military, and other declared enemies of the people. In addition, both groups sponsored a mounting wave of kidnappings. The ransoms collected helped support their military and political projects.

As the political situation moved toward open warfare, the economy again emerged as a problem for government planners. The 1973 oil crisis, when members of the Organization of Petroleum Exporting Countries used production and export caps in an effort to push oil prices to historic peaks, affected Argentina profoundly. Rising energy and import prices put enormous pressure on businesses. For consumers, prices of all goods increased quickly. Juan Perón had promised to hold inflation in check. By the end of 1974, government efforts to stall price increases in the wholesale and retail markets were falling apart.

Isabel Perón, following the conflicting advice offered by different branches of the government, sponsored a series of policy shifts that left the public confused. Businesses, pressed by government price and market controls on the one hand, and labor pressure for wage relief on the other, increasingly turned to clandestine agreements with their buyers, their suppliers, and even their workers. Consequently, although the government set down official price and wage limits, an increasing amount of the business activity took place in an unregulated "parallel" market.

In the first quarter of 1975, the economy neared collapse. Industrial production dropped, prices increased from month to month at rates higher than price escalations in the previous three years, and workers threatened to force additional concessions. In May, Economics Minister Celestino Rodrigo moved to bring conditions under control. He announced that the government would devalue the national currency by more than 150 percent in relation to the U.S. dollar. He also ordered price hikes for utilities and government services. The government put a limit on wage increases and published lists of prices for goods sold in the domestic market.

Critics labeled the new economic intervention as the *rodrigazo*—inviting comparisons with the cordobazo and equating the government's sudden conservative shift with the attacks of terrorists. The unions moved firmly in protest. Setting aside internal divisions, the CGT sponsored the first general strike against a Peronist government.

Dependent upon the political support of the union leadership, Isabel Perón moved toward a compromise. She publicly criticized Rodrigo's policies and promised new wage increases. Rodrigo resigned in protest. The unions' victory meant little, however. The economy had become nearly unmanageable. Inflation surpassed measurable levels. Economists, who compared the country's condition with that of Weimar Germany during the Great Depression, estimated that prices increased during 1975 near or beyond 1,000 percent and projected that the country faced a prolonged period of "hyperinflation."

Argentina was in shambles. The extreme right and left of the political spectrum had abandoned the political system. Political violence continued with the government unable to pose any solution to the deepening problems that challenged the country. President Isabel Perón had all but disappeared from public view. In September 1975, she had taken a leave of absence. With the presidency in doubt, competing factions within the Peronist movement fought for authority.

Eventually, with the backing of union leaders, Isabel reclaimed the presidency. What little authority she once held as Juan Perón's successor had evaporated.

In February, the Argentine Congress began proceedings to impeach the president. Another attempt to bring the economy under control through wage and price controls collapsed despite the support of pro-government union leaders. Public anger at the government increased. Even before the armed forces had taken any action, many observers believed that a military coup was both inevitable and welcome.

THE *PROCESO* (1975–1981)

Having lost control of the political system after the collapse of Onganía's "Argentine Revolution," the military planned their return to power with great care. Factionalism within the armed forces remained a major challenge. Just as in the 1960s, the officer corps of the three branches of the Argentine military was deeply split. One faction, anti-Peronist but committed to constitutional rule, occupied the space of the Azules. Taking a harder line were those who believed that politicians of all kinds represented a threat to the true nation. They wanted to create a strong and lasting dictatorship. With the military in control of society, this faction believed that they could turn back mounting threats not just to the Argentine nation but to Christian civilization.

When Onganía's government collapsed, the military's political position was weak. Although the armed forces lacked unity, the political and economic chaos that had descended upon Argentina after Juan Perón's death created a power vacuum that ambitious officers aimed to fill. Less than two years after surrendering power to its Peronist enemies, the military again returned to the political arena.

The first targets of the revived armed forces were the "subversives." Attacks, in particular those of the ERP, against military bases and personnel presented an immediate threat. Conditions led the national government to declare a state of siege at the end of 1974. This allowed the military to conduct operations against the populace. Army commanders declared an offensive against the ERP in Tucumán. Army units engaged ERP forces directly in the zones that the guerrillas had declared their own. Taking on police powers, soldiers identified and "neutralized" suspects, their bases of operation, and any suspected sympathizers. Communities and neighborhoods that the military had determined to be supportive of the ERP came under attack. Tucumán became a military camp. Even after the battle against the ERP had ended in 1976, military units continued to search for and eliminate "subversives" and sympathizers.

In other parts of Argentina, the military expanded its security operations. It coordinated its operations with police and government forces. Although guerrilla organizations continued to advertise their presence through bombings and assassinations, the army's offensive had achieved near total success by January 1976.

As Isabel Perón's government collapsed, the military took power. On March 24, 1976, army officers seized Perón. A junta announced its ambitions shortly afterward. General Jorge Rafael Videla stood at the head of the new government. He publicly declared that the military aimed at purging from the nation all elements that threatened its stability and future hopes. In some respects, Videla's statements echoed those of Onganía a decade before. Years of conflict and recrimination had led the military faction that had taken command of the country toward more extreme measures and solutions.

Although the military actions against the guerrilla had been successful, the dictatorship planned to go much farther. Using force, it hoped to purge from society the idea of subversion, along with the ideologies and political traditions that junta leaders connected with it. It launched *la guerra sucia* (the Dirty War). Antiterrorist operations pioneered by the quasi-official AAA increased. Using police and military personnel and resources, the dictatorship took into custody thousands of suspected enemies of the state. Union activists, leaders of community aid groups, even student activists who petitioned authorities for paper and pencils for use in school, became targets.

Working with dictatorships in Chile, Brazil, and Uruguay as part of a secret program labeled "Operation Condor," the dictatorship pursued its enemies in foreign countries. Sharing intelligence and trading exiles from one country for those who had fled abroad, the government was able to pursue, arrest, torture, and execute individuals who had evaded capture.

Following the orders of the state, security personnel "disappeared" the targets. State officials, when faced with inquiries from the relatives of the detainees, denied that the missing were prisoners. Instead, they reported that the missing were either abroad or in hiding. As the number of "disappeared" persons mounted, the government claimed that it held fewer than 500 terrorists in prison.

The broad sweep of repression discouraged public protest. Union leaders, who had played a major role in challenging past military regimes, were detained, tortured, and occasionally executed. Union activists became targets of the security forces and "disappeared" in the first months of the regime. Although isolated worker actions did take place, the dictatorship's attacks shattered the unions' collective power.

The press offered little opposition. Initially, government officials checked any criticism of their actions by imposing press censorship. The government quickly lifted its censorship decree and replaced it with repression. Attacks and disappearances made most journalists retreat from the topic of the campaign of terror.

In concert with its campaign of violence against society, the dictatorship imposed a rigid economic program. Economics Minister José H. Martínez de Hoz introduced new exchange rates and trade reforms that promoted agricultural exports and industrial imports. The policy shifts aimed at increasing export revenues and at the dismantling of inefficient industries. He also outlined a plan to privatize government-controlled industries and reduce government spending on social services.

The economics program as designed promised a major transformation of the economy and the society. In the eyes of its framers, the program attacked the legacies of Peronism. Success would right the balance in society and politics by eliminating the groups that Peronism had promoted artificially: state-sponsored industries and unionized workers.

In its first months, the Martínez de Hoz reform strategy appeared to bring stability to the economy. Dramatic increases in exports and a falling inflation rate came, however, at a heavy price. The country's industrial sector entered into a severe depression. Industrial output fell and then stagnated for two years. Industrial employment levels dropped along with wage levels. Although these measures cheered government officials, the impact of the policy shifts embittered broad sectors of the population.

In 1979, the dictatorship appeared to have achieved its aims. The horrific repression of the state's enemies had ended all political and military challenges. Economic trends gave policymakers confidence. The victory of the national soccer team in the 1978 World Cup, which the dictatorship hosted, provided a measure of international prestige. The *Proceso de Reorganización Nacional* (Process of National Reorganization) had reached its peak.

All too quickly the dictatorship's economic program began to unravel. International changes, which undermined the country's agricultural sector, and the lingering industrial depression within Argentina destroyed the financial standing of the country's banking system. Privatization plans, which were essential in any effort to cut fiscal deficits and balance the economy, had stalled. Military officers, who had assumed command of state industries and bureaucracies, refused to cooperate in dismantling the public sector. By 1980, inflation again jumped out of control. The apparent victory over the economic disasters of past governments evaporated.

While its economic program faltered, the dictatorship opened a dialogue with select civilian leaders. This effort symbolized the confidence and ambition of the Videla administration. In interviews with representatives from conservative parties and important institutions, it hoped to create support for the formation of a "Movement of National Opinion." Involving a limited number of participants who were sympathetic to the Videla administration, its policies, and the aims of the Proceso, the dialogue was designed to serve as the foundation for a future shift toward joint civilian-military rule.

A carefully planned transition that left Peronists and other major parties out of the process would have guaranteed a number of things. First, it would have blocked any return to the policies and practices that the military associated with Peronism. Second, it would have insulated the military from any legal or political challenges against its actions during the Dirty War. Third, it would have cemented a political role for the armed forces into place for a generation.

The dialogue launched in 1979 led to no substantial agreement, however. Isolated, the military followed its own rules and procedures in an effort to maintain its control over the country. Having agreed to hold the presidency for only five years, Videla transferred power to General Roberto Viola, the commander of the army, in March 1981.

Ultranationalist factions within the armed forces had tried to block Viola's ascension to the presidency. They believed that his views were too liberal. Their fears seemed to be correct. Deteriorating economic conditions led the new provisional president to seek a return to civilian rule. He announced discussions with the leaders of the major political parties, and rumors of a planned transfer of power to a civilian regime appeared.

This mobilized a challenge within the armed forces. Conservatives and nationalists, who feared any return to civilian rule, rallied behind General Leopoldo Galtieri. Using the excuse of the provisional president's poor health, Galtieri and his supporters forced Viola from power on December 12.

THE DICTATORSHIP'S COLLAPSE (1981–1982)

Galtieri embarked on a distinct track. With ambitions to become an independent political figure, he tried to build a popular following. He took credit for government food distributions. He focused public attention on issues of national honor and concern. Of these, two came to the fore: a lingering border dispute with Chile and control of the *Las Malvinas* (the Falkland Islands).

Argentina's southwestern border with Chile had been a subject of disagreement between the two countries since the nineteenth century. At the start of the Proceso, ultranationalists considered seizing the disputed territory, but fears over the costs of war with Chile stalled any move in this direction. In January 1982, Galtieri briefly revived the issue, claiming that the treaty arbitration neglected Argentina's national interests. When the issue failed to draw sufficient support within popular circles and from other military commanders, the dictator set it aside.

The Falkland Islands seemed to be a much more promising target. Great Britain had seized the islands in 1833. The value of the islands as coaling stations was clear in the nineteenth century. By the closing decades of the twentieth century, British control over the Falklands stood as an embarrassing reminder of the nation's imperial past. Intermittent negotiations over the issue of what country should control the island had stalled, and Galtieri's advisors believed that the British had little desire to protect their claims.

Galtieri saw a move to take the Falklands as worthwhile for two main reasons. First, as a military campaign, it would help unite the armed forces and, he hoped, solidify their support for his administration. Second, giving the long-standing claims of Argentine sovereignty over the islands, a successful invasion would make Galtieri and his government into heroes. Hoping to take the lead of a political movement that would end with his election to the presidency, Galtieri approved the invasion of the Falklands.

He and his advisors anticipated no serious response from the British. For insurance, they also believed that the U.S. government, which had expressed its appreciation of Argentina's support of its policies in Central America, would check any attempt by Great Britain to take back the islands.

An invasion of the Falkland Islands began on April 2, 1982. Army units also seized Sandwich and the South Georgian Islands located to the south and east. The British forces, small and poorly armed, offered almost no resistance. When the government broadcast news of its successful invasions, mass demonstrations in support of Galtieri and the dictatorship broke out in every Argentine city.

The British government, shocked by the invasion, demanded Argentina's immediate withdrawal. To the dictatorship's surprise, the British put into motion a counterinvasion. British attacks from the air and the sea began on April 25. Its naval forces established a cordon around the islands and blocked attempts to reinforce the Argentine positions.

On May 1, a second surprise occurred. The United States, after trying to broker a negotiated settlement, sided with its longtime ally. It condemned the Argentine invasion and offered the British logistical

Argentine soldiers carry military supplies during the ill-fated Falklands War, April 13, 1982. (Daniel Garcia/AFP/Getty Images)

support. Efforts by the United Nations to negotiate a settlement also failed. Backed by the United States, the British were determined to force the Argentine forces off the islands.

British forces began their attack on the Falklands on May 21. The well-trained British forces faced off against Argentine units that were mainly comprised of undisciplined recruits. After weeks of careful maneuvers that divided and then isolated the bulk of the defenders, the British made ready for a final assault on the Argentine positions. Recognizing the advantages that the British invasion forces attained and fearing the cost of an attack, the Argentine forces surrendered on June 14.

The Falkland Islands War shattered the political standing of the dictatorship. With the exception of the air force and a few units under army command, the Argentine forces put up no resistance against the British taskforce. On June 15, Galtieri offered his resignation in a public address carried by radio and television. Although he blamed foreign imperialists for the defeat, the news that followed the return of the captured soldiers undermined Galtieri's claims. The poor planning and cowardly performance of the government and the army officers who commanded the operation discredited the regime.

THE MILITARY SURRENDERS POWER (1982–1983)

Even before the full retreat from the last, disastrous days of military rule, elements of Argentine society had rallied in protest. The dictatorship had successfully neutralized the CGT. With the leading union officers under detention or "disappeared," worker protests and strike activity fell dramatically. The leaders of smaller unions did move into the void left by the elimination of the front line of the CGT.

Beginning in 1977, the union movement split into two main tendencies. Following the leadership of Saúl Ubaldini, who represented the beer workers, and Roberto García, who was president of the taxi drivers' union, the "Group of 25" mounted the first labor protests against the Proceso. Lacking press coverage and operating in the face of government terrorism, the "Group of 25" grew more combative. The group called brief general strikes in 1979 and 1981.

As their actions became bolder, the group gained sympathy and support from other union members and the population at large. As the traditional opponent of military dictatorships returned to form, new groups framed original challenges to the Proceso and the Dirty War. The most famous were *Las Madres de Plaza de Mayo* (The Mothers of the Plaza de Mayo, or *las madres*), who first started their weekly silent marches on April 30, 1977. As their demonstrations continued, las madres established international connections and received exposure abroad, which prevented any wholesale detention of the group. Weak counter-protests did occur. The military's supporters attacked the group and its leaders in the press. Individual members faced acts of violence and harassment. Ultimately, the government's efforts to intimidate the leadership of the group failed miserably.

The Falkland Islands disaster fostered a dramatic increase in popular protests against the regime. As a consequence, the military moved to salvage its political position and orchestrate a return to civilian rule. General Cristino Nicolaides, a retired army general, took power as the chief of the armed forces. He then named Reynaldo Bignone provisional president. This signaled two things: Even though Bignone was not involved in the junta and was thus an outsider, his appointment showed that the hard-liners still held sway; and since he represented the army, which had contributed the most to the failure in the war with Britain, his ascension meant that the army regarded the disaster as a product of personal ambitions, not institutional failure.

The new leaders set about the task of orchestrating a military evacuation from the executive branch. Their most important goals were a ban on prosecutions or punishments for the events of the Dirty War, a sharing of power during the undefined "period of transition," no civilian investigations into military actions, maintenance of the crippled condition of the unions as political organizations, and inclusion of the military leadership in any discussions over military and economic policy.

This agenda was an attempt to create a political pact that would insulate the military as an institution and protect military officers from reprisals. Since an estimated 300 to 400 officers played a role in developing the Dirty War as policy, and even more became involved when the antisubversion programs were implemented, the dictatorship's leaders pushed hard to stay in command of the political transition.

Most Peronist leaders accepted the military's demands. In 1982, after Galtieri's resignation, Peronist leaders fell in behind Deolindo Bittel. A shadow cabinet of PJ officials began preparing for their next turn at ruling the country. Bittel designed a plan for a transition period of two years, with the military still in command of the national government.

As Bittel and his advisors negotiated with the military, the surviving components of the Peronist movement fell into political competition. The effort to select a presidential candidate became a complicated affair, with each branch of the CGT and various wings of the party publicly parading a range of choices. Negotiations between the military, spearheaded by General Nicoliades, and labor unions, especially those loyal to Lorenzo Miguel, who headed the metallurgical workers union and served as president of the main CGT branch through the 1980s, developed into a major liability for the PJ.

Nicoliades and the junta promised Miguel that the military would help him take charge of a united CGT during the period of transition. In return, Miguel promised to use his authority within Peronist ranks to block any prosecutions of military personnel in connection with the Dirty War.

Miguel, Bittel, and other key Peronist leaders assumed that the transition would follow the pattern set in 1973. Their movement's links with the country's disastrous plunge into the Proceso and the Dirty War had, however, mobilized popular resentment. Rather than repeat the patterns of the past, the 1983 elections that ended the dictatorship gave the power to rebuild Argentina to a different party with a new and ambitious agenda.

9

Democracy's Fragile Return (1983–1991)

In 1983, most observers anticipated a Peronist electoral victory. It had been the country's majority party, and in the two last national elections it polled nearly twice as many votes as its closest competitors. All the parties had suffered under the weight of the military dictatorship. Their organizations were banned and their leaders attacked. The Peronists' advantage lay in the continued strength of the unions, which had served, and all believed would serve, as a political machine for the Peronist candidates.

The election put Raúl Alfonsín and the *Unión Cívica Radical* into power. Seen by a majority of the voters as the only party untarnished by the political and economic anarchy of the previous decade, the Radicals directed the return to constitutional rule. After a promising start, the depth of the country's economic and political problems undermined the Alfonsín government.

Breaking from the patterns of the recent past, civilian rule managed to survive. Constitutionally mandated elections handed power over to the Reformist wing of the Peronist Party in 1989. Under the charismatic rule of Carlos Saúl Menem, Argentina continued the slow and difficult process of political, economic, and social recovery.

THE RADICALS TAKE POWER (1983–1985)

In January 1983, the Argentine government carried a budget deficit equal to 14 percent of the country's GDP. Inflation reached an unmeasurable level, estimated as best as was possible at 310 percent. The balance-of-payments deficit, which had to become a surplus if Argentina was to escape its economic crisis, reached $6.7 billion. External debt moved past $43.5 billion. After the utter failure of civilian and military governments to manage the problems that plagued the country since World War II, many wondered if political instability and economic decline had become permanent characteristics.

Alfonsín had characterized himself and his party as the only ones capable of leading Argentina's reconstruction and reconciliation. This would prove problematic. The economic situation was overwhelming, and the costs necessary to deal with it—devaluation, privatization, promotion of exports, and limitations on imports—would not do much to make the regime popular in the short run.

As bad as conditions were at the start of 1983, by the end of the year when the Radicals took power, circumstances were much worse. The external debt continued to grow and surpassed $45 billion. Inflation during the final months of 1983 doubled the astronomical rates of January. Investment capital flowed out of the country. Transfers of cash, converted into dollars and then deposited in banks or invested safely abroad, passed $22 billion.

Alfonsín put Economics Minister Bernardo Grinspun in charge of the government's recovery plan. It seemed that he had few options. International creditors demanded a strict, orthodox approach to the country's economic disaster. The Argentine government had to cut its spending, put in place financial reforms to stabilize the value of the country's currency, and make Argentina an attractive place for investment. All this had to be accomplished while the government maintained its debt payments.

Grinspun and the Radicals believed a reliance on standard approaches would force the Argentine people to pay an excessive price for the financial disasters of the past. Instead, the government embarked on a creative and risky course. Rather than follow the standard course of devaluations and budget cuts, which would have cost the government a great deal in political terms, Grinspun announced that the government would sponsor wage increases and increased employment. It would also maintain its funding of social programs and supports of provincial governments.

The size of the debt made even the threat of default a major concern for the country's creditors. The directors of the IMF and private banks involved with the Argentine debt negotiations rejected Grinspun's recovery proposals, but they did not impose sanctions. Doing so, many believed, would lead to Argentina's suspension of debt payments, which would then spark a financial crisis that might spread throughout Latin America and beyond.

By refusing to compromise, Grinspun put off any forced settlement that would have halted the government's attempt to bring stability to the domestic economy. The Radical government believed that the time gained would pay off, that consumer confidence would return, and that spending would grow. As consumer purchases fueled rising demand for goods and services in the country, investors would reverse course and invest in industries and businesses. Once evidence of a recovery appeared, the government would then be in a position to bargain with international creditors for more time. As the anticipated recovery gained strength, Argentina would be able to better support its debt burden.

By the end of 1984, the government's economic program had satisfied no one. Wages continued to lag behind inflation, which remained excessively high. Producers found no rising demand for their products and as a result the industrial and service sectors of the economy remained in recession. Agriculturalists objected to taxes placed on exports and the lack of any coherent fiscal and trade policy. Farmers and ranchers threatened to reduce output, which would immediately have led to falling export and tax revenues. Overseas, IMF negotiators lost all patience with Grinspun and his proposals. After issuing warnings, the IMF and other funding sources suspended all new loans in May 1985 and demanded a firm schedule for existing debt repayments.

In the wake of the IMF challenge, Grinspun resigned. Alfonsín replaced him with Juan Sourrouille, who devised a new economic strategy. On June 14, 1985, the government announced its Austral Plan. The Austral Plan had four main components. First, the government introduced a new currency: The austral replaced the peso. Second, the government set firm and extensive wage and price controls. Third, the government set in motion a series of budget cuts and revenue increases that promised to reduce and ultimately end federal budget deficits within a few years. Finally, new regulations limited the ability of the government to issue currency to meet its expenses, which had helped fuel inflation in past years.

Government officials hoped that the plan would provide a break from the past. The replacement of the old currency set aside the name used for centuries. By forcing a conversion to a stronger currency whose value was set to the dollar, the change helped establish the wage and price freeze. Citizens were asked to report any business that tried to sell goods or services at prices above those authorized by the government. This step directly involved all Argentines in the economic plan, a move the planners hoped would help build public support.

Just as important, the new economic team believed the Austral Plan would force the economy to operate in a more disciplined and predictable fashion without requiring a cut in wages or price increases. In addition, by taking a dramatically new approach, the government hoped to gain renewed support from international creditors.

For a short time, the Austral Plan worked. During the initial months of the plan's implementation, inflation dropped from triple digit levels to an annual rate of less than 20 percent. The currency shift cut speculation and encouraged investment and savings. The government's apparent progress in achieving deficit reductions enhanced its reputation.

Groups on both ends of the spectrum, unions and the Argentine Rural Society, tempered their protests. The brief success of the Austral Plan helped the Radicals hold their own in the 1985 national elections. Although their share of the vote dropped four points, from 47.4 to 43.2 percent, the Radicals gained one seat and retained their majority in the Chamber of Deputies. In contrast, rival Peronists lost eight seats. The vote thus appeared to be a strong endorsement of the government. Observers recognized, however, that enormous challenges remained. The Radicals' political future depended upon the Alfonsín government's ability to manage the economy. At the same time, the success of its economic program required that the government's political standing remain strong.

THE MILITARY RESISTANCE (1983–1987)

Before leaving office, the armed forces took action to defend themselves from attempts to seek justice against those who planned and carried out the human rights violations that took place during the Dirty War. Publicly, they decreed the Law of National Pacification at the end of September 1983. The law sanctioned an amnesty for all military and police personnel involved in carrying out the war against subversion. With the crimes unlisted and the criminals unnamed, the decree tried to close the door on the military's war on society.

Political leaders attacked the military's action and promised that the decree would hold no weight after the coming elections. Privately, the military had sought assurances from the leaders of the Peronist Party and the unions. Although Lorenzo Miguel, whom Alfonsín had accused of being party to the agreement, denied the existence of any military-union pact, most critics accepted the accusation as fact.

The popular belief that the Peronists would cooperate with the armed forces and use the transition period to advance their mutual interests helped bolster support for the Radical Party in the October 1983 elections.

The push for justice had become a major issue even before the elections. After the Falkland Islands disaster, the Mothers of the Plaza de Mayo helped build a crusade to bring the architects and henchmen of the Dirty War to trial. Marches and mass demonstrations drew tens of thousands of supporters. A new group, the Grandmothers of the Plaza de Mayo, called for investigations into the disappearances of children who were rumored to have been taken along with their parents to detention centers. Foreign governments, led by prosecutors in Italy and Spain, petitioned the government on behalf of their citizens who had disappeared along with the unknown thousands of Argentines during the military terror.

Court proceedings against commanders who directed known detention and torture operations began in the summer of 1983. Before his election, Alfonsín stated that if elected he would not form a special tribunal to investigate military and police atrocities. Instead, he approved the use of the judicial branch to pursue cases against suspects. He urged the courts to focus on the officers who designed and directed

Beginning on April 30, 1978, the Mothers of the Plaza de Mayo maintained a silent, poignant protest against the "Dirty War," the military dictatorship's campaign of terror that kidnapped and executed as many as 30,000 people. (Bettmann/Corbis)

the Dirty War and those who committed human rights violations against the detainees.

At the same time, he recognized that the guerrilla organizations, through bombings, assassinations, and large-scale assaults on military bases and police stations, did bear some responsibility for provoking the Dirty War. He also suggested that soldiers who were caught up in the process by simply following orders did not deserve punishment.

After winning the presidency, Alfonsín did not move away from his promises. He revoked the amnesty decree imposed by the dictatorship shortly before the October elections. Although he supported the idea of bringing human rights violators to justice, he did not create any special commission to investigate past crimes and file indictments. He sought a moderate course.

Not surprisingly, his government's position did not satisfy the human rights organizations that push for justice. By allowing prosecutions, the Alfonsín government angered the military and their conservative supporters. Arguing falsely that the alleged crimes occurred during a justified and legally sanctioned war, soldiers and their supporters viewed the prosecutions as illegal and unwarranted.

The search for survivors of the Dirty War uncovered a number of mass graves. The bodies lacked identification and showed signs of death by execution. Human rights groups demanded that the government force the military to account for the dead. With pressure building, Alfonsín ordered military trials for the officers who directed the dictatorship between 1976 and 1983. He also ordered the courts to bring the leaders of the Montoneros and the ERP to trial. Behind the scenes, he authorized efforts to locate Dirty War protagonists in exile and seek their extradition.

Alfonsín and the Radical Party had declared that they would be in command over the military. The government's move against the criminals of the Dirty War, however, suggested to many that it approached the armed forces with caution and deference. Many believed that the military courts would acquit the defendants or ignore major crimes in an effort to maintain the standing of the armed forces.

Led by the Mothers of the Plaza de Mayo, a push for civilian judicial proceedings against suspected torturers and assassins gained force. Reacting to popular demands, Alfonsín asked Ernesto Sábato to chair the *Comisión Nacional Sobre la Desaparación de las Personas* (National Commission Concerning the Disappearance of Persons, or CONADEP). The commission supervised a wide-ranging investigation to collect information on the roots, the development, and the operations of the military and political machinery of the Dirty War. It also attempted to document the numbers, the identities, and the location of the persons "disappeared" by the agents of the Dirty War. After taking its charge in January, the commission completed its investigations and published a report of its findings in September 1984.

The creation of a commission by the Alfonsín government temporarily satisfied the demand of the public for justice. When CONADEP published its report, titled *Nunca más* (*Never Again*), the report's length and detailed descriptions inflamed public anger and increased pressure on the government. In response, the Alfonsín administration transferred the cases pending in the military courts to civilian ones. Trials involving the senior commanders who headed the government or the branches of the military during the Proceso began in April 1985. After months of court sessions, the judges sentenced General Jorge Videla and Admiral Emilio Massera to life in prison. Other defendants received lesser penalties.

Although the Alfonsín government was sincere in its desire for justice, its focus on the commanders continued to frustrate the groups that sought broader investigations and wider-ranging indictments. CONADEP had implicated more than 1,000 police and military officials in the crimes connected with the Dirty War.

The armed forces, in turn, grew more entrenched. The government had gone far beyond what the military command believed was justified in pursuit of human rights violators. At the same time, the government had tried to weaken the military by cutting its budget and by forcing senior officers into retirement.

The resolution of the border dispute with Chile, which had lingered since 1977, underscored the armed forces' political isolation. Ultranationalists still clung to the belief that any compromise with Chile over the islands that dotted the southern frontier of the continent represented a betrayal of Argentina's honor and national interests. The matter had been forwarded to the pope for final arbitration in 1978 and, as was the case with the arbitration decision rendered by the British government, Chile was rewarded with control of three islands that gave it access to the Atlantic Ocean.

Ultranationalists within the military believed that standing firm against the arbitration would demonstrate to the nation the military's importance. The debate over the issue would also distract public attention from the investigation of human rights abuses. Rather than confront the military directly, Alfonsín submitted the issue to a public vote. On November 25, 1984, more than 80 percent of those polled favored the arbitration ruling. The Peronist Party, which had recommended a boycott of the vote, suffered a major embarrassment when the count revealed that almost all the eligible voters cast ballots. But the gap between those who favored the settlement and those who backed the ultranationalist position delivered a stronger condemnation to the military. The weakness of its political standing was clear.

The armed forces and their civilian supporters refused to surrender. As a new round of indictments targeted military and police officials that CONADEP implicated in the Dirty War, the *Familias de los Muertos porla Subversión* (Families of the Victims of Subversion, or FAMUS) appeared. In an effort to counter the status of the Mothers of the Plaza de Mayo, they held regular masses at the national cathedral in downtown Buenos Aires and at other sites. The group had two aims: It put forward a list of assassinated police officers and soldiers to match the lists of the "disappeared"; and it wanted to serve as a focal point for the building of public support against the government's prosecutions of human rights violators.

Although the numbers involved in the pro-military protests remained small, the opponents of the court actions effectively made their point by evoking the ghosts of the pasts. Bomb detonations in the Federal Capital and other cities followed the issuing of indictments and judgments. Rumors of military protests and even coups began to circulate.

Sensing the growing unease among military officers, the Alfonsín government tried to appease the armed forces. In October 1985, against the recommendations of his economic advisors, Alfonsín backed a 25 percent wage increase for military personnel. In December 1986, the president announced legislation that would place a deadline for prosecutions relating to political and military crimes committed during the Dirty War. The proposal, named the *"punto final"* (literally, "end point"), passed the National Congress despite massive public demonstrations and international criticism against it. By the law's February 23, 1987, deadline, prosecutors filed 487 charges against more than 300 officers. Nearly 100 of those charged were still serving in the armed forces. The government had set the *punto final* in the hopes that it would bring a quick end to the prosecutions. Instead, the mass filings infuriated the armed forces and their supporters.

On April 14, Major Ernesto Barreiro declared his opposition to the prosecutions. Having been indicted, he refused to appear in court and instead rallied troops in his defense at a military base in Cordoba. On April 17, Lieutenant Colonel Aldo Rico organized an occupation of the Campo de Mayo army base in Buenos Aires in support of Barreiro. Appearing in camouflage, the rebels called for a change in the army high command and an end to the human rights trials.

The president ordered the army to capture the rebels. When units surrounded but then refused to attack the rebels, a serious crisis developed. Tensions within the military branches emerged. To demonstrate their loyalty, air force commanders requested permission to bomb the rebel positions. Junior officers, many of whom had participated in the Dirty War and in the Falklands operation, sided with the rebels. These officials represented a distinct faction within the military chain of command. They felt unfairly pressured by the court prosecutions and the budget cutbacks that threatened their careers. They also suspected that more senior officials, who had participated in the crimes of the past dictatorships but then retired rather than defend their actions, had abandoned the military and its interests. Alienated and angry, many junior officers also resented the Alfonsín government. They viewed the rebellions as an opportunity to push back the government's efforts to reform and politically isolate the military.

The rebel challenge unexpectedly mobilized massive demonstrations in support of democracy. The CGT called for a general strike that it would maintain in place until the rebellion ended. Leaders of the political parties, industrial and producer organizations, the unions, and even the Catholic Church signed a petition that pledged their support for popular government. As the crisis developed, thousands occupied the Plaza de Mayo and declared their willingness to block any attempt to put the military back into power.

Alfonsín decided to negotiate directly with the rebels. Secretly, he met with the rebel leaders on April 19 and convinced them to end their protests. Shortly afterward, from the balcony of the Casa Rosada before hundreds of thousands of supporters, he announced the end of the crisis. Alfonsín was cheered for his heroic intervention.

In the weeks that followed, the president ordered changes in the army command. Then, on May 5, he submitted to Congress the *Ley de Obediencia Debida* (Due Obedience Law). The proposal blocked prosecution of soldiers who committed violations of human rights during the Dirty War as a result of following the orders of their superiors. It quickly received congressional approval. The Due Obedience and *punto final* laws effectively blocked the prosecution of hundreds of officers.

Leaders of the organizations that had pushed for investigations and trials connected to the events of the Dirty War accused Alfonsín of sacrificing the country's interests. Although the president and his supporters denied the existence of any deal, the timing of the law undermined popular support for the government.

RADICALS OVERWHELMED (1985–1987)

Although the economy and human rights issues claimed the foreground during the first three years of the Alfonsín administration, the Radicals and their leader also tried to shore up their political strength at the expense of their main rivals. Recognizing the importance of organized labor as one of the Peronists' key political bases, the Radicals pushed for a number of reforms that aimed at weakening the CGT and at fostering independent, multifaceted leadership within the unions.

The condition of the CGT at the end of the dictatorship left it apparently open to such a challenge. During the last Peronist administrations, government and party officials worked with Lorenzo Miguel, the leader of the CGT, to weed out union leaders and activists who stood in the way of plans to unify and centralize Miguel's authority. The Dirty War and the Process of National Reorganization inflicted heavy casualties on the labor movement. Unionists who were loyal to Peronism fell victim to death squads and military repression. The independents faced attacks from the left and the right.

Within the CGT, as a result of the years of conflict and in the wake of the Peronist defeat, three factions fought for control over the union hierarchy. Miguel remained the recognized head of the faction labeled *"los 62 organizaciones"* (the 62 Organizations, or simply "los 62"). This was a coalition of older unions that were closely linked to the traditional centers of Peronism. Saúl Ubaldini continued to gain notoriety as a result of his activism during the dictatorship. He assumed leadership of *"los 25 organizaciones"* (the 25 Organizations) and became the CGT's secretary general. Ubaldini and his followers were more confrontational and less trusting of the veteran politicians within the Peronist movement. Finally, a third faction that engaged in negotiations with the Alfonsín government emerged after 1983. The government named Carlos Alderete, the head of the Light and Power Workers Union and the key leader of the new faction, the minister of labor in April 1984 to enhance his status and deepen the fissures that divided the union leadership.

When Alfonsín began his presidency, he quickly sent to the Chamber of Deputies a proposal to make the unions more democratic. Under the proposal, state officials would supervise union leadership elections and regulate the way unions spent the dues they collected from their members.

With the Radical Party in control of the Chamber, the proposal passed easily. The Peronists still held a majority in the national Senate, however, and there the reforms fell one vote short of approval. Eventually, the government and the CGT reached an agreement that led to a new round of elections within the country's unions. Although these contests, held after the compromise was signed in July 1984, were more open and competitive than previous elections, the candidates loyal to the Peronists still dominated the voting and the political allegiance of the unions did not change.

The attempt at reform invigorated the union movement. Beginning in 1985, the unions challenged the government's economic policy, and in particular its efforts to stall or slow down wage increases. Saúl Ubaldini, who played a crucial role in the unions' revival during the Proceso, replaced Miguel as the secretary general of the CGT. Ubaldini then directed a series of strikes, which grew in size and significance. The strikes targeted the Austral Plan and demanded reforms that favored workers and the poor.

Separate from the CGT's general strikes, public workers and pensioners mounted their own strikes and protests against the government's failure to protect their economic standing. With national elections looming, the government approved a 5 percent general salary increase for all workers and a 25 percent increase for the dismally paid public school teachers in October 1985.

The granting of wage concessions may have produced some benefits for the government in the short run, but their impact upon the Austral Plan was dramatic. Industrialists and employers demanded price increases to pay for the higher wage levels. Workers, emboldened by the concessions, demanded additional raises. The increases given to public workers increased the government's budget deficit.

To revive the Austral Plan, the government announced new policy shifts in February 1986. It outlined a plan for tax reform that promised an increase in revenues from existing taxes that property owners and businesses often ignored or avoided. To increase exports and build up foreign exchange reserves, it reduced export taxes. It announced plans to sell government-owned industries that, if successful, would have raised revenue and reduced government spending.

Pressures from industrialists, exporters, agriculturalists, and the unions led the government to restructure its economic policies again in April. In the place of wage and price freezes, which it had already broken months before, the government proposed administered price controls, which would allow price increases in the face of rising production costs.

At the same time, Alfonsín also sent to Congress plans to move the national capital south to Viedma, a city located on Patagonia's northern frontier. Presented as a bold step toward fostering the development of the sparsely populated Patagonia, the proposal made more political than economic sense: The shift would allow the government to reduce the number of public employees and potentially disrupt the Peronist neighborhood organizations that had worked closely with Peronist administrations in efforts to organize voters in the capital and Greater Buenos Aires.

The new round of reforms had little positive impact. By ending the strict wage and price controls, the April compromises destabilized the economy. Inflation rates grew, union protests increased, and industrialists and producers pressed for more concessions. Anticipating greater problems, the government's economic team tried to regain control. New fiscal and monetary controls, applied first in September 1986, were not enough to stall rising prices and growing budget deficits. The planners took more drastic action in February 1987: Labeled the *"Australito"* (literally, "little Austral"), the government imposed new wage and price controls. These, too, quickly collapsed.

For the remainder of Alfonsín's term in office, the government struggled against inflation and economic stagnation without success. The country's economic slide, combined with growing discontent over the issue of human rights, shattered public support for the government and the Radical Party. The 1987 national elections gave them a clear signal of their status. The Peronists captured a majority in the Chamber of Deputies and 16 of the 22 provincial races for governor.

Conditions worsened in the months that followed. Amid union protests and resistance from business to any attempt to control prices, the IMF threatened to cut off Argentina from any future aid. The Radicals had clearly lost control of the country. Rather than negotiate with a doomed government, all parties marshaled their energies and resources for the 1989 presidential elections.

THE PERONIST REVIVAL (1983–1988)

Political trends made it clear that the Peronists had again become the dominant political force in Argentina. Although many remained skeptical, recalling the disastrous performance of past administrations, the utter failure of the Radical government left the path to power clear. The Peronist Party had changed from 1983. The party's defeat in the first elections after the Proceso's collapse inspired a reform movement within Peronism. Between 1983 and 1985, the reformers could not overcome the organizational strength and ruthless tactics of the established leadership. But after the party's poor performance in the 1985 elections, the push for change gained strength.

The key leaders of the "Renewal" wing of the Peronist movement were Antonio Cafiero and Carlos Saúl Menem. Cafiero, a veteran politician, had tried to capture the party nomination for the governorship in Buenos Aires Province during the 1983 elections. Although the party did allow competing slates in the primaries, the party bosses picked the winners. The defeats of 1983 and 1985 forced the traditional, or orthodox, leadership from control of the party. Benefiting from the change, Cafiero was elected governor of Buenos Aires in 1987.

Menem was the son of Syrian immigrants who had become wealthy as a result of their successful winery. He became active in Peronist politics in 1955 and was first elected governor of La Rioja in 1973. A loyal supporter of the orthodox wing of the party that took command of the Peronist movement after Juan Perón's death in 1974, he was arrested by military authorities and held in prison between 1976 and 1980.

Cafiero emerged as the chief spokesperson of the Renewal wing in 1985. After his winning the governorship in Buenos Aires, most observers believed he would be the party's presidential nominee in 1989. Menem, who had established himself as an independent player in party issues, decided to compete with Cafiero for the nomination. The unions split their allegiance. Cafiero gained the support of the "Group of 25," which had helped organize the union challenge to the dictatorship and the Alfonsín administration. Menem captured the support of the "Group of 15," which was a faction within the CGT that had briefly offered support to the Alfonsín economic and union reform efforts. Cafiero leveraged his position by taking over as president of the Peronist Party. With loyalists firmly convinced that the party's nominee would capture the presidency, the campaign between the two leaders attracted wide attention.

Having been elected president of the party, Cafiero put in place the party's first direct primary. Party members were given the chance on July 9, 1988, to elect the presidential nominee and the candidates for other offices across the country. Party activists, mostly Renewal-wing loyalists, favored Cafiero. Menem, however, took his campaign directly to the party membership. He depicted himself as a charismatic leader who remained concerned with the traditional party goals of justice and honor for the poor and the humble. Running against Cafiero, whom many viewed as indistinguishable in policy terms from Alfonsín and the Radicals, Menem offered the voters a strikingly distinct choice.

Menem ran especially strong in the working-class districts surrounding Buenos Aires. Union officials and neighborhood party captains, who had helped rebuild the party's electoral strength in the 1970s and the 1980s, used their personal connection with the voters to deliver to the La Rioja governor the margin of victory.

ELECTIONS AND REFORM (1989–1991)

The Radical Party, having taken charge of Argentina in the wake of the Proceso, managed to revive popular trust in civilian government.

Unfortunately, economic and political circumstances provided them with few achievements that their candidates could use to build support during the 1989 campaign. Their effort to control the economy was shattered.

Each month's price increases surpassed the levels recorded during the entire year of 1985 or 1986. Argentines returned to the practice of hoarding U.S. dollars. By exchanging their wages and salaries from australes to dollars, speculators gained higher profits than those who invested in stocks and bonds.

Eduardo Angeloz, the governor of Córdoba, led the Radical Party ticket. Regarded as more conservative than Alfonsín, he could not overcome the strength of the Peronist Party's organization or the general disappointment with the failures of the outgoing administration. Voters on the right abandoned the Radicals and voted instead for minor parties.

On May 14, Carlos Menem captured over 46 percent of the national vote and ran ten points ahead of Angeloz. The Peronists gained large majorities in the Chamber of Deputies and the Senate, which returned them to the dominant position that they had held before the death of Juan Perón.

The fact that elections took place amid the general economic crisis struck many as impressive. In the recent past, economic chaos had opened the path for military coups. The transfer of power was scheduled for December 10. Menem and his advisors began planning their strategy as the Alfonsín administration tried desperately to gain control over prices and currency values.

When the Alfonsín government introduced the Austral Plan, it set the new currency's value on par with the U.S. dollar. In the days following Menem's victory, $1 traded on the open market obtained 175 australes in exchange. By early June, the exchange rate fell to 375 australes to the dollar. Such panic made it impossible for the government to operate as it had before. In its new price schedules, the government set maximum levels in dollars. Businesses openly accepted U.S. currency.

With wages lagging far behind the price jumps, and with unemployment emerging as a new problem, desperate mobs sacked grocery stores for food. Fights between store employees and looters led to riots in Rosario, Greater Buenos Aires, and elsewhere.

Lacking any popular support, Alfonsín decided to transfer power to Menem ahead of schedule. Initially, the Radicals tried to negotiate the terms of the transition to gain some influence over the new government's economic and fiscal policies. The negotiations failed, however. As conditions deteriorated, Alfonsín decided to resign at the end of June.

The Radicals had hoped that their government's legacy would be the establishment of political and economic foundations for long-lasting civilian rule. By turning over power to an elected successor, the Alfonsín government did accomplish one thing that had not occurred in Argentina for decades: The transfer of power was the first time since 1916 that rival parties had peacefully exchanged control of the government.

In economic terms, however, the Radicals had actually moved the country backward. The economy had contracted from the early 1980s. Industrial employment and output had dropped, the volume of goods and services traded in the domestic economy had fallen, and foreign trade lagged. After reducing the budget deficits during the Radical government's first years in office, the collapse of the Austral Plan had led to falling tax revenues that prevented any efforts to reduce budget shortfalls. Taking into account shifting currency values and price inflation, wages in 1989 were roughly 20 percent lower than they had been in 1986 and more than 35 percent lower than they had been in 1984. Finally, the national debt had jumped from 46.9 to 63.3 billion during Alfonsín's term in office.

When Menem took charge of the government in July 1989, what action his administration would take was unknown. He had been vague during the presidential campaign. He promised leadership but offered no concrete goals or strategies. As governor he allowed observers to draw comparisons between his style of leadership and those of the nineteenth-century caudillos.

Although many feared that he would attempt to create a populist state and follow the example set by his party's founder, conditions in 1989 made any attempt to imitate Perón's political program impossible. The government had no resources to offer its supporters, nor could it afford to run the industries already controlled by the state. It faced enormous pressure from international creditors and the general public.

Hemmed in by the circumstances, Menem announced an economic reform program. Appreciating the difficulties his government faced, he compared his plans to "surgery without anesthesia." The potential gains, he advanced, were great—true and lasting economic stability. The reforms' first phase would follow a path taken by other Latin American countries that had tackled economic reconstruction and reform in recent decades: Reduce the role of the state in the economy, open up the country to foreign trade and investment, and allow market forces to shape the course of economic recovery and expansion.

Circumstances gave the Menem administration advantages that its predecessors lacked. The excesses of the military dictatorships had removed the Peronists' staunchest enemies from the political arena. No military coup would block Menem from office or interfere with his attempts to govern the country. In turn, the incompetence of the Alfonsín administration weakened the main civilian opposition. Elected as a Peronist president, Menem could also count on support from most of the unions. The workers who had followed Saúl Ubaldini through the 13 strikes that he organized against the Alfonsín administration viewed the new government as being closely tied to their interests.

Consequently, none of the major forces that had competed for power in past decades challenged Menem. The conditions that Argentina had fallen into also helped clear a path for the new government. The hyperinflation that crippled the economy created a sense of panic as well as a willingness to let the new government take command of the situation. With all forms of political opposition checked, the economic emergency gave Menem and his advisors leverage far beyond what the Alfonsín administration had in either 1983 or 1985.

To give weight to his economic program, Menem named Miguel Roig, a past chairman of one of the country's most influential and profitable export firms Bunge & Born, as his economics minister. Roig, who was not a member of the Peronist Party, was a leading force in the implementation of the government's economic restructuring plan. The government announced drastic cuts in government spending. Layoffs of government workers and the privatization of inefficient state-owned industries would bring an end to budget deficits within two years. The government also promised to deregulate the economy and let the market determine wages and prices rather than the government.

The country's reaction to the steps that the government took in between July and September was positive. Inflation cooled and businesses reported improved conditions. Unfortunately, by the end of the year the slow pace of the reforms fueled renewed currency speculation and revived inflation.

Efforts to stabilize the banking industry and cut government spending further in January and in March 1990 brought inflationary spikes under control, but the government seemed to be reacting to a never-ending series of crises. In July, new decrees helped open up Argentina to imported goods and cut back government subsidies and market protections for domestic companies. As imports forced a stabilization of prices, the government authorized the rapid sale of dozens of state-owned companies.

The economic restructuring efforts did not show clear signs of progress during Menem's first year in office. His government's effort to slow inflation and reduce the role of the government in the economy did foster a major recession. Industrial and business activity continued to contract. The press criticized the government as hyperinflation continued and linked up with a deepening recession. In March 1991, Domingo Cavallo moved from his post as foreign minister to take charge of the government's economic reforms. Cavallo announced new and drastic steps to force economic stability. First, the government introduced the *peso Nuevo* (new peso) as the new currency, with each new peso worth 10,000 australes. The government then set the value of the peso equal to the dollar. To build confidence in the currency shift, the government allowed the public to freely exchange pesos for dollars. Working with Congress, it established restrictions on the Central Bank's operations that built up its reserves and blocked it from printing money to cover government deficits.

To open up the country's economy even more, Menem signed a treaty with Brazil, Paraguay, and Uruguay that formed the *Mercado Común del Sur* (Common Market of the South, or Mercosur). This treaty began a multiyear process that would end with the complete linking of the member countries' markets for industrial and agricultural goods during the period 1995–1999.

The Cavallo Plan succeeded in a key area: By effectively tying the country's currency to the dollar and by limiting the money supply, it stopped inflation. The plan's costs, however, were significant. As foreign competition and government cuts eliminated jobs, displaced workers found few opportunities for employment. Stability did not bring sustained economic growth. Although Menem earned credit for keeping his promises, the impact of his government's economic reforms remained unclear. In the years that followed, Menem embarked on a course that enhanced his power but left many political and economic challenges unresolved.

10

False Hopes
(1991–2001)

After more than a decade of economic and political crises that seemed unmanageable, the success of Carlos Menem and his government surprised many. He had mounted a campaign for the presidency that echoed Peronism's oldest traditions. In public appearances, he offered few specifics. Instead, counting on the strength of the Justicialist Party, the backing of union leaders, and the loyalty of his followers, Menem used the slogan "Follow me." To what end no one could predict.

After assuming the presidency, Menem authorized a strong and effective stabilization program that brought Argentina's economy into line within two years. Groups that feared he would try to make himself into a populist autocrat cheered the actions that led to smaller government, fiscal surpluses, and a push to modernize both the private and the public sectors.

Others, however, became alarmed at the costs of the reforms that Menem had authorized. Although the government had managed to cut inflation and promote economic growth, through its efforts it had also fostered rising unemployment and marked disparities between the wealthy and the poor. Evidence of widespread corruption within the government produced wider criticism. Despite the administration's apparent achievements in the economic arena, as a result of his political ambitions and errors Menem would leave his legacy clouded and his country divided and in crisis.

REFORMS AND SCANDALS (1991–1994)

President Carlos Saúl Menem had inherited a bankrupt government and a divided country when he took office in December 1989. The new administration promised stability and honesty, but as was the case with the Alfonsín government, economic realities and the resistance of entrenched interest groups stalled reforms almost as soon as they appeared.

With Economics Minister Domingo Cavallo leading the push, the Menem government embarked on an ambitious and risky set of new policy initiatives in 1991. Linked together, the currency, trade, tax, and budget reforms brought the economic situation under rapid control.

The Menem government did have a number of advantages that helped it achieve policy successes that had eluded previous governments. First, the seriousness of the crisis made aggressive actions necessary. Second, the memory of how economic turmoil set the stage for political violence and the imposition of military dictatorships in past decades encouraged the public to support the government. Many feared that failure would lead to disaster. In control of the government and the party, Menem had a stronger hand in dealing with national and provincial legislatures. Peronist blocks in the legislatures helped orchestrate broader and deeper political support for his efforts. Finally, the fact that Menem was a Peronist gave him leverage that others lacked. He could count on the sustained support of union leaders and members as he led the push for economic restructuring and reform.

Union leaders and party officials, who had helped organize massive protests against the military dictatorship and the Alfonsín administration in previous years, split over what to do in reaction to the Menem government's actions. This limited the size and scale of popular protests as the costs of the changes became clear.

As the government implemented its economic restructuring package, union leaders met and worked to end their differences. Representatives of the various factions initially agreed to share control of a united CGT beginning in 1992. As soon as the news of this agreement became public, disagreements over strategy and tactics reappeared, and new fractures divided the federation. Leaders who believed that a successful Peronist government would serve the workers' interests in the long run tried to block strikes and other forms of protests. Others, who had fallen out with the new president, formed a new organization: the *Congreso de Trabajadores Argentinos* (Argentine Workers Congress, or CTA). Grouping together the most active unions, the CTA launched a series of actions that protested the government's labor regulations and economic reforms. Lacking support of the larger CGT, the CTA protests did not present a major threat to Menem and his proposals.

The Argentine public voiced its opinion of the Menem government's record in the country's national elections. In 1991, when the economic restructuring policies were just underway, Menem's Justicialist Party ran well throughout the country and captured 40.7 percent of the vote. This was four points lower than its 1989 total, but it still ran well ahead of its closest rival, the Radical Civic Union. Observers regarded the election as a cautious endorsement of the Menem government.

By 1993, voter support for the government had grown. Overall, the Justicialist Party candidates captured over 42 percent of the national vote. The party ran especially strong in Buenos Aires Province, and it won a plurality in the Federal Capital for the first time in decades. The key factors that produced the Justicialist Party's electoral success were its neighborhood recruitment efforts, which turned out consistently large numbers of party loyalists for each election, and the Peronist and independent voters' broad satisfaction with the economy.

The government's ability to control inflation through monetary and trade reforms brought relative stability to the economy. This achievement by the government's economic team benefited candidates of Menem's party throughout the country.

The reforms did have costs. Their implementation produced both problems and scandals. Cuts in government spending were an essential part of the government's economic policy. The Menem's advisors tried to reduce the government's budget mainly in two ways. First, the government cut public sector employment. Ministries and agencies eliminated positions and encouraged retirements in an attempt to shrink the number of people working directly for the government. The government also cut more employees and its payroll when it sold off publicly held companies. Overall, reduced spending and the privatization of public agencies, services, and companies between 1989 and 1993 eliminated over 302,000 public sector jobs at the local, provincial, and national levels.

Second, the national government negotiated cuts in subsidies and transfers to provincial governments. These cash transfers, which supported provincial government operations and the implementation of public programs in the country's interior, had reached almost $8 billion in 1989. By 1992, they fell to $4.4 billion.

The budget cuts in these areas led to a jump in the number of persons without work across the country. In many provinces, the state was at the center of the economy. Budget cuts affected both those who worked in government offices and those who worked in the shops and businesses that the government and its workers supported through contracts and purchases.

Government actions also produced unemployment in other, unanticipated ways. The privatization program quickly led to layoffs as new owners reduced their companies' payrolls. As imports rose in response to tariff reductions, Argentine industries lost market share. Many closed, while others modernized. These shifts in the industrial sector pushed more people out of the workforce.

The impact of these actions was alarming. Government officials recorded an unemployment rate of 6.9 percent in 1991. The rate rose to 18.6 percent by 1995, which was the highest rate ever recorded in Argentina. At the time, only Nicaragua had more of its economically active population idle. In addition, the number of persons unable to find fulltime employment, persons labeled by government statisticians as "underemployed," passed 11 percent.

Scandals also marred the government's reform effort. When he took office, Menem appointed to positions of authority a large number of non-Peronists along with a number of supporters from his home province of La Rioja. These outsiders often took advantage of their circumstances. The privatization of government-owned companies became notorious. María Julia Alsogaray, a leader of the *Unión del Centro Democrático* (Union of the Democratic Center, or UCeD), directed the sale of EnTel, the country's telephone system, and SOMISA, the national steel company. As the negotiations neared conclusion, charges that Alsogaray accepted kickbacks and colluded with buyers to skim cash from the sale contracts appeared. Prosecutors filed charges and Alsogaray was forced to resign her posts. Similar charges of illicit profiteering, bribery, kickbacks, and collusion marred almost every privatization deal.

Another focal point of scandal involved President Menem's in-laws. The Yoma family used their control over customs operations and their connections to the president as a means of enriching themselves. A number of investigations between 1992 and 1995 connected them to a variety of crimes that ranged from bribery and extortion to drug trafficking.

The scandals often crossed borders. In 1994, when a disagreement over national boundaries led to a brief war between Perú and Ecuador, Argentina covertly shipped weapons and ammunition to Ecuador. Public inquiries made by the press and political rivals led the Menem government to state that it had pledged to remain neutral. When news of the sale leaked out in July 1996, Defense Minister Oscar Camilión stepped down in the wake of judicial action that removed his immunity from prosecution. Eventually two directors of the state's military arms manufacturer Fabricaciones Militares were arrested and convicted of illegally conducting the sale.

Menem did order anticorruption probes and the creation of special commissions to clean up his government, but these actions had little effect. New revelations of corruption and scandal discredited every step that the government took to improve its image. More stunning blows to the president's reputation came as the result of international terrorism. In 1992, a bomb set off outside of the Israeli embassy in the Federal Capital killed 29 persons. Two years later, a second bombing that targeted a Jewish Community Center nearby killed 90. Despite international attention, capital police and national security forces failed to turn up suspects in either attack. Investigations conducted by the government implicated corrupt police officers and foreign nationals. Prosecutions of Argentine suspects ended in 2004 without any convictions. In 2006, new indictments accused the Iranian government and Hezbollah terrorists as those responsible for the bombings. As the 20th anniversary of the Jewish Community Center attack passes in 2014, the investigation has not progressed.

ILLUSIONS END (1994–1996)

Concerns over the impact of the government's policy did not significantly weaken Menem's political position. During his first years in office, he and his supporters had strengthened their standing within the Justicialist Party. While the government slashed spending in many areas, funds for neighborhood organizing that flowed through *Unidades Básicas* (Community Organizing Center or Neighborhood Office), which connected city and suburban neighborhoods block by block to the government and the ruling party. Organizers in charge of each community center, known as *punteros* or *caudillos del barrio* (neighborhood bosses) channeled cash, food, resources, and political connections to those in need, who in turn became the foundation of the Peronist movement during the 1990s. Working with support from the government and the Justicialist Party, these community centers helped dissipate organized opposition to the Menem administration's policies.

Hoping to establish a more secure political position, Menem pushed for constitutional reforms in 1994. A key provision of the reform proposals involved the presidency. When he was elected in 1989,

Argentine President Carlos Menem waves to the crowd along with his first wife, Zulema Yoma. (Daniel Garcia/AFP/Getty Images)

the restored constitution of 1853 limited him to one term in office. The president and his supporters hoped to push through a revision that would allow Menem to stand for reelection. The Radical Party, led by ex-president Raúl Alfonsín, did not want to extend Menem's political career. However, rather than have the reform forced upon them by a Peronist-dominated Congress, the Radicals entered into negotiations with Menem's representatives in 1993. The resulting "Olivos Pact" led to a constitutional convention that drafted a number of reforms that quickly became law.

Menem was given the chance to run again, but the amended constitution reduced presidential terms from six to four years. It also limited the presidential right to issue regulatory decrees, which Menem had used broadly and often in the place of legislative action and review. Senators, previously selected by provincial legislatures, were to be elected by popular vote. Instead of two senators for each province and for the Federal Capital, three would serve, with the third senator representing the party that captured the second-most number of votes in each contest.

The year 1995 opened with a single focus: Would Carlos Menem become the first president reelected in the country since 1952? The apparent success of the national government's economic policies, still directed by Economics Minister Domingo Cavallo, convinced many that the president was unbeatable.

Menem's strongest challenger was José Octavio Bordón, an ex-governor and a senator from Mendoza Province. Bordón had been an active member of the ruling party, but he had lost faith in Menem. He criticized what he saw as Menem's autocratic style and also attacked the government's economic reforms as being beneficial for the rich but costly for the poor. He also joined the "Group of Eight," a Peronist congressional faction that protested the president's pardon of those charged with crimes related to the Dirty War, in a call for justice.

Bordón broke from the Justicialist Party and ran as the candidate of the *Frente por un País Solidario* ("Front for a Country in Solidarity," or FREPASO). FREPASO developed as a coalition of progressive and reform-oriented parties that had splintered the country's left-wing votes in past elections.

The challenge initially appeared promising. The Radical Party had lost direction as a result of its poor showing in recent congressional elections. The "Tequila Effect," an economic downturn caused by a financial crisis in Mexico that reduced foreign investment and restricted credit throughout Latin America in December 1994, appeared to have stalled the Menem government's economic reform push. Having averaged a 7 percent rate of growth since 1991, Argentina now faced another recession: Estimates of the expansion of Argentina's gross domestic product fell to an annual rate of 0.5 percent by the end of the third quarter of 1995. The collapse of the Mexican stock market created a run on investments from abroad in all of Latin America. Argentina was one of the region's most affected markets: Between December 1994 and March 1995, more than $4 billion of deposits flowed out of the country.

In the weeks before the election, the apparent opportunity faded. The government's economic team successfully negotiated new loans from abroad that put off an economic crisis. That the government avoided a financial panic bolstered public support for the administration. In turn, the FREPASO candidate presented no clear alternative. Bordón seemed to endorse the government when he publicly promised to continue the successful economic policies put in place under Menem.

Rather than taking a risk with someone new, Argentine voters turned out firmly on May 14 for the status quo. Menem captured 49.5 percent of the vote and avoided a runoff. Bordón ran a distant second, collecting 29.6 percent of votes cast. Horacio Massaccesi, the Radical Party's candidate, garnered just under 17 percent.

After the election, the Menem government announced new, tighter financial policies and the more sales of government-held assets. These actions did little to spur the economy. On June 22, protests by government workers in the city of Córdoba led to predictions by journalists of a "social explosion." With recorded unemployment running at an estimated record high of 14 percent at midyear, President Menem reiterated his campaign promise to create 330,000 new jobs. The promise remained unfulfilled as the year passed.

Turmoil erupted within the government in August. Domingo Cavallo, who had taken charge of the government's economic restructuring program in 1991 and had played a key role in building domestic and international support for its actions, leveled a broad attack at Menem, stating that the government was in the hands of "mafias" who used it for their own enrichment. Cavallo remained in charge of the Ministry of Economics, since the president and his advisors believed that removing him from service would threaten Argentina's relations with international creditors and create doubts concerning the country's economic reform effort.

Cavallo's accusations, however, sparked a major political shift. Menem faced mounting attacks from all sides. Peronists, angry at the president's efforts to centralize power within the Justicialist Party as well as with the political system, challenged his new policy initiatives. Leaders of rival parties renewed their criticism of government corruption. Union leaders launched strikes in protest over the deepening recession, low wages, and lack of jobs.

Argentina remained in a recession through 1996. Hoping to revive the economy, Menem pushed for greater authority. On February 7, the Congress granted emergency powers that allowed the president to decree tax increases and spending cuts. Menem then declared a new series of reforms that reduced military spending and cut social services and workers' benefits.

Behind the scenes, tensions between Menem and Cavallo continued to build. Serious disagreements over what policy steps the government should take during the first half of 1996 divided the economics minister from other cabinet officials. A final break over the implementation of a tax on banking operations, which Cavallo viewed as inflationary and counterproductive, led to Cavallo's dismissal on July 26. While the president tried to calm the fears of investors and creditors by promising to keep his government committed to economic reform, Cavallo set about organizing a political opposition movement that would challenge the Peronist Party from the right.

Continued recession, lingering unemployment, and government policies aimed at weakening worker rights finally revived labor activism. On August 8, to protest economic conditions and demand action to check unemployment, the country's three national labor organizations—the General Confederation of Labor, the Argentine Workers Movement, and the Argentine Workers Congress—collectively staged a general strike. In the face of government threats to potential demonstrators, more than 80 percent of the country's workforce stayed home from work. A second general strike, highlighted by a march to the Casa Rosada, shut down the country for 36 hours on September 26 and 27.

Adding to Menem's problems, ghosts of the past dictatorship reappeared. The confession in March of Adolfo Scilingo, an ex–lieutenant commander in the Argentine navy, that he participated in "death flights," where military officials drugged suspects accused of subversive activities and dropped the unconscious victims from planes into the Atlantic Ocean, revived calls for a more thorough investigation of human rights abuses that occurred during the period 1975–1986, when military governments detained and "disappeared" thousands.

Scilingo was the first person involved in the flights to admit guilt. His statements, broadcast on television within Argentina and later internationally, spurred a new effort to seek prosecutions of suspected human rights violators. Although military officials initially accused Scilingo of lying to journalists, his action led to a round of confessions from others who had participated in similar operations.

New human rights groups within Argentina and abroad pushed for justice. Growing out of the Mothers of the Plaza de Mayo, the Grandmothers of the Plaza de Mayo raised entirely new charges against the officials of the defunct dictatorship. Many of the detainees were pregnant or, after being raped by their captors, became pregnant during their incarceration. The Grandmothers sponsored investigations into the fate of the babies rumored to have been born in the detention centers. As a result of independent investigations, the group uncovered evidence of illegal adoptions arranged by military and security officials. The Grandmothers sought court action to return to them the children of their "disappeared" relatives. In a related move, prosecutors in Italy and Spain brought charges against officials who had detained, tortured, and killed Spanish and Italian citizens who had been caught up in the violence of the Dirty War.

Over the protests of military officers, foreign prosecutors successfully used the evidence collected by the Argentine CONADEP in 1984 to convict a handful of the most notorious criminals who had escaped prosecution in Argentina.

THE PERONISTS FRACTURE (1997–1999)

After seven years in office, President Carlos Menem and his advisors appeared to be overwhelmed. Their economic reform effort had kept inflation in check since 1991, but that seemed to be their only clear success.

After initial signs of economic growth, the country's fortunes continued to ride on their agricultural industries. When the harvests were large and when prices peaked, grain exports brought tax revenues, increased foreign exchange, and helped balance the country's foreign trade. When bad weather or falling prices cut into farming's profits, other economic sectors—especially manufacturing—reminded everyone of how little progress the country had made.

After facing nearly a decade of recession, Menem's popular support had withered. Protests from all sides mounted. The president claimed that a press conspiracy had developed. Reporters, who focused on the negative, were united in an effort that aimed at destroying his administration, he claimed.

More accurately, Menem's leadership style had left him isolated. He had used decrees to avoid compromises with the national legislature. He used the government's resources to reward cooperative union and party leaders and to punish those who challenged his authority. As the public lost patience with the slow pace and high costs of his government's policies, he became the target of mounting anger.

On January 25, 1997, José Luis Cabezas was found dead in his automobile in the city of Pinamar. Cabezas, a photojournalist, had been investigating Alfredo Yabrán, the head of the country's private postal and telegraph company. Other reporters, who had become alarmed at a growing number of threats and actions made against political journalists, labeled the crime as an execution and demanded a thorough investigation.

To many, the circumstances of the killing evoked memories of the political assassinations that darkened Argentina during the Dirty War (1975–1983). Journalists organized a national protest of the killing, highlighted by marches in Buenos Aires during the week after the killing and a year-long publicity campaign on television and in the newspapers. Eduardo Duhalde, the governor of Buenos Aires, helped push the investigation forward in February by offering a $100,000 reward for any information that would break the case.

Arrests were made in within weeks of the killing. The first detainees were connected with gangs that operated in the coastal vacation cities of Buenos Aires Province. Provincial authorities first suggested that robbery or blackmail might have been the killers' motive for the crime. Further investigation, however, undermined these theories and implicated others.

The use of phone records and the testimony of informants tied a number of ex–police officials from Buenos Aires Province with the execution. The testimony of those detained suggested a link to Yabrán. The crime became the year's major event as revelations in the press detailed communications between the assassins and Yabrán's lieutenants and exposed other, unrelated connections between Yabrán and members of the provincial and national governments.

Yabrán's suicide on May 20, 1998, cut short the investigation. Why Cabezas became a target remains unclear. Investigators suggest that Yabrán worried that the photojournalist had learned too much about alleged smuggling and money-laundering activities he and his associates ran within the postal service. Other theories were more ominous. The crime and the twisted nature of its investigation revived concerns about government corruption and political violence.

Popular protests against the Menem administration grew in number and intensity as the decade closed. In Jujuy, Río Negro, and other interior provinces, where the reductions in state spending and the privatization of state businesses hit hardest, groups of protesters engaged in a series of blockades of national highways. Although most protests began and ended peacefully, in February and in June the national government sanctioned the use of federal troops to clear highways.

The country's public school teachers organized a separate protest. Calling for higher wages and increased spending on public education, the teachers left their classrooms and instead manned the "*capra blanca*" (white tent) that they set up across from the Congress in the capital. The CGT advertised its support of these protests in a series of actions that culminated in a general strike on August 14. A new series of popular protests swept the country. Road occupations occurred in Salta, Río Negro, and again in Jujuy. Student protesters occupied buildings and fought with police on the grounds of the national universities in La Plata and the Federal Capital.

The scandal surrounding the Cabezas case and the mounting protests against the government's economic policies undermined Menem's political standing. At the beginning of the year, rumors suggested that Menem might seek a new reform of the constitution that would have allowed him to seek an unprecedented third term in office. During the months that followed, challenges within and outside the ruling Justicialist Party, in particular continued charges made by ex-minister Domingo Cavallo of political corruption within the Menem government, took their toll. By August, Menem's approval rating had fallen to 18 percent in a poll conducted by the national daily *Clarín*.

RISING IN CHALLENGE (1997–2000)

Although Menem won a second term by a comfortable margin in 1995, the divided nature of his political opposition had played an important part in the campaign. The Radical Party ran a strong second in the congressional balloting, but its efforts to defeat Menem crashed. FREPASO, the coalition of left-wing and reformist parties that fell in behind Bodrón, would have captured the presidency if it had formed an alliance with the Radicals. Its slate of congressional candidates, however, ran poorly in most areas. Their presence on the ballot largely helped return a Peronist majority to the Chamber of Deputies and the national Senate.

Learning from the past, FREPASO and Radical Party leaders opened discussions of an electoral alliance in 1997. In August, the two groups joined in the *Alianza para Trabajo, Justicia, y Educación* (Alliance for Work, Justice, and Education, or *Alianza*). In its first national trial, the Alliance ran well in the October national congressional elections. Although the Peronists held fast in interior provinces, victories in the Federal District, Buenos Aires, and other core provinces gave the Alliance a majority in the Chamber of Deputies.

In the wake of the electoral defeat, the Peronists seemed leaderless. Menem had held onto public attention by engineering a push for another constitutional amendment that would have permitted him to run for a third consecutive term as president, but this angered many party loyalists, in particular the governor of Buenos Aires, Eduardo Duhalde. Having won election in 1995, Duhalde hoped to use a successful reign as governor of the country's leading province as a step toward winning the presidency. Menem's ambitions to hold onto power, especially his push to match Juan Domingo Perón's three successful campaigns, stalled Duhalde's efforts.

The Cabezas case damaged the governor's political standing as well. Yabrán had close connections with the governor and with President Menem. As the investigation into the photojournalist's assassination first focused on corrupt provincial police officials and then turned toward Yabrán, both Peronist leaders found themselves forced to make excuses for their past meetings with the troubled businessman. The case's resolution left many questions unanswered. Duhalde, linked with the string of corruption cases that marked the Menem administration, found his political standing with independent voters damaged.

Menem ultimately failed in his attempts to open a road to a third term. As his second term neared its end, the Alliance selected Fernando de la Rúa as its candidate. De la Rúa had been active in the Radical Party since the 1980s. He had competed with Raúl Alfonsín for the party's presidential nomination in 1983. His reputation grew after he was elected mayor of the Federal District in 1985. He ran a scandal-free administration that he cited in his efforts to create a contrast between himself and the rival Peronists.

During the months leading up to the October 25 election, de la Rúa and his allies rallied the groups that had been most negatively affected by the Menem administration's policies. Unexpectedly, the opening of new trials against the officers who participated in the Dirty War helped the Alliance build its popular base. President Menem's pardons of convicted human rights abusers, both military officers and guerrilleros, had angered many. Lawyers representing the Grandmothers of the Plaza de Mayo had managed to bring independent cases to trial. Citing the illegal adoptions that investigators had first uncovered three years before, General Jorge Videla, Admiral Emilio Massera, and other junta leaders were charged with kidnapping. Ruling that these crimes were unrelated to the human rights violations covered by the Punto Final Law of 1984 and the pardons decreed by President Menem in 1990, the courts convicted the ex-officials and imposed new prison sentences.

The debate over the trials put the Peronists on the defensive. De la Rúa and the Alliance promised to respect the courts and win justice for the victims. Combined with its promises to help those harmed by the recession and the government's budget cuts, the popularity of the Alliance candidates grew. As a result, de la Rúa captured almost 48 percent of the national vote and ran well ahead of Duhalde. The Alliance maintained its majority in the Chamber of Deputies, but the Peronists managed to hold onto their control of the national Senate.

In accepting the presidency, de la Rúa promised to run a government that was free from corruption. He also promised to work with all parties and build consensus behind his planned reforms. He outlined a new economic policy that would provide employment opportunities and living assistance for the poor. He also called for the creation of an anticorruption office within the government to serve as a protection against future scandals.

The new government took power in December. By January 2000, a series of events interrupted the de la Rúa administration's operations. First, the new president was forced to seek medical treatment for a pulmonary condition that was at first believed to be grave. Weeks of tests and hospital stays, which preoccupied de la Rúa, prevented the government from moving ahead on its own slate of reforms. Then, the economy presented a greater challenge. The country remained in a recession that had reached desperate levels. Industrial employment continued to drop and unemployment estimates remained above 15 percent. Despite the expansion of MERCOSUR and trade pacts with Latin American and Asian countries, export volumes and revenues lagged below levels set in previous years. Argentina continued to depend on grain exports. Relatively low market prices and an average harvest meant lower earnings for farmers and dropping tax and tariff revenues for the country.

Eventually, the government moved ahead with its legislative agenda. A key proposal targeted labor regulations. The government wanted to ease restrictions on employers and increase its ability to revise workplace regulations independent of the country's unions. The proposal passed the Chamber of Deputies and, after a round of negotiations and revisions, the national Senate. Shortly after the vote, however, Senator Antonio Cafiero, a leading Peronist who had lost his party's presidential nomination to Carlos Menem in 1988, revealed that government officials had bribed senators to win their votes for the labor law. The de la Rúa government denied the charge, but ongoing investigations implicated key officials with attempts to fix the vote. Federal prosecutors brought indictments against de la Rúa and seven cabinet officials. The charges remained in place until December 2013, when the courts cleared the president and his ministers.

Facing a fiscal emergency, de la Rúa agreed to put into place austerity measures that further cut government spending and bolstered fiscal reserves. In return, the International Monetary Fund (IMF) provided a bridge loan to help the government manage its debt for the remainder of 2001. As economic conditions remained dismal, the specter of a debt default loomed. Such an action would lead to an international crisis similar in scale and impact to the 1994 crisis that Mexico's debt moratorium had produced. A contraction of foreign investment and loans would cripple the national government and plunge Argentina into depression.

In protest over the government's austerity measures and the alleged vote-rigging scandal, Vice President Carlos Alvarez resigned in October. Leader of the FREPASO coalition, Alvarez played an instrumental role in attracting voters from the left of the political spectrum. The remaining members of FREPASO abandoned the Alliance in March 2001.

De la Rúa's administration started with ambition and hope. In less than a year, the government's popularity plummeted. Congressional elections delivered a clear message. With the Alliance splintered, candidates allied with the administration ran poorly. Peronist Party slates, while receiving fewer votes than they captured in 1999, carried a larger percentage of the total. They increased the number of seats controlled by the party. Almost a quarter of the voters turned in blank ballots. Unlike the Radical Party's protest votes more than a century before, these blank ballots dismissed all political alternatives.

After the vote, popular protests increased in size, frequency, and severity. *Piqueteros* (protesters), operating as part of community-based groups or in connection with a range of specific concerns that helped identify and mobilize those involved, blocked transit routes, occupied factories, or staged demonstrations in public squares. Unions that represented both the industrial and service sectors staged marches, rallies, and strikes. The protests focused the country's attention on unemployment, poverty, and the lack of opportunity that developed during the Menem administrations and then worsened since the de la Rúa's inauguration.

By December 2001, international and domestic economic conditions continued to deteriorate. In desperation, President de la Rúa brought back Domingo Cavallo to direct the government's economic policy team. With the value of the Argentine peso dropping and investment capital moving more rapidly out of the country, Cavallo announced a strict set of restrictions. Labeled as the *"corralito"* ("little corral"), the government limited individuals' access to their savings and other bank accounts. The government put a cap on withdrawals and currency transfers. Cavallo believed that if the government could effectively slow the rate and cap the volume of money moving out of private bank accounts, it might find a way to stabilize the economic situation. With enough time to develop a new strategy, the government might then secure its international credit lines, make its debt obligations manageable, and reorder its fiscal priorities.

The Argentine people reacted immediately. Mass protests occurred across the country. Within weeks, as the economic crisis worsened, looters raided grocery stores. Residents in the Federal Capital marched from residential neighborhoods to the Congress and the Casa Rosada. With spoons, ladles, and other utensils they clanged cooking pots and pans as a way of demanding from the government actions that addressed their basic needs.

In response to challenges from the streets, de la Rúa declared a state of emergency on December 18. Police moved in challenge to the protesters. The confrontation turned violent. On December 20, police action left five protesters dead in the Plaza de Mayo. Cavallo resigned from the government. President de la Rúa called for the formation of a unity government, with representatives from across the political spectrum. Opposition groups, their ranks expanding, ignored his request. Out of options and with a dwindling political base, de la Rúa resigned on December 21.

As was the case in 1989, when economic conditions and political protests paralyzed the Alfonsín administration, the year 2001 ended with Argentina facing a profound political crisis. In this instance, no successor stood ready to jump into place. The Argentine Congress inherited the burden of running the government. Ramón Puerta, who had only become the president pro tempore of the national Senate in November, became the provisional president in accordance with the chain of succession that the Argentine Constitution mandated. His reign lasted two days. To provide greater stability, Congress selected Adolfo Rodríguez Saá, then governor of San Luis Province, to serve as provisional president.

Saá confronted the political unrest and economic crisis immediately. In one of his first actions, he ended the country's external debt payments and accepted the consequences of default. He announced the creation of a new currency and promised emergency aid to municipal and provincial governments. His support within the Peronist movement withered quickly. On December 30 he left the capital. He turned in his resignation only a week after he took office.

Facing a new constitutional crisis, Puerta resigned from his leadership post in the Senate so that he would not be pressed into service as president a second time. Congress selected a new interim leader: Eduardo Duhalde.

Unlike Saá or Puerta, Duhalde's service as vice president under Menem in 1989 gave him valuable experience that he could apply in the face of the deepening crisis. He also still commanded a strong base of political support in Buenos Aires Province, where he had served as governor from 1991 to 1999. While his path to office gave him little authority, his experience and his political strength within the Peronist movement gave Duhalde sufficient political power to step into the presidency.

It appeared that Argentina had cycled back to where it was in 1989. Economic conditions ripped apart what was left of the social safety net that had supported much of the population. Conditions abroad exacerbated the domestic situation. Protests continued: Those in the Federal Capital intensified.

Duhalde formed an interim government and promised to stay in command until the crisis ended. The debt default remained in place. Interest payments to the debt held by the IMF continued, which allowed the interim government to negotiate for relief from this major creditor. The negotiations faltered, however, and talks with IMF representatives produced no settlement. The government imposed new restrictions on bank accounts and announced a plan to convert savings accounts and certificates of deposits into bonds. Account and deposit holders obtained court rulings that forced open access to their savings, which in turn threatened to undermine the government's efforts to confront the crisis.

The *piquiteros* continued their campaign for economic justice. In urban areas, the *punteros* in command of residents associated with their *unidades básicas* organized their own local protests. With weak or nonexistent ties to the interim government, the community groups pursued their own ambitions and interests.

Government programs that provided stipends for unemployed workers did little to quell their opposition. Factional strife within in the Justicialist Party made it increasingly difficult for Duhalde as the months passed. Carlos Saúl Menem reappeared as a political force and announced his intentions to win a third term as president.

To those protesting in the streets, conditions did not appear to have improved during Duhalde's year in office. The debt default and the devaluation of the currency did, however, reduce the fiscal challenges that the national government faced. Improved demand for Argentina's farm exports—in particular, soybeans that found a nearly insatiable market in China—and increasing commodity prices helped the government increase its tax revenues. This allowed government officials to channel funds toward national and provincial obligations and establish a better fiscal foundation by the start of 2003.

The circumstances made it impossible for Duhalde to extend his hold on the presidency. He devoted his energies and what leverage he commanded within the Peronist movement toward preventing Menem's return to power. As a first step, he ordered an open election in which candidates from all parties competing for the presidency. The April balloting ended with Memen running ahead of all other challengers. The ex-president's 24.5 percent share of the total left him facing a runoff. Néstor Kirchner, governor of Santa Cruz Province who had gained the backing of Duhalde and his allies, appeared likely to move ahead of Menem in the second round of voting as other candidates offered their endorsements. Before the runoff could take place, Menem withdrew his name from consideration.

Menem's action left Kirchner, a relatively unfamiliar candidate from a Patagonian Province, in line to be the next president. Without a political mandate, Kirchner assumed office on May 25, 2003.

11

Peronism's Third Turn (2002–2014)

Scholars and pundits often compare Argentina with the United States. Its resource base and its diverse geography invite this. Its history, especially since 1930, presents important distinctions. The Great Depression set in motion a series of changes that transformed Argentina's international relations and its social structure. Beginning in 1945, the Argentine government tried to take the country in a new direction. Juan Perón built a new political movement, one that would dominate national politics in the decades that followed. Peronism's key legacies established during its first generation in power were state-led industrialization, which created a diverse industrial sector dependent on imported inputs, and a large, political active working class. As the world economy challenged the financial standing of Argentina's industrial base, Peronism's rivals tried to find a different way to fuel economic growth.

The military and civilian governments of the 1950s and 1960s tried to separate the workers from the benefits created by economic growth. The unions' strength and their active resistance undermined these efforts and left Argentina deadlocked politically and economically.

During the Proceso, the government tried to annihilate the political base of Peronism and eliminate its economic and political foundations. The resilience of the movement and the excesses and tragic errors that dictators inflicted upon the country led the military to once again abandon the political arena.

Democracy returned, but Alfonsín and the Radical Civic Union were not able to create enough of a political base to hold onto power. Menem promised a new direction, but his administration's abandonment of government-controlled industries and services, along with the workers they once employed, marooned millions. Workers trained for the jobs of the post–World War II economy found no place in the Menem administration's neoliberal future. Political protests and economic stagnation forced upon Argentina the fundamental question: What should the government do for a working class that could not find work?

KIRCHNER'S ARGENTINA

Néstor Kirchner had no political base outside of Santa Cruz, his home province where he had served as governor since December 1999. Duhalde's backing and a broad desire inside and outside of the Peronist movement to support anyone other than Menem qualified him for the presidency.

To build popular support and secure the position of his new administration, Kirchner took action in a number of areas: the cultivation of support within Peronism, a restored nationalism, a revival of the campaign for justice for victims of the Dirty War, and relief from the economic crisis.

His overtures to the Justicialist Party's traditional supporters blended all of these initiatives. The Peronist movement had drifted from its roots since 1983. Kirchner stepped into the political void and rallied Peronists. He promised to put the people back to work. He labeled the country's international creditors as enemies who held back Argentina's efforts to build an economy that worked in the interests of the many, not the few. He challenged the United States and its efforts to dominate the hemisphere's markets and limit the policy choices of its neighbors. Within and beyond Argentina, he aligned the country and his policies with progressive neighbors: Hugo Chávez in Venezuela, Luiz Inácio Lula da Silva in Brazil, and Evo Morales in Bolivia. He promised to make the state work once again as a protector of the poor, the humble, and the oppressed. Kirchner's rhetoric echoed Perón, not Menem.

Presenting a clear contrast to those who preceded him, Kirchner's campaign for a revived Peronism struck a popular cord. He linked symbolic actions to his call for change. Traditionally, Peronist leaders directed state investment in the economy. Although he did not push for a complete reversal, Kirchner ordered the nationalization of a number of services and companies that the state had sold to private investors in the 1990s.

For Kirchner, the reassertion of state power in the economic realm increased his popular standing. If you pressed its supporters, Peronists would define their movement in many ways. Before Menem's two terms in office, almost every Peronist would agree that nationalism was a central characteristic of the movement. When Perón first took command of the government after World War II, the effort to make Argentina a leading power in economic, military, and diplomatic terms was a central ambition. Linked to this was a desire to make Argentina self-sufficient and independent. These broad goals justified the state-run industrialization program, the expanded control and regulation of the country's rural industries, and the public purchase of and investment in Argentina's transportation infrastructure between 1949 and 1949.

When the Menem administration adopted policies that privatized the public sector's control of industries, utilities, and services, the president asserted that the future of the movement and the country depended upon the opening of Argentina to globalization, competition, and international investment.

Menem's emphasis on cooperation and engagement internationally aligned the government's diplomatic and military policies with those of the United States. Most notably, in contrast to Argentina's traditionally neutral or non-aligned stance during international crises, his government supported the U.S. Desert Shield and Desert Storm operations that pushed back the Iraq military from Kuwait in 1990 and 1991, and participated in the United Nations intervention in Bosnia in 1994.

While he characterized his actions as being in line with Peronism's traditions, their impact, especially the sale of public sector companies, attacked the movement's historical foundations. In most respects, Menem's privatization of state-owned properties and services, combined with a reduction in the amount of money transferred from the federal to provincial governments, had more in common with the actions of the Proceso's Economics Minister José Martínez de Hoz. The sale of government-owned operations, such as the national telecommunications firm ENTel, the national postal system, or the Aerolíneas Argentinas—a government-supported airline—stripped away public sector jobs and expenditures. The privatizations and attempts to attract foreign investment in both the 1970s and the 1990s reduced industrial and service sector employment directly connected to the state.

Policymakers in both the late-1970s and the 1990s asserted that their actions would make Argentina more open and attractive to external sources of investment and innovation. This shift would help the country keep pace with rapid changes taking place around the world. In their view, this gave the country a better chance to modernize and grow, which in the medium term would benefit the privileged and the poor, the workers and the elite.

In both cases, the policies helped destroy the economic standing of Peronism's most loyal supporters—the service sector and industrial workers. The failure of the Menem administration to secure for Argentina a path toward sustained economic expansion meant that those who lost their jobs when their plant, office, or industry privatized found no alternative means of making a living. Progress and innovation did not occur. Rural exports remained the essential foundation of the economy. Unemployment and poverty, especially in the interior provinces, became more pronounced. In sum, the Menem administration's push to change Argentina ended in failure.

Kirchner reversed the policies of Menem in both the areas relating to government support for the poor, the unemployed, and disadvantaged and the areas relating to the privatization of industries and utilities.

These actions did not resurrect the government as the country's key economic actor. Public sector employment remained less than it was in the 1970s. In turn, the government did not repurchase every privatized company or operation. Lack of capital would have prevented such a move had Kirchner proposed it. Stripped of the need to direct and support what had become inefficient and uncompetitive companies gave the government more room to maneuver in the face of international and domestic pressure over the country's debt default and currency devaluation in 2002.

Shortly after taking office, the president ordered the nationalization of *Correo Argentino*, the country's postal system. This decree started a series of actions that reclaimed privatized rail lines, port facilities, airlines, and *Aguas Argentinas*, which controlled water and sewage services in the capital and Greater Buenos Aires. Kirchner's government did not nationalize YPF, the country's oil and natural gas company, but it did establish ENARSA (*Energía Argentina Sociedad Anónima*, or Argentine Energy, S.A.), a publicly funded corporation dedicated to the search for and exploitation of new oil and gas fields within the country and offshore.

The channeling of funds toward the reconstruction of government aid programs was more significant. Using *unidades básicas, piquitero* groups and other official government agencies, the Kirchner administration rebuilt connections between the administration and the population. It extended and established formal public assistance programs: Household subsidies that the Duhalde administration created in 2001 remained in place; "Argentina Trabaja" ("Argentina Works") funded neighborhood credit programs and public works projects; and it expanded public pension programs. As government programs and social spending expanded, popular support for the government grew.

The government strengthened its support of unions. The settlement of a long-standing conflict with public school teachers exemplifies this shift. In 1993, the Menem administration announced plans to expand compulsory education from the then required 7 years to 10 years nationwide. At the same time, it announced plans to increase opportunities for private education and cut back on supplemental and support programs for teachers and schools. It also expanded a push to shift funding obligations for education from the federal to provincial governments. When fiscal conditions forced additional cutbacks in 1997, teachers faced salary reductions and the elimination of stipends that help teachers pay for materials that they used in the classroom.

The teachers' union, the *Central de Trabajadores de la Educación de la República Argentina* (CTERA or Confederation of Education Workers of the Argentine Republic) organized a national strike, marked by the erection of a *carpa blanca* (white tent) in front of the Argentine Congress and a hunger strike by union leaders and teacher volunteers, who took turns fasting over the course of 30 months. The tent became a focal point of protest, with labor leaders, opposition politicians, intellectuals, and celebrities making appearances at the site to help build public support. With the passage of the Federal Educational Finance Law in December 1999, which promised that federal spending on education would increase to 6.6 percent of the country's annual gross domestic product (GDP), the teachers declared victory and ended their strike.

The rapid disintegration of the de la Rúa administration left the promise of increased funds for education unfulfilled. The CTERA joined other unions in a series of protests, demonstrations, and strikes during de la Rúa short run in power. The Duhalde government, which focused its energies on surviving the recession and finding a proper, constitutionally sound path toward the election of a successor government, left these issues unaddressed.

Kirchner moved quickly to resolve the impasse. His government established a new guaranteed funding base for public education, set at a minimum of 6 percent of the country's estimated gross national product each year. It also, with the passage of a new National Education Law, repealed the 1990s' push to decentralize and privatize public education. The national government reclaimed its control over public education and reasserted national standards in relation to teacher salaries, school administration, and educational standards. Finally, it passed legislation that mandated the establishment of new vocational schools that promised better opportunities for students who sought technical or career training.

Kirchner moved aggressively against those responsible for human rights violations during the "Dirty War." In contrast to the Alfonsín and Menem administrations, his administration sought prosecution not accommodation or compromise. In August 2003, the Argentine Congress approved the administration's repeal of laws that limited prosecution of military and police authorities involved in state terrorism and related crimes. Prosecutors revived old cases, which the accused tried to block in the courts. Kirchner's clear stance established strong alliances with a range of groups, most notably the Grandmothers of the Plaza de Mayo and their supporters.

With the debt default unresolved, the Kirchner government had some leverage with the country's international creditors. Publically, the president refused to accept compromise. His public stance allowed government negotiators to seek better terms from the IMF. In 2005, the government announced a new deal with the IMF that restructured its payments and swapped over $100 billion past due for government bonds. A growing budget surplus allowed the government to set aside the deal and pay off its debt to the IMF at the year's end. On December 15, 2005, Kirchner announced that Argentina would settle its account with the IMF with a $9.81 billion payment.

Elections allowed Kirchner to measure the political success of his efforts. In 2005, congressional contests nationwide provided an opportunity for the president to move himself away from Eduardo Duhalde and toward the construction of his own political base with Peronism. He established the *Frente para la Victoria* (Front for Victory or FPV) and ran a slate of allied candidates across the country.

The key contest took place in Buenos Aires Province. Kirchner's wife and advisor, Cristina Fernández de Kirchner, stood for election as senator. Hilda Beatriz "Chiche" González de Duhalde, the wife of the provisional president who had served as minister of social welfare, challenged Fernández de Kirchner. The Kirchners' FPV slate captured 45.7 percent of the vote in Senate contests and a large plurality of the vote in Chamber of Deputies slates. Fernández de Kirchner took charge of the national Senate. Rival Peronist factions captured only 4 of the 24 seats up for vote. Alliances with regional parties and the results from 2003 left the FPV with working majorities in both congressional houses. Free from the influence of Duhalde and the shadow of Menem, President Kirchner asserted that the election served as a mandate for his policies.

Presidents, under the restrictions set by the Argentine Constitution, could seek reelection. Those who served two consecutive terms were then barred from serving again. Consequently, Kirchner announced that he would not seek reelection. Instead, Fernández de Kirchner would take up the leadership of the FPV. This created the opportunity for *los K*—as the media labeled the country's first couple—to take turns as president in future elections.

Underlying Néstor Kirchner's political success, the Argentine economy continued to expand. The South American Common Market, with parallel agreements that tied Venezuela, Chile, and Bolivia to Argentina, Brazil, Uruguay, and Paraguay, fueled manufacturing, exports, and employment and provided oil, gas, and mineral imports that bolstered Argentine industries. Grain exports, especially soybeans, and climbing market prices provided revenues from export taxes that the government channeled into its popular programs. By 2007, the political unknown from Patagonia had become the most popular Peronist leader since the 1940s.

Kirchner's popularity and his administration's achievements translated into political power. The FPV dominated another electoral round. With the opposition in disarray, Fernández de Kirchner captured 45.3 percent of the presidential vote—double the total of her closest rival. The election left the FPV and its allies in control of 48 Senate seats and 160 seats in the Chamber of Deputies, which extended their majorities in both houses.

TRADING PLACES

A veteran politician, the new president faced the challenge of moving the ambitious and apparently successful programs of Kirchner's administration forward. The most serious challenge came from the countryside. Before the 2007 election, relations between the Kirchner government and farmer organizations were tense. The government had become concerned about the cost of wheat and its impact on the cost of food. To protect consumers, it implemented price ceilings and export limits. These interventions led farmers to shift some of their production to other grains as they protested policy restrictions that interfered with their operations.

Shortly after taking office, Fernández de Kirchner announced a change in the rate charged for soybean and sunflower seeds. The consistently strong demand for them presented an opportunity for the government to increase the amount of revenue that export taxes produced.

Farmers, led by the *Federación Agraria Argentina* (Argentine Agrarian Federation, or FAA), the *Sociedad Rural Argentina* (Argentine Rural Society, or SRA) and other agricultural organizations, threatened a rural strike. President Fernández de Kirchner had little leverage. Taxes on exports still represented the most important source of tax revenue. If a disruption of farming production caused only a partial drop in the size of the harvest, the resulting loss of funds would interfere with the government's operations. The leaders of the rural protest asserted that their actions would not interfere with the supply of food for Argentine consumers. They promised that their strike would focus on the production and transport of soybeans and other grains destined for export and leave food production and provision with the domestic market unaffected.

President Fernández de Kirchner moved forward. She used an executive decree to implement the tax increases. The decree also put into place a new cap on profits that farmers could earn from exports. In response, the farmers went on strike. Farmers across the Pampa region drove tractors and trucks off their fields and blocked transit routes in protest. Despite the promise not to hurt Argentine consumers, the work stoppage in the countryside disrupted shipments of grain for both the domestic and international markets. Soybean production dropped from approximately 46 million tons in 2007 to 32 million tons in 2008. Wheat and corn production fell as well. Since work stoppages affected the supply of feed grains, beef production fell and produced shortages in urban markets.

The standoff continued for months. Protests in support of the farmers, organized by opposition parties, occurred in the capital. In response, the FPV staged its own demonstrations in support of the government's actions. By June, with no alternative, the government negotiated a truce. The government agreed to seek congressional approval of the export tax increases if the farmers ended their strike.

President Fernández de Kirchner's FPV had majority control of both the Chamber of Deputies and the Senate. The bill moved through the Chamber, but it failed to pass the Senate.

The administration's failure to win congressional approval for its export regulations signaled a political shift against the new government. Fernández de Kirchner seemed more reactionary than innovative, and this encouraged both a revival of support for opposition parties and a splintering of the Peronist movement. Economic conditions made the situation more challenging. Export revenues, as a result of

Farmers expressed their opposition to the government's export tax and trade policies in December 2006 by blocking major highways with tractors. (AP Photo/ Diarios y Noticias)

the farmer strike and as a result of shifting demand in Brazil, China, and other key markets, fell. Inflation, which complicated business operations and threatened the gains that workers had made since 2003, grew to alarming levels. The high rates of growth that had lifted the country out of recession during Néstor Kirchner's presidency slowed.

The government's first reaction troubled observers and critics: Official reports that provided statistical measurements of monthly and quarterly economic trends presented inaccurate estimates of lower inflation, unemployment, and poverty rates as well as higher tax revenue collections. The rigged official reports did little to help the government. By the end of her first year in office, President Fernández de Kirchner's popularity dropped to 23 percent.

As news reports that criticized the government increased, the president challenged the media directly. During President Kirchner's term, the government had a close relationship with leading media companies. For example, Néstor Kirchner, in 2007, approved of the Clarín group's purchase of cable companies that gave it 80 percent of the market in the Federal Capital and a majority share nationally. The relationship became antagonistic during the farmer strike. In its newspapers, television broadcasts, and on radio, reports from the group's outlets questioned the government's actions. The Kirchners, in response, accused the Clarín group of using their market dominance to spread propaganda against the government.

The president and her allies increased the pressure as the conflict deepened. In 2009, Fernández de Kirchner proposed strict limits on the market share that private media companies could control. The government launched surprise inspections and audits of the group's corporate offices. Its union allies staged a strike that disrupted the distribution of newspapers on November 6. When the group's news reporters published stories that alleged government corruption, the Kirchners' supporters falsely accused Ms. Ernestina Herrera de Noble, the widow of the Clarín group's founder and its largest shareholder, of adopting children taken from *desaparacidos* (missing or disappeared ones) during the *proceso*.

While its conflict with the media developed, the government expanded its social programs. Existing tax revenues put limits on what the administration could do. In response, it took control of private pension funds in November 2008. The Menem government established a private pension funding system, the *Administradoras de Fondos de Jubilaciones y Pensiones* (Pension and Retirement Funds Administrators, or AFPJ), in 1994. The value of these funds had grown to $30 billion by 2008, despite losses caused by the 1999–2001 recession.

The Fernández de Kirchner administration promised to pay a fixed pension benefit for those whose had accounts nationalized through this action. Access to the funds helped the government cover its obligations and increase spending on a range of public programs.

As one of its first actions, the administration created a new welfare fund to support poor households. It launched the *Asignación Universal por Hijo* (Universal Child Allocation) in November 2009. This program, directed toward households led by unemployed or underemployed persons with low incomes, provided a stipend for children who enrolled in and maintained regular attendance in school. It also mandated vaccination programs.

In the wake of the challenges that came in 2008, the subsequent year did not make things easier for the president. A global recession slowed international trade. Brazil's move to devalue its currency made Argentine exports more expensive and less competitive in this key market. A drought hit the country's core farming regions, reducing harvest yields in a year of record production in the United States. Congressional elections in July cost the FPV its majority control of both the Chamber of Deputies and the Senate.

The Fernández de Kirchner government muddled through. Diversions became common. It revived Argentina's sovereignty claims over the Falkland Islands. The British government rejected these claims with little comment. In April, its representatives presented before the

United Nations a claim to offshore mineral rights in the ocean surrounding the Falkland Islands and Antarctica. In December, with the support of rival Peronist factions, the Argentine Congress approved a resolution that asserted the country's authority over both the Falkland and Georgian Islands. These appeals did little to revive the president's popularity.

Turning again to fiscal concerns, the Fernández de Kirchner administration established a reserve account, initially set at $6.7 billion, at the *Banco Central de la República Argentina* (the Argentine Central Bank, or BCRA). Chartered as an independent institution, supposedly free from political influence and interference, the move gave the government access to the bank's reserves. This allowed the president to use the reserves to cover revenue shortfalls and fund programs, operations, and debt service. When bank president Martín Redrado criticized the action as a violation of the bank's charter and the Argentine Constitution, President Fernández de Kirchner issued a decree that stripped Redrado of his title and authority.

Opposition parties had trouble building an effective coalition to challenge the FPV. By 2010, the opportunity passed. Underlying the shifting political conditions, Argentina's economic fortunes improved. Large harvests and increased export volumes strengthened the government's fiscal standing. While inflation remained a concern, the government asserted that unemployment continued to fall and poverty rates improved. With fears of another recession lifted, the government was able to coopt enough votes in Congress to maintain a working majority in both houses.

The Kirchners went on the political offensive. Progressive decrees, exemplified by the government's legalization of same-sex marriage in July, depicted the FPV as progressive. Behind the scenes, Kirchner promoted "La Campora," and Peronist youth organization. Named in honor of Hector Cámpora, the president who briefly held power before Perón's reelection in 1973, the group mirrored in part the *Juventud Peronista* (Peronist Youth) that operated as a popular auxiliary for the Justicialist Party through the 1970s. Formed in 2003, its first major actions came in the organized protests that supported Fernández de Kirchner during the 2008 farmers' strike.

Kirchner used La Cámpora to recruit and train a new generation of loyalists. By 2010, these recruits were ready to run for provincial and national congressional seats and take up positions in provincial and national ministries. Máximo Kirchner, the presidents' son, led the group. Calling themselves "Cristina's soldiers," La Cámpora's members promised to push the Kirchners' ambitions forward.

Néstor Kirchner's death on October 27 shocked the country. It also derailed the ambition of *los K.* and their supporters. Kirchner and Fernández de Kirchner could no longer trade turns in the presidency. The president moved ahead after ending her mourning. She announced plans to seek reelection in 2011. This move put the opposition in disarray. Despite her mixed record in office, Fernández de Kirchner easily won reelection and the FPV regained majority control in the Chamber and the Senate.

THE PERONIST MOVEMENT LOSES MOMENTUM

The election put the FPV at the center of power. Its authority was far from strong. As 2011 closed, economic conditions again turned against Argentina, which forced the administration to implement wage and price controls and currency regulations that angered many. For a time, the government appeared leaderless: A health scare, triggered by a false diagnosis of thyroid cancer, drove President Fernández de Kirchner into seclusion in December.

Kirchnerismo (Kirchnerism) had stalled as well. Continuing with its nationalist theme, President Fernández de Kirchner ordered the expropriation of YPF. Repsol, a Spanish firm, had acquired a majority stake in the firm in 1999 after the Menem government privatized it six years before. It initially promised to fight the move in court, and it threatened to withhold imports of crude oil and natural gas. With the government willing to use currency and trade controls to undermine the company, Repsol officials negotiated a compensatory settlement made public in February 2014.

With no one in position to succeed the president, the governing Peronist faction seemed destined to splinter before the next presidential elections in 2015. Potential leaders emerged, but then fell out of favor with the president. Its policy initiatives remained dependent on the performance of the farming sector. When exports climbed, the government secured sufficient revenue to fund its public programs. When exports fell, the government relied on misinformation and nationalist appeals to distract the country from its fiscal problems.

Another health scare, caused by a fall months before, forced the president to undergo brain surgery in October 2013—weeks before congressional elections. The FPV candidates won 40 seats in the Chamber of Deputies but lost 3 Senate seats. The vote tally revealed a dramatic loss of popular support. In 2011, FPV candidates captured 57 percent of the votes cast. The 2013 total dropped below a third of the total.

Opinion polls suggested that the president's popularity matched the declining performance of her party.

The declining fortunes of *los K* did not revive the political opposition. The Radical Civic Union, once a major force nationally, never recovered from the disastrous collapse of the de la Rúa administration. Although it retained isolated pockets of strength and continued to seek alliances with other opposition parties, it lacks the organization and the resources necessary to effectively compete in national elections. More important, the Radicals and leaders of other opposition parties offer no clear alternative to the blend of nationalism and public welfare spending that the Kirchners established.

Economic conditions became grim by December 2013. Police officers in 14 provinces staged strikes in protest of insufficient wages. News of the strikes encouraged looting in cities across the country, which forced the government to mobilize army units to restore order. Foreign investment, in reaction to the government's nationalist stance against Repsol and in recognition of the fundamental problems facing the country, dropped. The government, which had tried to maintain its official exchange rate for pesos through 2013, abandoned the effort in 2014. Pulling back from its operation in currency markets to protect its reserves, the year opened with the largest devaluation since 2001.

In June, U.S. courts undermined Argentina's efforts to deal with its foreign debt. In 2001, when the Argentine government defaulted on its bond payments in the midst of a profound economic crisis, the value of the bonds plummeted. As government officials negotiated with creditors, eventually reaching a settlement with 92 percent of bondholders in 2003, a group of hedge fund investors that had acquired a small portion of the defaulted bonds at discounted price refused to accept anything short of full payment.

President Fernández de Kirchner called the holdouts "vultures." While the holdouts held less than 6 percent of the defaulted debt, a New York district court ruled on October 26, 2012, that not only did Argentina owe the fund repayment at the bonds' full price, but that the country could not make payments to any creditors until the dispute reached resolution.

Arguing that the ruling would undermine its financial standing and disrupt other international credit agreements, Argentina appealed the ruling. In June 2014, the U.S. Supreme Court rejected the appeal and ordered the country's representatives to work out a settlement. When negotiations reached an impasse, Argentina's foreign debt again fell into default.

Inflation, lingering unemployment and underemployment, financial instability, and a foreign debt crisis: The final years of the Fernández de Kirchner administration seemed to be a repeat of the close of the Menem era.

INTO THE NEW MILLENNIUM

When its liberal *porteños* asserted their independence from Spanish authority in 1810, they acted with the belief that their country was destined for greatness. In the opening years of the twentieth century, foreign observers believed, Argentina had overcome the political turmoil of its past.

The country then appeared ready to realize the ambitions of its founders. Immigrants were flooding the country and helping it make its land productive. A growing foreign trade was enriching the country. Its capital, Buenos Aires, quickly became a rival to the great cities of Europe.

Today, Argentina retains the potential that led observers to predict great things. Its agricultural resources rank among the richest in the world. It continues to play an important role in the world's grain markets. Its scientists and researchers are developing new seeds and techniques to capitalize on its natural advantages. Ranchers and farmers, individually and as part of corporations, associations, and confederations, react quickly to new opportunities and expanding markets. In many respects, however, Argentina is a shell of its former promise. It has traditionally had one of the world's best-educated populations.

Since the 1970s, resources have flowed out of the country's public educational system. The reinvestment in public education, one of the key achievements of the Kirchner administration, has funded the opening of new schools and improved the salaries of teachers. It has not completely repaired the damage that the dictatorship and the Menem administration's privatization and decentralization schemes caused. Its universities, which have also received increased funding since 2003, still lack sufficient funds for maintenance and equipment.

For good or for ill, Argentina's economic problems during recent decades have forced dramatic changes, parallel to those taking place in other countries. During the period 1995–1999, small shops and businesses have closed in record numbers: According to government estimates, over 4,600 small businesses in the Federal Capital alone went out of business.

Unemployment, underemployment, and poverty became significant problems during the 1990s. The recession that hit bottom in 2001 made these problems worse. Government programs in recent years have helped address the needs of the poor and displaced in part, but cash transfers and public work programs relieve symptoms. They do not provide a solution to the structural challenges that idle much of Argentina's active workforce.

Imports have pushed local producers out of many manufacturing activities. Surviving businesses have had to increase the scale of their operations. More and more companies rely on technology and machinery to do the work that was once done by hand. As is true in every economy open to international competition, Argentine workers need to build skills and ready themselves for the competition that a global marketplace has presented before them.

The challenges that have mounted in recent years are much greater in the interior of the country. For decades, provinces in the northeast and the south depended upon the public sector. The government was the major employer in most provinces as private investment and foreign trade focused their attention on the capital and the core Pampa region.

Privatization and the entrance of multinational corporations into the country's mineral industries have brought some opportunity to the Andean and Patagonian regions, but the new enterprises have not taken the place of the shrinking public industries and government payrolls.

Protests over economic conditions first occurred in Tucumán in the 1970s. Interrupted by military repression, they recurred in the 1980s and the 1990s. Mass demonstrations, led by piqueteros, introduced a new cycle of popular rebellion in 2001. The Kirchner administration's engagement with the protesters created a brief political peace. Each downward cycle in Argentina's export trade, and the subsequent drop in funds available for redistribution, disrupts the truce. The protests of 2014 have led many to speculate about President Fernández de Kirchner's chances of surviving until elections choose her replacement.

The Kirchner and Fernández de Kirchner administrations addressed the issue of human rights directly and with some success. The blanket amnesties and bans on court inquiries relating to the crimes committed by military and security officials during the *proceso* ended. With the government's active support, human rights organizations secured indictments that led to convictions of many of the officers who directed the "disappearance" of thousands decades ago.

The selection of Cardinal Jorge Mario Bergoglio to serve as pope reminded Argentina of what remained unexamined. Pope Francis, during the 1970s, served as the provincial superior of the Society of

Jesus in Argentina. The chief officer of the Jesuit order during the "Dirty War," his critics asserted that circumstances must have put him face to face with the homicidal commanders of the dictatorship then in power.

Investigations of Bergoglio's personal history led some researchers to question some of his actions during that dark period. In the view of some critics, he appeared to have played a part in the detention of two Jesuit priests who the government accused of subversive activities. The priests were tortured but survived and regained their freedom months after their arrest.

Many came to the defense of the new pope. A review of the CONADEP investigations and recollections of those involved in a range of human rights investigations absolved Bergoglio of any involvement. The claims and challenges reminded Argentines that after four decades much in relation to the "Dirty War" remained unexamined and unresolved.

Politically, the precedents set after 1983 are historic. Rather than fall into violence, rival parties have handed over power in an orderly and peaceful fashion. Even in the midst of the profound crisis of 2001, respect for constitutional practices and popular mandates remained intact.

When Argentina entered into an economic and political crisis after World War II, commentators compared the situation to a riddle. How could a country with so much promise fall into such a state? Their question was misplaced. Argentina is a country with significant natural resources and enormous potential. It is also a country with deep regional, political, and material divisions. Its current state is a product of a history that appears to have benefited the few rather than the many. Reversing this is no simple challenge.

Notable People in the History of Argentina

Alberdi, Juan Bautista (1810–1884). Born in Tucumán, he was a member of the literary and political circle known as the "Generation of 1837." His opposition to the dictatorship of Juan Manuel de Rosas forced him into exile, but after Rosas's fall from power in 1852, Alberdi became one of the country's most influential figures. His treatise *Bases y puntos de partida para la organización política de la República Argentina* (*Bases and Starting Points for the Political Organization of the Argentine Republic*) served as the intellectual basis of the national constitution of 1853. Through his writings, he encouraged European influences and immigration as a means of bringing civilization and development to Argentina. His views were often reduced to a single, defining phrase: "Gobernares poblar" ("To govern is to populate").

Alem, Leandro Nicebro (1842–1896). A political activist from his youth, first as a supporter of the political interests of the city of Buenos Aires and, after 1893, as the cofounder of the *Unión Cívica Radical* (Radical Civic Union), which grew into Argentina's first national popular-based political party.

Alfonsín, Raúl Ricardo (1926–2009). An activist and leader within the *Unión Cívica Radical,* (Radical Party, or UCR) he became the party's leader after 1981. He captured the presidency in 1983 and directed the country's transition from military to civilian rule. Having overcome threats from rebel military factions that challenged the government's efforts to bring participants in the Dirty War to justice, in 1989 he resigned his post, just months before the scheduled end of his term, because of an economic crisis.

Ameghino, Florentino (1854–1911). A scientist who gained fame for his independent research into geology, paleontology, and archeology, he and his brother Carlos established the foundation for the development of the physical sciences in Argentina through their fieldwork, lectures, and published works.

Aramburu, Pedro E. (1903–1970). An army general who rose through the ranks during Juan Perón's first presidency, he gained national attention as a participant in the coup against Perón in 1955. He then replaced the coup leader, Eduardo Lonardi, as provisional president. He remained politically active in the armed forces after he turned power over to Arturo Frondizi in 1958. In 1970, a cell of the Montoneros kidnapped and assassinated him, which was one of the most notorious acts of political violence during the ban against the Peronist movement (1955–1972).

Avellaneda, Nicolás (1836–1885). Born in Tucumán, he helped lead the process of organizing the political and economic foundations of the country between the fall of Rosas and the War of the Triple Alliance (1865–1870). He served as president (1874–1880) and emerged as a leader of the conservative *Partido Autonomista Nacional* (National Autonomist Party).

Belgrano, Manuel (1770–1820). Born in Buenos Aires but educated in Spain, he served as the secretary of the Viceroyalty's Trade Council (*Consulado*) between 1794 and 1810. His reports and essays helped build support for trade reforms and economic promotions. He emerged as a central figure in the struggle for independence. After helping construct a revolutionary government in 1810, Belgrano commanded the campaign against Asunción in the following year. His army's defeat at the Battle of Tacuarí ensured the separation of Paraguay from the United Provinces of the Río de la Plata.

Borges, Jorge Luis (1899–1986). Renowned for his poetry and short fiction, Borges became the country's most famous modern author.

The story collections *Dreamtigers, The Book of Imaginary Beings,* and *Dr. Brodie's Report* are his best-known publications. His writings, original and complex in structure, helped shape the spread of "magic realism" in Latin American literature.

Calfucurá, Juan (d. 1873). Political and military leader of the Araucanian peoples during the post–Independence era, he helped build links between tribal groups that transformed the native peoples of the Pampa region into a feared and effective military force. His political and military successes led Juan Manuel de Rosas to negotiate treaties that rewarded Calfucurá and maintained a truce between the tribes and the increasing number of settlers and ranchers who pushed south and west across the Pampa after 1820. After his death, the system of alliances that he created collapsed, which eased the military conquest of the region by Argentine forces during the 1878–1979 "Conquest of the Wilderness."

De la Rúa, Fernando (1937–). He emerged as a leader of the *Unión Civica Radical* (Radical Civic Union, or UCR) in 1982, as the party moved to select its candidates for national office at the end of Argentina's last military dictatorship. Although Raúl Alfonsín defeated him in the UCR's primary elections in 1983, he later gained national prominence after being elected senator representing the Federal District. He then was elected mayor of the Federal Capital in 1996. He captured the presidency in 1999 as the candidate of the *Alianza para Trabajo, Justicia, y Educación* (Alliance for Work, Justice, and Education, or Alianza), which was a coalition of the UCR and FREPASO. In the face of an economic crisis and mounting popular protests, marked by food riots and highway blockades, he resigned from office in December 21, 2001.

Echeverría, Estebán (1805–1851). The recognized leader of the "Generation of 1837," he was Argentina's first great literary figure. Born in Buenos Aires Province, he studied philosophy, Latin, and literature at the University of Buenos Aires and in Europe. His poetry and short fiction blended European romanticism with topics of local import, and his work won acclaim immediately. His political vision, which centered on the creation of a unified Argentina, led him to challenge the Rosas dictatorship. Pressured into exile, he continued to write and publish works that became central to Argentine literature. His most important writings are *Dogma socialista* (*Socialist Dogma*) and *El matadero* (*The Slaughterhouse*).

Farrell, Edelmiro J. (1887–1980). Born in Avellaneda, on the outskirts of the Federal Capital, he achieved the rank of brigadier general in 1943. Since the 1930s, he had been active in political intrigues within the armed forces, and as a member of the ultraconservative officer group GOU he played a leading role in the 1943 coup. Factional struggles led to his ascension to the presidency in 1944. An ally of Juan Perón, Farrell authorized Perón's demotion and detention in 1945 and later supervised the election that brought Perón to power the following year.

Frondizi, Arturo (1908–1995). As a lawyer and university lecturer, Frondizi emerged as a critic and rival of the Peronists during the 1950s. He ran for vice president on the Radical Party ticket in 1951. His economic nationalism and vocal challenge to the regime helped him become a leader of the anti-Peronist opposition and, in 1958, a successful presidential candidate at the head of the *Unión Cívica Radical Intransigente* (Intransigent Radical Civic Union, or UCRI). Caught between the unions, which pushed for economic gains, and the military, which wanted the government to take a hard line against Perón's supporters, his administration fell victim to a military coup in 1962.

Galtieri, Leopoldo Fortunato (1926–2003). A career military officer, he gained prominence as a member of the military dictatorship that planned and implemented the Dirty War. He assumed the presidency in 1981. To build popular support, he ordered the invasion of the Falkland and South Georgian Islands in 1982. The invasions led to a disastrous war with Great Britain. In the wake of the defeat, Galtieri resigned from office. After the return to civilian rule in 1983, Galtieri faced charges for violating human rights. A presidential pardon cleared him of an initial series of convictions. Investigations into the kidnapping of children related to victims of the Dirty War led to new charges in 1999 and 2000, and civil charges in 2002.

Garay, Juan de (1528–1583?). A veteran of numerous military campaigns in the Andes, he moved to Asuncíon in 1568 and led expeditions to establish and fortify a number of sites, including Santa Fe (1573) and Buenos Aires (1580).

Gardel, Carlos (1890–1935). Propelled by radio broadcasts and films, he became the symbol of the Tango. Decades after his death in a plane crash, his recordings remain popular in and beyond the country.

Hernández, José (1834–1886). Born in Buenos Aires but raised on an estancia leagues south of the capital, he began a literary career as a journalist. As the editor of *El Río de la Plata,* he became a critic of Domingo Sarmiento and the promotions of the national government. His epic poem *Martín Fierro* (1872) and its sequel *La Vuelta de Martín Fierro,* which romanticize the gauchos and rural life in the years before rapid development transformed Argentina's countryside, represent seminal literary works that reflect on and help define Argentine culture and history.

Illia, Arturo Umberto (1900–1983). A medical doctor, he became a Radical Party activist in Córdoba during the 1930s. He was elected president representing the *Union Cívica Radical del Pueblo* (People's Radical Civic Union, or UCRP) in 1963. His administration was plagued by a lack of popular support. Union strikes and economic instability, combined with political polarization, made it difficult for him to govern. As Argentina fell into political crisis in 1966, he was pushed from power by a military coup.

Juárez Celman, Miguel (1844–1909). Born in Córdoba, he became an ally of Julio Roca after 1880. He captured the presidency in 1886 and used his power to promote the development and settlement of the country's interior. Corruption and favoritism marked his administration, which his enemies called the *"Unicato"* (one-man rule)— a reference to his autocratic style. When economic doubts led to a collapse of foreign loans, known as the "Baring Crisis" (1890), his regime faced a major recession and a popular rebellion. Pressured by Roca and his supporters, he resigned. The collapse of his administration fostered a political crisis that culminated with the Sáenz Peña Electoral Reform Law (1912) and the eclipse of the National Autonomist Party as the country's dominant force.

Justo, Agustín P. (1878–1943). Born in Entre Ríos, he pursued a military career and became active in the Radical Party. President Marcelo T. de Alvear named him minister of war in 1922. Disagreements with supporters of Hipólito Yrigoyen led him to join in the 1930 coup, and he served briefly as a cabinet member of General José F. Uriburu's dictatorship. He led the formation of the Concordancia and in rigged elections became president in 1932.

Lanusse, Alejandro Agustín (1918–1996). Born in Buenos Aires, he had a successful military career, interrupted in 1951 when he participated in a failed coup attempt against the Peronist regime. Released from jail in 1955, he reclaimed his rank and rose to commander-in-chief of the army. He participated in the ousting of Juan Carlos Onganía in 1970. Factional struggle led to the fall of provisional president and coup leader Roberto Levingston and to Lanusse's promotion to the presidency in 1971, after which he approved Juan Perón's return from exile and supervised the 1973 elections that brought the Peronist Party back into power.

Liniers y Brémond, Santiago de (1753–1810). Born in France, he commanded the naval squadrons that policed Buenos Aires harbor during the final decades of the colonial era. When a British invasion led the Spanish viceroy to flee Buenos Aires in 1806, he helped organize the formation of defensive militias that defeated the invaders. The cabildo granted him the title of acting viceroy and full military command, which he used to organize a second successful defense of the city in 1807. He continued to serve as interim viceroy until 1809.

Mármol, José (1817–1871). Famous throughout Latin America for his romantic poetry and novels, he spent his most productive years in exile. He used his writings to criticize the brutality of the Rosas dictatorship. His most important works are the poem "El peregrino" and the novel *Amalia.*

Mendoza, Pedro de (1487–1537). Granted the right to lead an expedition of exploration and settlement into the Río de la Plata region, he founded the Puerto de Nuestra Señora Santa María del Buen Aire in 1536, which became known as Buenos Aires. The isolation of the settlement and the attacks of Native Americans forced the survivors to abandon the site in 1541.

Menem, Carlos Saúl (1930–). He served as president of Argentina from 1989 to 1999. Born in La Rioja, he joined Peronist youth organizations and became a party activist at the end of Juan Perón's second term in office. During the decades when the Peronist Party was banned from political participation, he developed a local power base in his province. Elected governor of a La Rioja in 1973, he was later forced from office and held prisoner by the military dictatorship that ruled over the country between 1976 and 1983. With the return to civilian rule, Menem again won the governorship. He allied himself with Peronist reformers and won election as the country's president in 1989. During his two administrations, he supervised economic reforms that led to the privatization of state-owned industries and an influx of foreign investment. He also worked to improve Argentina's relationships with the United States, Europe, and the rest of Latin America. A constitutional amendment allowed him to win a second term in office.

Mitre, Bartolomé (1821–1906). Born in Buenos Aires, he served in the militias that fought against Rosas in the 1840s, and with Urquiza in the campaigns that eventually ended the dictatorship. He played a number of important roles in the era of national consolidation. By the end of the 1850s, he emerged as a leader of Buenos Aires and its ambitions to remain independent from the rest of Argentina. After the Battle of Pavón, in which the Argentine Confederation's armies defeated those of Buenos Aires, Mitre helped forge a compromise. His stature and influence helped him become the first president of the newly formed Argentine Republic in 1862. In 1869, he founded *La Nación,* which remains one of the country's leading national newspapers. He published political essays and historical studies and remained politically active. He led a revolt against the national government when his 1874 bid for reelection to the presidency failed. In 1889, he founded the *Unión Cívica* (Civic Union) and was elected to the national Senate in 1894.

Moreno, Mariano (1778–1811). Born the son of a Spanish colonial official, he studied law and the philosophies of the European Age of Enlightenment in his youth. He emerged as a proponent of liberal reform as a participant and legal advisor to the cabildo of Buenos Aires. In 1809 he authored the *Representación de los hacendados* that served as a rallying point for those seeking a break from Spain. During the first years of the Independence struggle, Moreno was a leading figure in the debates over the creation of a new, liberal government.

Newton, Richard B. (d. 1868). Arrived as a youth from Great Britain, he became one of Argentina's most influential ranchers. He represents a generation of Europeans who became wealthy through the development of sheep and cattle ranches. Historians credit him as being the first to use barbed wire fencing, which made possible selective breeding of sheep and cattle. He was also one of the founding members of the Argentine Rural Society.

Onganía, Juan Carlos (1914–1995). He served as the leader of the *Azules* (Blues) faction within the armed forces in the 1960s. He attained the rank of commander-in-chief of the army in 1962 and then, in 1966, supported the coup against President Arturo Illia. In the wake of the coup, a military junta named him the country's provisional president, who then directed the "Argentine Revolution" that proposed a conservative reordering of society. Efforts to challenge his government's restrictions on political activism and the rights of labor produced violent confrontations that culminated in the *cordobazo* of 1969. The military forced him from power in 1970.

Palacios, Alfredo Lorenzo (1879–1963). Born in Buenos Aires, he studied law and then pursued a career in politics. He was a cofounder of the Socialist Party and served as the congressional voice for labor between 1902 and 1943. He was an active critic of the Peronist regime.

Pellegrini, Carlos (1846–1906). Born in Buenos Aires, he was a leader of the *Partido Autonomista Nacional* (National Autonomist Party) beginning in the 1870s. After service in the national Congress and in various ministerial posts, he became president in the wake of President Miguel Juárez Celman's resignation in 1890. After using fraud and force to ensure the election of Luis Sáenz Peña, he became an important proponent of electoral reform.

Perón, Eva María Duarte de (1919–1952). Having made a living as a radio actress, she served as a key political ally of Juan Perón. She married Perón in 1945 and then assisted in efforts to orchestrate the support of organized labor during and after Perón's presidential election. Although she held no official posts, she channeled public funds through the *Fundación María Eva Duarte de Perón* (María Eva Duarte de Perón Foundation, established in 1948), later known as the *Fundación Eva Perón*. Called "Evita" by her supporters, she helped coordinate the campaign for women's suffrage in 1947. Even after her death, she remained a symbol for the Peronist Party's commitment to the poor and the working classes.

Perón, Juan Domingo (1895–1974). The son of poor European immigrants, he was Argentina's most important and controversial political leader in the twentieth century. He began his training for military service in 1911. In 1930, he participated in the coup against President Hipólito Yrigoyen. He helped form the GOU, the *logia* within the army that pushed for a nationalist revolution during the Concordancia and that played a key leadership role in the 1943 coup. Working under General Farrell, he became a prominent leader in the military government and led the effort to build political support for the regime. He was elected president in 1946 and reelected in 1952. Until his ouster in 1955, he used the government to transform Argentine politics. Relying on support from unions, the military, industrialists, and the Catholic Church, he directed efforts to industrialize Argentina. The failure of his programs pitted his most loyal supporters against liberals and ultranationalists. Forced into exile by a military coup, he worked to maintain his dominance over the Peronist movement. Conflict between unions, revolutionaries, and the national government led to his return in 1972 and his reelection as president in 1973.

Prebisch, Raúl (1901–1986). Born in Tucumán, he became famous as the director of the Economic Commission for Latin America within the United Nations in 1948 and the founding director-general of the United Nations Conference on Trade and Development (UNCTAD) in 1964. His work in economic theory, in particular in *The Economic Development of Latin America and Its Principle Problems* (1950), led to the development of the Singer-Prebisch Thesis. This thesis challenged the assertion that open international trade worked to the mutual benefit of industrial and primary producers. It became the basis of the Structuralist Theory and the Dependency School of International Development. His scholarship and work with the UN promoted "Import-Substitution Industrialization" (ISI) as an economic modernization strategy for Third World countries.

Pueyrredón, Juan Martín de (1777–1850). Beginning with his participation in the military actions against British invasions in 1806 and 1807, he became an important Independence leader. He served as supreme director of the United Provinces of the Río de la Plata between 1816 and 1819.

Rivadavia, Bernardino (1780–1845). Born in Buenos Aires, he was one of the most important leaders during the Independence era. A proponent of the Unitario cause, he worked as a cabinet member and, ultimately, as president of the United Provinces of the Río de la Plata. He organized the Constitutional Convention of 1826, helped briefly solidify the new country's finances, and pushed for efforts to hold onto the territories that once comprised the viceroyalty of the Río de la Plata after the break from Spain. His aggressive promotion of national at the expense of local interests rallied the Federalist movement that pushed him from power.

Roca, Julio Argentino (1843–1914). The dominant political figure of his generation, he was born in Tucumán and gained national prominence through military service. As the commander of the "Conquest of the Wilderness," he annihilated Native American resistance to the settlement and economic development of the Pampa region in 1879. He was twice elected president: first in 1880 and again in 1898. In and out of power, he worked to maintain the political primacy of the country's elite during the "Golden Age."

Rosas, Juan Manuel de (1793–1877). Raised on a cattle ranch, he developed his leadership talents as a youth against British invaders and Native Americans. After leading forces loyal to Supreme Director Juan Martín de Pueyrredón in 1818, he organized militia patrols of the southern frontier against Native American raids. Disagreements with Unitario leaders led him to raise an army against the government in 1827. Instrumental in Federalist victories in 1827 and 1829, he was declared governor of Buenos Aires Province. He then established a dictatorial regime that used force and terror to maintain its authority in the decades that followed. His government survived wars with competing caudillos and foreign invaders, but in 1852 a confederation of rivals forced him from power.

Sábato, Ernesto (1911– 2011). After having lost a professorship in 1945 because to political reasons, he embarked on a literary career and is regarded as one of the country's most accomplished authors. The novel *El túnel* was his first major achievement. After the end of the country's last round of military dictatorships, he directed the *Comisión Nacional Sobre la Desaparación de Personas* (National Commission on Missing Persons, or CONADEP) that investigated human rights abuses that occurred during the Dirty War. He remained an active commentator on the political and cultural turmoil that the country experienced in recent decades.

San Martín, José de (1778–1850). Regarded as the national hero and the country's most celebrated military officer, he received his education and training in Spain at the end of the colonial period. He resigned his commission in the Spanish army in 1811 and returned to Argentina. There, he helped organize the Independence forces. He planned and directed the invasions of Chile, in 1817, and

Perú, in 1820, which secured the independence of South America. Disagreements with Simón Bolívar, who led Independence forces in Venezuela, Colombia, and Perú, and disappointment over the warfare that engulfed the United Provinces of the Río de la Plata in the 1820s led him to live out his life in European exile.

Sarmiento, Domingo Faustino (1811–1888). Regarded as the chief promoter of public education in South America, he was born and raised in San Juan. His support of the Unitario cause forced him to flee into exile. In Chile, he was active as a government official and as a journalist. His writings helped establish him as one of the staunchest critics of the Rosas dictatorship. After Rosas's fall, he actively participated in the construction of the Argentine Republic. He was noted and attacked for his promotion of modernization programs that followed European and North American models. He served as governor of two provinces, as secretary of education, as ambassador to the United States, and, in 1868, as president. His most famous work is *Facundo*, a blend of fiction and political tracts that contrasted the barbarity of the Argentine interior with the civilized, progressive influence of urban life.

Solís, Juan Díaz de (d. 1516). The Spanish Crown authorized him to explore the southern reaches of the Americas in hopes of finding a passage to Asia. Embarking on a voyage in 1515, he led the first Spanish explorations of the Róo de la Plata estuary in 1516.

Torre, Lisandro de la (1868–1939). Born in Rosario, he helped form the *Unión Civica Radical* (Radical Party) in 1890. After parting with Hipólito Yrigoyen, he founded the *Partido Progresiva Demócrata* (Progressive Democratic Party) that became a major force in Santa Fe Province. His provincial base allowed him to play an important role in national affairs as a member of Congress. During the 1930s, he led congressional investigations into government corruption and favoritism, challenged the Justo administration's foreign policy, and led an investigation of price fixing by foreign-owned meat-packing plants.

Urquiza, Justo José de (1801–1870). Born and raised in Entre Ríos, he became an important rancher and merchant during the Federalist era. Leading the opposition to Rosas's trade policies, he took charge of the military forces that defeated Rosas and ended his dictatorship in 1852, and then claimed leadership over the Argentine Confederation until 1861.

Videla, Jorge Rafael (1925– 2013). As the country fell into violence in 1975, he gained prominence as the army's commander-in-chief. Working through President María Estela Perón, he supervised the "Dirty War" against real and suspected enemies of the state. Estimates of the people who "disappeared" during the military's campaign of terror range from 10,000 to 40,000. In 1976, he became provisional president and directed the "Process of National Reorganization," which aimed at forcing political peace. He resigned his post in 1981. Convicted of crimes against humanity in 1984, his life sentence was lifted by a presidential pardon. In 2000, prosecutors charged him along with other military leaders of the Proceso and the Dirty War with crimes related to the kidnapping of children of those detained and executed during his presidency. Charges mounted in the years that followed. He was ultimately convicted of human rights violations in 2010 and 2012. Given a life sentence, he died in prison.

Yrigoyen, Hipólito (1852–1933). A founder of the *Unión Civica Radical* (Radical Party), he became the dominant political leader of his generation and the first politician to capitalize on the Sáenz Péna Law of 1912 that mandated universal male suffrage and the secret ballot. His Radical Party used the newly enfranchised to capture control of the national government in 1916. As president, he blended nationalism and paternalism in an attempt to build and maintain a dominant political movement. Divisions within the party weakened his authority after his first term in office, but he successfully won reelection in 1928. The Great Depression undermined his government and left him with few defenders in the face of the military coup that forced him from office in 1930.

Glossary of Terms and Abbreviations

AAA (*Alianza Argentina Anticomunista,* **the Argentine Anticommunist Alliance**)**:** A government-sanctioned death squad, created during the brief presidency of Isabelita Perónto, to wage war against real and suspected enemies of the state.

Anti-Personalistas: Members of the UCR who challenged Hipólito Yrigoyen's control over the part during the 1920s. Members of this faction also supported the Concordancia of the 1930s.

Asiento: Literally, "permission," the term refers to the 1702 grant that gave Great Britain control of slave sales in Spanish America.

Azules ("Blues"): Refers to a faction within the military that supported civilian rule but not under Peronist leadership.

Blandengues: A militia first formed in the colonial era to protect against Native American raiding parties in the Pampa region.

Cabildo (**Town council**)**:** The term *"cabildoabierto,"* which translates as "open council," refers to the popular assemblies that directed the political centers of the Independence movement between 1808 and 1825.

Caudillo: Political authorities of the early and mid-nineteenth centuries who used military force and political violence to dominate regions and provinces prior to the achievement of national unification.

CGT (*Confederación General del Trabajo,* **or General Confederation of Labor**)**:** This is the umbrella organization that plays a leading role in the union movement.

Cimarones: Authorities and ranchers used this term as a label for wild cattle. Also used as a name for escaped slaves.

Colonos: Literally, colonists, one of the labels applied to grain farmers in the Pampa region.

Colorados: Translated as "Reds," in the nineteenth century it was associated with Rosas and other Federalist leaders. In the 1950s, it referred to the hardline anti-Peronist faction within the armed forces.

CONADEP: *Comisión Nacional Sobrela Desaparación de Personas* (National Commission Concerning the Disappearance of Persons). Headed by Ernesto Sábato, this commission in 1984 conducted an independent investigation of the human rights violations that military and security forces committed during the Dirty War.

Concordancia: A political pact between the National Democratic Party, the Anti-Personalist Radicals, and the Independent Socialists that ruled over the period 1932–1943 through electoral fraud, censorship, and repression of their political enemies.

Consulado: Merchant councils. Under the centralized and heavily regulated trade established at the beginning of the Spanish colonial era, this merchant monopolized trade from Cádiz in Spain and in concert with allied merchant councils in Veracruz, Lima, and Mexico City. After trade reforms in the late eighteenth century, merchant councils in each port worked with Crown officials to monitor trade.

Cordobazo: Title of the popular protests that rocked the provincial capital of Córdoba in May 1969.

Criollo: An American-born male of European descent.

Descamisados **("Shirtless ones"):** Peronists and their rivals used the term in reference to the poor and working-class supporters of Juan Domingo Perón.

Encomienda: Initially meaning a responsibility taken up by a person of authority acting in the name of the Spanish Crown, it became a system of exploitation in colonial Spanish America. The holder of the encomienda, a Spaniard referred to as the "encomendero" had the right to use the labor and resources of a community to meet his needs. In theory, the encomendero was responsible for the protection of the communities under his charge. It was also the encomendero's responsibility to see to the Christianization of the locals. In practice, the Spanish took much and provided little in return. In most of the Americas, the encomienda system led to the destruction of Native American communities in a few generations.

ERP (*Ejército Revolutionario del Pueblo* or Revolutionary Army of the People): Based in Tucumán but active throughout the country in the 1960s and 1970s, it was one of the key revolutionary groups active in the years before the Dirty War.

Estancia: A cattle ranch. Ranch owners are called *estancieros*.

FPV (*Frentepara la Victoria* or Front for Victory): The wing of the Peronist movement that emerged as the political base for first president Néstor Kirchner in 2003 and then for President Cristina Fernández de Kirchner during her two terms in office.

Gaucho: A term, sometimes used in the distant past as a strong insult, that refers to the rural population that served the ranches of the colonial era and the early nineteenth century. Became a symbol of independence for nationalists by the end of the nineteenth century.

GOU: An acronym for *"Grupo de Oficiales Unidos,"* which was a secret military group, or "logia," that sought the advancement of nationalist political objectives at the expense of civilian rule. GOU members, including Juan Domingo Perón, participated in the 1943 coup.

Guaraní: The American people native to the northeastern corner of Argentina.

Guerra sucia **(The Dirty War):** This was a declared war against "subversives" that exploded into a campaign of terror against innocent civilians between 1975 and 1983. Between 15,000 and 40,000 people fell victim to the armed forces' counterinsurgency campaign.

Guerrilla: Translated as "little war," the term in the Argentine context refers to the armed conflict between the forces of authority and secret groups that pushed for revolution during the 1960s and 1970s.

IAPI (*Instituto Argentino de Promocióndel Intercambio* or Argentine Institute of Growth and Trade): Created in 1946, it controlled prices and exports of agricultural goods. Profits that its operations produced supported government investments in industrialization and social welfare programs.

JP (*Juventud Peronista* or Peronist Youth): Formed as a youth auxiliary to the Partido Justicialista, it became a focal point in the struggle between politicians and guerrilleros during the 1960s.

Justicialismo: The term applied to the eclectic ideological program of the Peronist movement.

Mazorca: Literally, an ear of corn, this was the name of the political police force that Juan Manuel de Rosas used to enforce his will over the province of Buenos Aires after 1829.

MERCOSUR (*Mercado Comúndel Sur* or Common Market of the South): The trading zone launched in 1995 that links Argentina to Brazil, Paraguay, and Uruguay.

Mestizo: People of mixed heritage, descended from European and Native American ancestry.

Montoneros: A term that first referred to the cavalry forces used by caudillos in the nineteenth century. In the 1960s, a guerrilla organization adopted the term and grew into one of the main revolutionary forces in Argentina during the 1970s.

Pampa: The broad central plain that is the economic, agricultural, demographic, and political core of the country.

PAN: The abbreviation for the Partido Autonomista Nacional (National Autonomist Party), which formed in the early 1870s in opposition to the political ambitions of Bartolomé Mitre and his supporters. It was a dominant force in the country's "Golden age" (1880–1910).

Piquiteros: Political protest groups, which first appeared in 1996 but became a central part of the popular demonstrations that undermined the de la Rúa administration in 2001. The term is taken from the English word "picket."

PJ (Partido Justicialista, or Peronist Party): Formed in support of Juan Domingo Perón after World War II.

Porteño: A term used in Argentina for a person who lives in the city of Buenos Aires.

Proceso: This refers to the *Proceso de Reorganización Nacional* (Process of National Reorganization), which was the label for the political program of the military dictatorship that ruled Argentina between 1976 and 1983.

Renovadores: The "Renewal" faction within the Peronist Party. This group helped the Peronists return to national leadership after electoral defeats in 1983 and 1985.

Saladero: A rural operation that slaughtered cattle and then produced dried and salted beef for sale in the local and regional markets.

SRA (Sociedad Rural Argentina, or Argentine Rural Society): An organization formed in 1866 to promote the interests of ranchers nationally.

UCR: Initials of the *Unión Cívica Radical,* or Radical Party, which formed in 1890 and remains one of Argentina's most important national political organizations.

UIA (*Unión Industrial Argentina* or Argentine Industrial Union): This is a federation of business and factory owners active in Argentine politics.

Unidades Básicas **(Community Organizing Center or Neighborhood Office):** Grassroots offices or centers that serve as the basis of Peronist political organizing and activity. During periods of Peronist rule, government officials typically channel funds for community and social services through these offices, which creates linkages between the state and communities across the country.

Unitario: A partisan of the central government in the city of Buenos Aires that tried to control the United Provinces of the Río de la Plata between 1816 and 1829. It then became the term for enemies of Rosas who hoped to unite the region's provinces into a single country.

Vaquería: Refers to the expeditions sanctioned during the colonial era to gather and slaughter wild cattle.

Yerba mate: Argentines use the dried leaves of this plant to make *mate,* a hot, caffeine-rich drink.

YPF: *Yacimientos Petrolíferos Fiscales,* the state-run petroleum company.

Bibliographic Essay

GENERAL WORKS

For readers who wish to explore one or more topics relating to Argentina's history, the best place to begin one's research is *Argentina, 1516–1987: From Spanish Colonization to Alfonsín* (Berkeley: University of California Press, 1987), by David Rock. Rock and other experts provide chapters on distinct historical periods in Leslie Bethell (ed.), *Argentina since Independence* (New York: Cambridge University Press, 1993). To launch a bibliographic search relating to a wide range of topics, consult the bibliographic essays devoted to Argentina in Leslie Bethell, ed., *The Cambridge History of Latin America*, vol. 11 (New York: Cambridge University Press, 1995). Argentine themes, topics, and issues appear frequently in Jose C. Moya, ed., *The Oxford Handbook of Latin American History* (New York: Oxford University Press, 2011). Leading Argentine scholars—Lyman Johnson, Susan Socolow, Jeremy Adelman, James Brennan, and Donna Guy—authored essays on Colonial Spanish South America, the Independence era, Labor History, and Gender and Sexuality that often highlight the Argentine experience.

The Argentina Reader: History, Culture, Politics (Durham, N.C.: Duke University Press, 2002), edited by Gabriela Nouzeilles and Graciela

Montaldo, provides selections and translations of key primary and secondary texts that cover major eras and themes of the country's experience across centuries.

Focused on economic issues, themes, and topics since the nineteenth century, Gerardo della Paolera and Alan M. Taylor (eds.), *A New Economic History of Argentina* (New York: Cambridge University Press, 2003) provide a starting point for investigations of key issues that shaped the country and its international standing. Roberto Córtes Conde provides a broad and engaging overview of Argentina's economic performance and related social shifts in *The Political Economy of Argentina in the Twentieth Century* (New York: Cambridge University Press, 2009).

For information on more recent publications, consult *The Handbook of Latin American Studies* (available online: http://lcweb2.loc.gov/hlas/). This research guide published by the Hispanic Division of the Library of Congress appears annually. The volumes alternate between those that focus on literature and the humanities and those that focus on the social sciences.

For those with access to research libraries, a number of high-quality journals publish articles and essays on Argentina regularly. The best are *The Hispanic American Historical Review, The Latin American Research Review, The Americas,* and *The Journal of Latin American Studies.*

I have listed the following works that I relied on during the writing of this text. In local libraries, you will find other books of value.

PRE-COLUMBIAN AND COLONIAL HISTORY

Articles that reflect up-to-date scholarship concerning the original inhabitants of Argentina appear in Stuart Schwartz (ed), *Cambridge History of the Native Peoples of the Americas,* v. 3 (New York: Cambridge University Press, 2000). This work includes an extensive bibliography and thorough coverage for all the country's regions and peoples through the era of national consolidation.

Scholars in Argentina have recently produced a large volume of original and important writings on the colonial economy. Their findings are beginning to appear in translation. For an introduction to this rapidly evolving field, see Samuel Amaral, *The Rise of Capitalism on the Pampas: The Estancias of Buenos Aires, 1785–1870* (New York: Cambridge University Press, 1998). See also Jonathan Brown, *Socioeconomic History of Argentina, 1776–1816* (New York: Cambridge University Press, 1979).

Nicholas Cushner has explored Jesuit mission operations in many parts of Latin America. For information on the Jesuits in Argentina, see

Jesuit Ranches and the Agrarian Development of Colonial Argentina, 1650–1767 (Albany: State University of New York Press, 1983). Concerning the rise of Buenos Aires, see Susan Migden Socolow, *The Bureaucrats of Buenos Aires, 1769–1810* (Durham: Duke University Press, 1987). See also John Lynch, *Spanish Colonial Administration, 1782–1810* (Westport: Greenwood Press, 1969).

INDEPENDENCE AND ROSAS

Many narratives of the Independence era treat Argentina's experience as part of the collective struggle to separate the Americas from Spain. Both John Charles Chasteen, *Americanos: Latin America's Struggle for Independence* (New York: Oxford University Press, 2008) and John Lynch, *The Spanish American Revolutions* (New York: W. W. Norton, 1973) stand out. For works that focus specifically on the Río de la Plata region, see David Bushnell, *Reform and Reaction in the Platine Provinces, 1810–1852* (Gainesville: University of Florida Press, 1983), and Tulio Halperín Donghi, *Politics, Economics, and Society in Argentina in the Revolutionary Period* (New York: Cambridge University Press, 1975). See also Mark Szuchman and Jonathan Brown, *The Revolution and Restoration* (Lincoln: University of Nebraska Press, 1994).

Juan Manuel de Rosas is a controversial figure in Argentina. An outstanding work on the dictator and his historical significance is John

Lynch, *Argentine Dictator: Juan Manuel de Rosas, 1829–1852* (Wilmington, DE.: Scholarly Resources Inc. 2001). Concerning the rival caudillos that worked with and against Rosas, see Ariel de la Fuente, *Children of Facundo: Caudillo and Gaucho Insurgency during the Argentine State Formation Process* (Durham, NC: Duke University Press, 2000).

Jeremy Adelman, in *The Republic of Capital* (Stanford: Stanford University Press, 1999), provides a clear explanation of the interplay among merchants, governments, and markets in and beyond Buenos Aires and how these agents shaped the creation of the Argentine Republic.

Hilda Sábato, in *Agrarian Capitalism and the World Market: Buenos Aires in the Pastoral Age, 1840–1890* (Albuquerque: University of New Mexico Press, 1990), provides information on the foundations of Argentine ranching during the Rosas dictatorship. Concerning the development of urban life and society, see Mark Szuchman, *Order, Family, and Community in Buenos Aires, 1810–1860* (Stanford: Stanford University Press, 1988).

NATIONAL CONSOLIDATION
AND THE GOLDEN AGE

Scholars have become much more interested in the consolidation of a constitutional order and a more powerful national state during the second half of the nineteenth century. David Rock, in *State Building and Political Movements in Argentina, 1860–1916* (Stanford: Stanford University Press, 2002), provides a detailed and nuanced analysis of how three political movements directed the political development of the country during this era. Books by Adelman and Sábato, mentioned earlier, explore the economic foundations of this period. The standard work on the growth of grain farming is James Scobie, *Revolution on the Pampas* (Austin: University of Texas Press, 1964). Concerning landowners, with a focus on the leading families in Buenos Aires Province, see Roy Hora, *The Landowners of the Argentine Pampas: A Social and Political History 1860–1945* (New York: Oxford University Press, 2001). Richard Slatta explores the social aspects of this process in *Gauchos & the Vanishing Frontier* (Lincoln: University of Nebraska Press, 1983). For a comparison of Argentina with Canada and its farming industry, see Jeremy Adelman, *Frontier Development: Land Labour and Capital on the Wheatlands of Argentina and Canada* (New York: Oxford University Press, 1994). Immigration provided much of the human capital that helped Argentina grow as dramatically as it did during the Golden Age. José C. Moya provides a strikingly original historical overview and analysis of the subject in *Cousins and Strangers: Spanish Immigrants in Buenos Aires, 1850–1930* (Berkeley: University of California Press, 1998).

Sarmiento was a central figure in the political, cultural, and literary history of these eras. See Tulio Halperín Donghi, Iván Jaksic, Gwen Kirkpatrick, and Francine Masiello (eds.), *Sarmiento: Author of a Nation* (Berkeley: University of California Press, 1994). For comparative insights relating to state formation in Argentina, Colombia, and Uruguay, see Fernándo López-Alves, *State Formation and Democracy in Latin America, 1810–1900* (Durham, NC: Duke University Press, 2000).

THE INTERWAR PERIOD (1910–1945)

No text deals specifically with the impact of World War I on Argentina, but Bill Albert, in *South America and the First World War* (New York: Cambridge University Press, 1988) covers the topic well.

The Radical Party is a major political force in this period. Concerning its trajectory, see David Rock, *Politics in Argentina, 1890–1930: The Rise and Fall of Radicalism* (New York: Cambridge University Press, 1975). See also Rock (ed.), *Argentina in the Twentieth Century* (Pittsburgh: University of Pittsburgh Press, 1975), which includes articles on the economic and political aspects of the period. Sandra McGee Deutch explores the conservative reaction against Yrigoyen and the Radicals in *Counterrevolution in Argentina* (Lincoln: University of Nebraska Press, 1986).

For an overview of the political influence and activities of Argentine ranchers, see Hora, *Landowners of the Argentine Pampas*, cited earlier. See also Carl Solberg, *The Prairies and the Pampas: Agrarian Policy in Canada and Argentina, 1900–1930* (Stanford, CA: Stanford University Press, 1987).

External shocks encouraged the development of domestic industry, which in turn became linked to important social and material shifts during this period. Yovanna Pineda provides an excellent examination of this topic in *Industrial Development in a Frontier Economy: The Industrialization of Argentina, 1890–1930* (Stanford, CA: Stanford University Press, 2009). See also Fernándo Rocchi, *Chimneys in the Desert: Industrialization in Argentina during the Export Boom Years, 1870–1930* (Stanford, CA: Stanford University Press, 2005).

The army asserts its authority over politics during this period. For a detailed discussion of the topic, see Robert Potash, *The Army and Politics in Argentina, 1928–1945: Yrigoyen to Perón* (Stanford, CA: Stanford University Press, 1969). The conservative ideologies of the era provide the intellectual foundation for later, more extreme interventions against civilian rule. To explore this topic, read David Rock, *Authoritarian Argentina: The Nationalist Movement, Its History and Its Impact* (Berkeley: University of California Press, 1993).

While the political role of Argentina's unions grows after 1945, Joel Horowitz provides useful background information in *Argentine Unions, the State, and the Rise of Perón, 1930–1945* (Madison: University of Wisconsin Press, 1990).

SINCE WORLD WAR II

Juan Domingo Perón is the dominant political leader of the last half-century. Joseph Page presents a careful and detailed narrative of the president's career and activities in *Perón: A Biography* (New York: Random House, 1983). A number of works about Evita Perón remain in print, but most are flawed. Alicia Dujovne Ortiz provides an entertaining and dramatic overview of the subject in *Eva Perón: A Biography* (New York: St. Martin's Press, 1996). One can find a useful introduction to the multiple facets of Peronism in James Brennan (ed.), *Peronism and Argentina* (Wilmington, DE: Scholarly Resources, 1998).

One of the best works that serves as a point of departure for most historians studying Argentina's recent history is Carlos Waisman, *The Reversal of Development in Argentina* (Princeton, NJ: Princeton University Press, 1987). Although he concentrated on Peronism and its impact, his text also makes essential connections between the 1930s and the post-war era. On the period 1955 to 1990, see William Smith, *Authoritarianism and the Crisis of the Argentine Political Economy* (Stanford, CA: Stanford University Press, 1991).

A number of books focus on distinct social and political groups. Concerning the role of the Catholic Church, see Michael Burdick, *For God and Fatherland: Religion and Politics in Argentina* (Albany: State University of New York Press, 1995). Labor and its struggle to shape the country's politics is a key subject of recent decades. James Brennan focuses on the years between Perón's second and third terms in office in *Labor Wars in Córdoba, 1955–1976* (Cambridge, MA: Harvard University Press, 1994). On the military in the years leading up to the *cordobazo*, see Robert Potash, *The Army and Politics in Argentina, 1945–1962: Perónto Frondizi* (Stanford, CA: Stanford University Press, 1980). See also David Pion-Berlin, *Through the Corridors of Power: Institutions and Civil-Military Relations in Argentina* (University Park: Pennsylvania State University Press, 1997).

New books concerning the Proceso and the Dirty War appear regularly. The report of the independent national commission appointed by President Raúl Alfonsín is a good starting point: *Nunca más* (New York: Farrar, Straus, Giroux, 1986). Paul Lewis explores the motivations and actions of the guerrilla organizations and the military in *Guerrillas and Generals: The Dirty War in Argentina* (Westport, CT.: Praeger, 2002). Concerning the military's use of torture and its impact on culture and society, see Marguerite Feitlowitz, *Lexicon of Terror*, rev. ed. (New York: Oxford University Press, 2011). Gerado Munck focuses on the key battle between organized labor and the dictatorships in *Authoritarianism and Democratization: Soldiers and Workers in Argentina, 1976–1986* (University Park: Pennsylvania State University Press, 1998). Thomas Wright provides a valuable overview and useful comparisons with a neighboring case in *State Terrorism in Latin America: Chile, Argentina, and International Human Rights* (Lanham, MD: Rowman & Littlefield, Inc., 2006). There are a number of books that explore the Falklands War in great detail. See, for example, Lawrence Freedman and Virginia Gamba-Stonehouse, *Signals of War: The Falklands Conflict of 1982* (Princeton, NJ: Princeton University Press, 1991).

For information on the political history of recent decades, with a focus on the evolution of the Peronist movement, see James McGuire, *Peronism without Perón: Unions, Parties, and Democracy in Argentina* (Stanford, CA: Stanford University Press, 1997). Concerning the transition from dictatorship to democracy, see Monica Peralta-Ramos and Carlos Waisman (eds.), *From Military Rule to Liberal Democracy in Argentina* (Boulder, CO: Westview Press, 1987). *Argentine Democracy: The Politics of Institutional Weakness,* edited by Steven Levitsky and María Victoria Murillo (University Park: Pennsylvania State University Press, 2005), provides a serviceable starting point for the exploration of the political scene since 1990 Javier Auyero provides a close examination of the clientilist structures and practices that tie the poor to the Peronist state machinery in recent decades in *Poor People's Politics: Peronist Survival Networks & the Legacy of Evita* (Durham, NC: Duke University Press, 2000). Auyero continues his illuminating exploration of the popular base of political power in *Routine Politics and Violence in Argentina: The Gray Zone of State Power* (New York: Cambridge University Press, 2007).

Economically, Argentina's fate seems closely tied to export revenues and its ability to service its foreign debt. Paul Blustein provides a narrative of Argentina's negotiations with the International Monetary Fund and other creditors during the crucial 1989–2001 period in *And the Money Kept Rolling In (and Out): Wall Street, the IMF, and the Bankrupting of Argentina* (New York: PublicAffairs, 2006).

Index

About the Author

DANIEL K. LEWIS is a professor of history at California State Polytechnic University in Pomona and an associate dean in the College of Letters, Arts, and Social Sciences. His research focuses on grain farmers, the state, and changing economic and political conditions between the two world wars in Argentina.

Other Titles in the Greenwood Histories of the Modern Nations
Frank W. Thackeray and John E. Findling, Series Editors